Achieving 100% Compliance of Policies and Procedures

Achieving 100% Compliance of Policies and Procedures

➤ Use business process improvement methods, streamlining tools, and quality tools to minimize variation and ensure compliance

➤ Enhance quality and flexibility; increase profitability, and competitiveness

➤ Build an organization receptive to change for an evolving policies and procedures infrastructure and improved customer satisfaction

➤ Establish continuous improvement plans for achieving savings of millions of dollars using business process streamlining methods, flow charts, procedure writing, and cost benefit analyses

---

A descriptive case study links
each chapter and includes
flow charts and procedures

Stephen B. Page, MBA

BookMasters, Inc.
Mansfield, Ohio

Address Printing questions to:

Steve Page
PO BOX 1694
Westerville, Ohio 43086
United States of America
Email: info@companymanuals.com
FAX: 801-382-1968

Ordering Information

Individual Sales: This book may be ordered through the author's web site at http://www.companymanuals.com/compliance/index.htm or through the above address.

Orders by U.S. trade bookstores and wholesalers: Please contact the author at the above address for pricing and shipping terms.

Library of Congress Cataloguing in Publication Data
Page, Stephen B. (1949 -)
>   Achieving 100% Compliance of Policies and Procedures. Includes case studies, flow charts, procedures, references, glossary of terms, appendices, and index.
>   ISBN: 1-929065-49-3

>   Published September 2000

Although I have extensively researched all sources to ensure the accuracy and completeness of the information contained in this book, I assume no responsibility for errors, inaccuracies, omissions, or any other inconsistency. Any slights against people or organizations are unintentional.

About the Author

Stephen B. Page is the author of four books. He holds a Master of Business Administration (MBA) in Management from the University of California at Los Angeles (UCLA). He has been employed by multinational companies including Eastman Kodak, Boeing Aircraft, Litton Industries, Qwest Communications, and Compuware. Stephen has thirty years experience in writing, analyzing, publishing, communicating, training, measuring, and improving business processes, policies, procedures, and forms. Stephen has written 250 company manuals in both printed and electronic formats, 6000 policies and procedures, and designed both manual and electronic form systems. Additionally, he has had first hand experience with the implementation of ISO 9000 Quality Standards and the Capability Maturity Model (CMM).

With his certification as a software engineer (CSQE), Stephen is competent in systems audits, Statistical Process Control (SPC), and quality tools. He is also certified in records management (CRM) and forms management (CFC). He has received many company-sponsored "Certificates of Accomplishment" including the Capability Maturity Model (CMM), ISO 9000 Quality Standards, Total Quality Management, Value Engineering, Six Sigma, and Management skills.

Stephen has written 10 trade journal articles. His most current article, "*Research: The Key to Quality Policies and Procedures,*" can be read in the *Quality Progress* trade journal (American Society of Quality), January 2000 edition. He is a skilled presenter and communicator. Stephen has presented three seminars on the subject of printed and electronic policies, procedures, and forms.

Stephen has worked in various industries including consulting, manufacturing, telecommunications, financial banking, and retail. He was the national chair for a Standards Manual for the Business Forms Management Association (BFMA); he was also the BFMA member of the year in the Los Angeles Chapter in 1987.

> *"I love to write. This is my fourth book and it is a culmination of my 30 years of experience. This 'how-to' book explores the area of compliance and continuous improvement because these are two areas where procedures analysts typically overlook or put aside until they have time to work on them. I wrote this book to help procedures analysts understand the importance of measures, measurements, metrics, numbers, variation, achieving compliance, and doing continuous improvement activities."*
>
> *Stephen Page*

Books by Stephen B. Page

Title	Publisher	©	URL: Http://
Achieving 100% Compliance of Policies and Procedures ISBN: 1929065-49-3	BookMasters, Inc. Mansfield, Ohio	2000	www.companymanuals.com/ compliance/index.com
Establishing a System of Policies and Procedures ISBN: 1929065-00-0	BookMasters, Inc. Mansfield, Ohio	1998	www.companymanuals.com/
Putting Secrets for the Weekend Golfer (a putting procedure) ISBN: 0312-15197-7	St. Martin's Press New York, New York	1997	Available through booksellers like Amazon.com or Barnes and Noble
Business Policies and Procedures Handbook (Replaced: Out-of-Print)	Prentice-Hall, Inc. Englewood Cliffs, New Jersey	1984	Replaced by "Establishing a System of Policies and Procedures"

How to Contact This Author

Stephen B. Page can be reached through the U.S. Mail, Email, Web Site, and FAX:

Stephen B. Page
PO BOX 1694
Westerville, Ohio 43086

Email: info@companymanuals.com
URL: http:// www.companymanuals.com/compliance/index.htm
FAX: (801) 382-1968

Contents

PART THREE:
INCORPORATING IMPROVEMENTS
AND ACHIEVING COST SAVINGS

Introduction

This book is about business processes, policies and procedures, and how they are measured and improved to ensure variation is minimized, quality is improved, cost is reduced, and customer satisfaction is increased. Plans and tools are provided to enable you to achieve, or work toward, 100% compliance of your business processes, policies, and procedures. Sample procedures and flow charts are used to help you understand how policies and procedures should be communicated, trained, published, measured, improved, and revised to take advantage of recommendations obtained through user/employee feedback responses, continuous improvement tools, audits, and focused streamlining efforts.

A major case study is used as an example in nearly every chapter to show how the principles and themes of this book are applied from the beginning of a procedure to the point where it is improved and published a second time. A Purchasing System was selected as the center of the case study for this book. Chapter 3, "*Focusing on a Case Study to Apply the Principles of this Book*" begins with an explanation of how and why a purchasing system was selected as a study topic for this book. A detailed flow chart and procedure are presented in the case study.

This case study is unique because it represents a real business process, flow chart, and procedure used in a company in California (Dataproducts Corporation, Woodland Hills, California). The principles of writing effective policies and procedures, communications, training, compliance, process improvement, and cost benefit analyses are applied to the case study. In Chapter 11, "*Conducting Profitable Continuous Improvement Activities*," a new flow chart and revised procedure of the original case study are presented to reflect streamlining efforts and the results of statistical studies presented in this book. In Chapter 12, "*Saving $1 Million with Cost Benefit Analyses*," a cost benefit study is conducted that results in millions of dollars being saved by selecting the most economical, cost efficient, and productive solution to the case study presented in Chapter 3.

This book goes beyond other books that teach you to write and publish policies and procedures and go no further. I provide answers to important questions that procedures analysts often face when writing, coordinating, publishing, communicating, training, measuring, improving, and revising policies and procedures. The questions to ask yourself are:

1. What can we do to ensure senior management endorses the efforts of the Policies and Procedures Department?

2. How can we be certain that management has included continuous improvement efforts in the company vision and strategic goals?

3. What can we do to ensure our users are involved with the writing, coordinating, and publishing of policies and procedures?

4. How can we be certain our target audiences (i.e., users) are following (or complying with) our published policies and procedures?

5. What can we be doing to be certain that our published policies and procedures reach all individuals identified in the target audiences?

6. How can we improve our analysis and research efforts of policies and procedures to ensure they will have a high degree of effectiveness even before they are approved and published?

7. How do we know if our communication and training efforts are being effective?

8. How do we ensure information communicated to our target audiences during training is also assimilated within their work environment?

9. What can we do to ensure our employees receive mentoring or coaching following training?

10. How do we know whether our policies and procedures meet or exceed 100% of the requirements of the managers, process owners, subject matter experts, and users?

11. How do we communicate the value of measuring business processes, policies, and procedures to target audiences?

12. How can we use statistics and quality tools to minimize variation of our published policies and procedures and get on the path toward achieving 100% compliance?

13. How can we be confident we have increased productivity, profits, sales, and customer satisfaction with our improvement efforts?

14. What can we do to help our organization become more receptive to learning and to sustaining change?

15. What can we do to help our company evolve into a "proactive" organization? How can we learn more about the culture of our organization and how we can influence the behavior of individuals?

16. What can procedures analysts do to become respected and recognized in his company, among his peers, and in his industry?

17. What can procedures analysts do to improve their skills and knowledge to help write effective policies and procedures and establish communication, training, compliance, auditing, and improvement plans?

18. What does the future hold for procedures analysts?

Publishing policies and procedures in any organization is not as easy as it may seem. While it may be simple to write policies and procedures, print them, and distribute them, it will have been a waste of time if users are just going to let these documents sit on a desk, in an in-basket, in a stock of papers, filed away in a manual, or deleted from an email or hard drive without ever being read!

Writing policies and procedures that are effective is more than just publishing documents that meet the requirements of management, process owners, and users. Writing policies and procedures that are easily understood and applied involves analyzing, writing, publishing, training, communicating, measuring, auditing, and continuously improving business processes and published policies and procedures.

ACHIEVING 100% COMPLIANCE IS AMBITIOUS!

The title of this book, "*Achieving 100% Compliance of Policies and Procedures,*" may seem ambitious to some readers but 100% compliance is achievable under the right circumstances. All organizations should have standards for acceptable compliance levels, the highest being companies who have achieved "Six Sigma" or 99.99966% compliance. These standards should be reflected in the organization's mission and vision statements as a commitment of management to the policies and procedures infrastructure and the goals and objectives of the policies and procedures department.

A SHORT SUMMARY ABOUT SIX SIGMA

"Six Sigma" is the most powerful breakthrough management tool ever devised, promising increased market share, cost reductions, and dramatic improvements in bottom-line profitability for companies of any size. Six Sigma is a process that enables companies to increase profits dramatically by streamlining operations, improving quality, and eliminating defects or mistakes in everything a company does, from filling out purchase orders to manufacturing airplane engines. While operational quality programs have focused on detecting and correcting defects, Six Sigma encompasses something broader — it provides specific methods to re-create the process itself so that defects are never produced in the first place (Harry, 2000).

Most companies operate at a 3 to 4 Sigma Level that equates to 66,807 defects per million for Level 3 and 6210 defects per million for Level 4. The cost of defects is roughly 20 to 30% of revenues for 3 to 4 Sigma. With Six Sigma approaching, there are fewer than 1 defect per 3 million opportunities and the cost of quality drops to less than 1 percent of sales. Other organizations may accept lower margins of error. The focus is not so much on the number of defects per million opportunities as it is on a systematic road map to reduce variability in a process. Six Sigma focuses on the process that creates or eliminates defects rather than the defects themselves, though defects typically decrease as the process improves.

THE PROCESS TO "ACHIEVE 100% COMPLIANCE" IS THE TRUE GOAL

Most companies who have worked diligently to achieve 100% compliance or other admirable goal such as certification as an ISO Quality Standards company, a Maturity Level of 2 or greater in the Capability Maturity Model, the Malcolm Baldrige Award, or Six Sigma will tell you that the process of trying to achieve these goals is most important. Focusing on the process to achieve difficult goals will yield many rewards like higher quality products and services, increased customer satisfaction, improved employee morale, improved business processes, policies and procedures, enhanced communication and training strategies, and a more integrated organizational infrastructure and culture. Even if you do not achieve your strategic goals, you should achieve high compliance levels by going through the processes and activities that are necessary to satisfy the stated goals of these programs. For instance, if Six Sigma is your goal and you achieve a compliance level of 90% and cannot just seem to get any higher, your organization will have experienced major changes and improvements that will only benefit your organization as you move forward. Your goal now is not to let your high compliance level slip, or go down.

GETTING TO 100% COMPLIANCE

How close you can get to 100% compliance, or how much variation (achieving 100% compliance means there is no variation) exists in your business processes or published policies and procedures, depends on the following four factors:

1. Nature of your Organization's Business. If your organization is in a business where any error is critical (e.g., nuclear facility, hospital, or airlines), then achieving a compliance range of 99.99966% (i.e., Six Sigma) to 100% should be your goal. If your organization's business is without life or death consequences, then achieving a comfort level of something less than 100% compliance might be satisfactory to management. These organizations can probably tolerate larger "margins of error" in their business processes and published policies and procedures. If lives are at stake, achieving the highest possible compliance is always the goal.

2. Organization's Vision and Mission. Depending on the organization's strategic goals, management may or may not wish to spend the time and money needed to achieve higher levels of compliance or goals like Six Sigma or ISO 9000 Quality Standards. Management may be satisfied with lesser compliance targets like 85% or even 75%. These figures equate to their comfort level. The procedures analyst should work closely with senior management to ensure the vision and mission statements reflect the company's position on achieving compliance for business processes, policies, and procedures. Management's commitment is critical to the success to the efforts of the Policies and Procedures Department.

3. Content of Policies and Procedures. Depending on the subject matter of a policy or procedure, achieving a compliance level of 100% may not be possible. For instance, if a procedure describes how to process a single

form, achieving 100% compliance may be possible because you can potentially control the size and behavior of an audience. If a procedure encompasses a large system, then achieving higher levels of compliance will be more difficult because the size and composition of an audience may not be known. When the total user population is unknown, collecting data for metrics and improvement programs will not be representative of the population.

Users tend to pay more attention to policies and procedures that personally affect their well being like benefits or compensation policies and procedures. Compliance is more likely to be closer to 100% if the content affects the pocketbook of a user. More effort is required for communication and training when the target audiences cannot see a direct benefit.

4. Organization's Receptivity to Change. The receptivity of an organization to change is often overlooked by procedures analysts. Successful implementation of policies and procedures depends on the organization's culture and attitude toward change. With many businesses being "reactive" in their approach to business, their attitude is typically "resistance to change." Guidelines are presented in this book to assist the procedures analyst with activities necessary to reduce the organization's "resistance to change" mentality and put into place business processes and procedures to help the organization evolve into a "forward-thinking" or "proactive" organization. Refer to Chapter 13, *"Preparing an Organization to be Receptive to Change,"* for further discussion on these topics.

➤If 100% compliance becomes a reality, then the goal is to maintain that level! Often the excitement of reaching a goal quickly wanes and when measurements are taken a second time, the compliance percentage drops off. Unfortunately, this happens frequently with those organizations that have achieved certification under ISO Quality Standards or the Capability Maturity Model (CMM). There is a strong momentum to achieve these victories the first time but it can become tedious and boring to keep up with the same level of effort to maintain the current status. The organization must find ways to keep the momentum flowing. The procedures analyst can play an important role by assisting senior management with these efforts. If the procedures analyst is not already involved, he can ask to be assigned to this company initiative.

RESISTANCE TO CHANGE MENTALITY

Procedures analysts and management often complain that people resist change and that it is difficult to implement a policies and procedures infrastructure. Unfortunately, these people rarely see themselves that way. Often, they see themselves as open and ready to accept new challenges and opportunities. From a systems viewpoint, it is often the organization's infrastructure, and not its people, which is rigid and inflexible, often leading to angry and frustrated employees. If people cannot approach problems, talk openly, or give opinions, then this prevailing attitude can cause withdrawal and people who do not care. The clearer the tie between what an organization is doing and their results, the more energy, commitment, and excitement they will generate during a change process. If the tie to results is fuzzy, the organization's strategic goals will eventually meet with resistance, apathy, or total ignorance. As a procedures analyst, your goal should be to start and end every effort at change with communication about performance improvement (refer to Chapter 4, *"Establishing a Communication Strategy"*). This message about performance improvement should include the importance of the change and how it impacts the bottom-line of the organization, i.e., profits, sales, revenues. The message could also include how the change affects productivity, quality, and even the employee's quality of life. This tie to results will ensure stronger commitment and participation when changes do occur.

When managers misunderstand what change requires, they issue edicts, make bold cuts, and provide new marching orders for people to follow. These managers believe that their actions will produce change. Very often, change is only superficial, temporary, or imagined. Real change requires dramatic, committed, and insightful leadership. Change is easier to accomplish when people are working with you to make it happen than when they are resisting change. Management must understand that it takes teamwork and working with employees to ensure any change is a smooth process. The procedures analyst knows this well: *He elicits the cooperation of employees, management, and sponsors early in the process of developing and coordinating business processes, policies, and procedures* (refer to Chapter 2, *"Writing Effective Policies and Procedures"*). This early buy-in to the new or revised business processes, policies, or procedures will prove helpful in achieving compliance.

Leaders should focus on understanding the business processes that slow or diminish change. Encouraging people to try harder, to become more committed, and to be more passionate, does not have a lasting effect. Sustaining change requires understanding and reinforcing growth processes and addressing the limits that keep change from occurring. Change cannot happen abruptly — people do not like to be suddenly faced with change. Change has to be continuous, slow, incremental, and closely monitored. This new content cannot be perceived as a threat to their culture, or environment in any way. The ironic truth is that the faster and more thoughtlessly people jump at change, the more carelessly they treat its effects, and the less flexible they become.

Change happens to all of us and to our organizations as well. Most of the time, however, we manage as if change has not happened or does not matter. We keep doing the same things we did yesterday, and when changes occur that force deviations from what we expect, we try to force situations back into their old patterns again. We have a hard time admitting that change has happened and that it matters. If we acknowledge that change matters, it means we have to change the way we do things, or the way we think about things, which can be difficult.

Today, virtually every firm has an improvement process under way. The efforts vary in concept, direction, intensity, and reward, but they are focused on achieving better performance. Organizations are chasing lower costs, higher quality, better service, higher levels of customer satisfaction, lower inventories, shorter cycle times, or some combination of these elements of business.

> The companies that succeed will be those that anticipate change and develop strategies in advance.

Change is inevitable as we are fast becoming a global marketplace. Technological change has continued to accelerate. Competition has increased and intensified. Companies now compete on global markets against global competitors. Customer expectations are rising. Attitudes and values are changing. Most importantly, our minds are changing, stretching to comprehend and cope with the implications of a world economy undergoing truly revolutionary change. As organizations fight to become recognized in their industry and strive to become number one, competition grows more intense. Continual change is needed to stay even or get ahead of the competition. Organizations need to recognize that "continual change" is here to stay and management must persistently work toward building a new mind-set open to accepting change. Organizations need to think and redesign their business processes and the manner in which they carry out their business. Benefits of improved business processes, policies, and procedures have moved beyond operational and tactical effectiveness to strategic effectiveness and positioning. The companies that succeed will be those that anticipate change and develop strategies in advance. This puts a premium on certain qualities of an organization like adaptability, flexibility, responsiveness, decisiveness, and speed. Organizations have no choice but to be anticipators and managers of change. Organizations can increase their flexibility and ability to anticipate change in a number of different ways. The development of effective core resources — financial, technological competencies, people, and so on strengthen the capacity of an organization to face new challenges. When executives talk about organizations, they frequently focus on the elements of organizational design, or the formal structures and systems that they develop to execute strategies. What has become clear is that organizational architecture can be a source of competitive advantage to the extent that it motivates, facilitates, or enables individuals and groups to interact more effectively with customers, work, and each other. The forces that are causing the rethinking of organizational architecture have become fairly evident: *Increasing competition, massive social and technological change, increasing government participation in economic affairs, and the evolution of global markets and thus global competition. Perhaps most important, the rate of change is increasing.* Organizations, therefore, need to increase their capacity to deal with uncertainty.

VALUE OF ORGANIZATIONS THAT ARE RECEPTIVE TO CHANGE

As organizations realize the value of creating a company that is receptive to change, changes that are made will have a higher chance of acceptance. As policies and procedures are written, published, communicated, trained, and deployed, they will be more readily accepted if the impact on the company's culture is kept in mind. If the organization has been conditioned to learn and to accept change, the likelihood of better-than-average compliance will increase.

> The best change processes are those that people invent for themselves.

The current approach to disseminating policies and procedures typically combines teaching with coercion, even though we would like to call it participative change. Self-initiated change based on real participation is something else entirely: *It is change from within.* This is why published policies and procedures do not always work. They are changed from outside: *It is somebody else's idea of how change should happen, or how change should feel.* If people are told to follow blindly simply because a policy or procedure has been approved, published, and distributed, this would be a mistake. Policies and procedures must be properly coordinated with process owners, users, and management before even thinking about publication and compliance reviews. People must be involved in the analysis and research phases when business processes are being studied to be truly participative. People usually do not oppose the content of proposed change, but it is the method by which the policies and procedures are disseminated, that tends to upset them. There have been many great business processes, policies, and procedures that failed at the onset because of an inadequate or nonexistent early coordination and deployment process that is unplanned.

This need for organizations to change should not be confused with actual change. Actual change takes real participation, emotion, and understanding. Change is more than training, slogans, creating a cross-functional team, or establishing a quality assurance department. Change is a new way of looking at the world. There is a big difference between a self-initiated change and change that comes at people from a training class, an email, or a voice mail message broadcast.

> Continuous quality improvement is not a linear process, but a cyclical process for achieving optimal performance and customer satisfaction (Harry, 2000).

Written policies and procedures are the direct result of a change in one or more business processes. Whether the change is a new process being deployed, a change in technologies, a revised form, or a simple paragraph change, the same steps used to create, publish, train, communicate, measure, report, and improve compliance of policies and procedures will be used. As this cycle continues and improvement activities are continuously implemented, the number of users complying with policies and procedures increases. Ideally, each incremental change will result in a higher compliance level. Continuous quality improvement is not a linear process, but a cyclical process for achieving optimal performance and customer satisfaction. Policies and procedures tell people that they need to change.

This book is based on the premise that the procedures analyst has written effective policies and procedures that can be measured and improved. Step-by-step guidelines are provided for writing effective policies and procedures for achieving 100% compliance and for ensuring continuous improvement profitability. Complete details for setting up a system of policies and procedures are contained in my earlier book, *"Establishing a System of Policies and Procedures."* Both books, this one and my earlier book about setting up a system of policies and procedures, are necessary to develop the framework for the policies and procedures infrastructure as well as ensuring that efforts are directed to ensuring that published policies and procedures are accepted by all the users.

Each of the 14 chapters of this book focus on achieving 100% compliance of policies and procedures through the following four themes and principles:

1. <u>Writing effective and well-coordinated policies and procedures that can be measured</u>. If the policies and procedures are designed and coordinated correctly the first time, there is a high probability that the first time compliance is measured, the policies and procedures will be at a compliance level that is acceptable by management.

2. <u>Focusing on the cyclical nature of continuous quality improvement</u>. Conducting continuous improvement activities is another major goal of this book. There are a variety of reasons that policies and procedures change. The procedures analyst must be alert to these changes in order to provide updates to policies and procedures as quickly as possible to ensure managers can make timely and appropriate decisions.

3. <u>Providing ongoing communication and training strategies</u>. A central theme in this book is to methodically and repeatedly seek out improvements and to promote current policies and procedures. Instead of communicating and training a topic only once, additional efforts need to be taken to ensure the topic is put before the users in the form of regular communications throughout the life cycle of the policy or procedure.

4. <u>Preparing an organization to be receptive to change</u>. The organization's culture and environment are often overlooked by procedures analysts and by strategic planners. The procedures analyst must develop a strong relationship with senior management to ensure they remain committed to the policies and procedures infrastructure. The procedures analyst must be closely involved with the culture, people, and environment of the organization to ensure that any change is positively received. Refer

to Chapter 13, *"Preparing an Organization to be Receptive to Change,"* for a complete discussion of this subject.

PLAN OF THE BOOK

This book is grouped into three parts for a total of 14 chapters: (1) Developing a Policies and Procedures Infrastructure; (2) Designing and Carrying out a Compliance Plan; and (3) Incorporating Improvements and Achieving Cost Savings. Each part builds on the previous one. First, the policies and procedures are written, implemented, communicated, and trained. A review plan is established that helps you to monitor external and internal changes that might affect the content of business processes, policies, and procedures. Next, the content of the policies and procedures is checked, measured, and audited. Quality tools and statistics are introduced to assist you develop metrics. And finally, profitable improvement activities are accomplished, and the cycle repeats itself. The cycle continues as policies and procedures are revised, published, communicated, trained, measured, and improved. Two chapters are added to this third part that focus on a "proactive" organization and the future of procedures analysts.

Each chapter contains relevant references. Flow charts, procedures, diagrams, tables, figures, and forms are placed along with the relevant text within each chapter. At the end of each chapter there are four important sections to assist you with learning the information within each chapter including (1) A checklist for change, (2) Applying what you have learned, (3) Achieve 100% compliance, and (4) References. At the end of the book, there are three appendices, a glossary of terms, and an index.

A case study presented in Chapter 3, *"Focusing on a Case Study to Apply the Principles of this Book,"* is used throughout the book as the main example to explain the fundamentals of achieving 100% compliance. The case study and its components (a procedure and flow chart) are referenced in nearly every chapter. In Chapter 11, *"Conducting Profitable Continuous Improvement Activities,"* the case study is revised based on the recommendations presented in this book. In Chapter 12, *"Saving $1 Million with Cost Benefit Analyses,"* time and cost studies are explained in detail to illustrate how major labor and material savings can be achieved through improvements. The book is structured so that each chapter builds on what you have learned in the preceding one. In Chapter 14, *"Looking to the Future,"* the procedures analyst is shown how to do an assessment of his career and of his skills and competencies as they relate policies and procedures' disciplines.

PART ONE
Developing a Policies
and Procedures Infrastructure

CHAPTER 1. Using a "Policies and Procedures Improvement Cycle" (PPIC) as the basis for achieving 100% compliance of business processes, and published policies and procedures. Deming's Plan-Do-Check-Act (PDCA) Cycle is used as the basis for this cycle.

CHAPTER 2. Importance of writing effective and well-structured policies and procedures that can be measured and improved. A 40-step process is presented to show the steps needed to coordinate, design, write, and publish policies and procedures. A standard writing format is recommended for the structure of all policies and procedures with an organization. The concept of a baseline is addressed.

CHAPTER 3. A case study is presented that is used in nearly every chapter to illustrate the principles and themes of this book. A flow chart and procedure based on the case study are presented and become "working" examples for each chapter.

CHAPTER 4. Importance of establishing a continuous communication strategy that the procedures analyst can use when disseminating published policies and procedures. Examples are presented for designing and implementing continuous communications to ensure the audiences are continually reminded to refer to and use the business processes and published policies and procedures. Twenty communication methods are presented and compared.

CHAPTER 5. Development of an effective training strategy for teaching users within target audiences. The difference between learning and training is discussed. The importance of mentoring and coaching employees is introduced as a necessary supplement to training to ensure learning takes place. Nine training methods and techniques are presented.

CHAPTER 6. Using a review and communication control plan to monitor new laws, tax changes, organizational changes, communication and training strategies as an effort to ensure procedures analysts keep current with company events, both internal and external.

PART TWO
Designing and Carrying out
a Compliance Plan

CHAPTER 7. Development of a compliance plan to use checklists, check sheets, scatter diagrams, run charts, control charts, histograms, Pareto charts, and systems audits to measure the compliance and stability of business processes, policies, and procedures.

CHAPTER 8. Development of a "Self-Assessment Checklist" for audiences to "self-inspect" their work when doing business processes, policies, and procedures.

CHAPTER 9. Selecting and designing appropriate continuous improvement tools (also called "quality tools") to measure business processes and published policies and procedures. Five examples of quality tools are used to illustrate the information presented in the case study. This information is used in Chapters 11 and 12 to show how improvements are actually made.

CHAPTER 10. Designing and doing systems audits to identify system failures and operating deficiencies in business processes, policies and procedures. A questionnaire is presented that asks pertinent questions about the case study. These audits are also used to support the conclusions of the other compliance methods.

PART THREE
Incorporating Improvements and
Achieving Cost Savings

CHAPTER 11. Findings from plans that were developed in earlier chapters are referenced and discussed to develop an improvement plan and establish a cross-functional team to study the results and responses from target audiences. Streamlining methods are presented that are used to make improvements to business processes and published policies and procedures. Solutions are reviewed and an idea is formed that results in the case study being re-engineered; a new flow chart and procedure are presented.

CHAPTER 12.   Cost benefit analyses are used to show how significant cost savings can be achieved through improvements to policies and procedures. A cost comparison of the original procedure (i.e., in the case study) and the new, re-engineered, procedure is illustrated. The results of the cost comparison are explained with possible ways to use and present the information to management.

CHAPTER 13.   Building a "proactive" organization to be receptive to change and continue to evolve. Guidelines for the procedures analyst for assisting senior management evolve toward or become a "proactive" organization are presented. Twelve ideal goals for a model "proactive" organization are presented as a starting point for management to establish a similar set of goals. The goals represent the minimum goals for senior management.

CHAPTER 14.   Examining a career path for the procedures analyst. He is shown how to take an assessment of his core competencies and skills; he is also shown additional activities he could be doing to become the best procedures analyst in his company and industry.

AUDIENCE

This book is aimed at business professionals who are responsible for writing, coordinating, publishing, communicating, measuring, auditing, and improving policies and procedures for their department or organization. This book is useful to employees at any level including managers, supervisors, team leaders, team members, and areas responsible for administration, human resources, forms management, quality assurance, quality control, information technology, web technology, finance, accounting, auditing, documentation, or technical writing. Employee involvement could be in the form of analysis, research, writing, coordination, approvals, publication, communications, training, measurements and data collection, or cost benefit analyses. Employees may also be called to attend or participate in events that involve business processes, policies, and procedures including team meetings, department meetings, company meetings, interviews, surveys, quality reviews, presentations, and so on.

THE INFLUENCE OF "Establishing a System of Policies and Procedures"

This book on "Compliance and policies and procedures" would have been difficult to write without my first two books on the subject of setting up a system of policies and procedures. My first book, *"Business Policies and Procedures Handbook,"* addressed setting up a system of policies and procedures for printed manuals; it was written in 1984. My second book, *"Establishing a System of Policies and Procedures,"* written in 1998 replaced my first book. This second book includes sections on writing policies and procedures for a network and the Intranet — it is still current and provides the building blocks, or framework, for developing a policies and procedures infrastructure.

This third book is a continuation of the second book as it provides guidelines for achieving 100% compliance by minimizing variation, improving quality, and assuring business processes, policies, and procedures are cost effective. This book does <u>NOT</u> replace the second book. This third book is a "how-to" book for measuring business processes and published policies and procedures, ensuring variation is minimized, enhancing quality, reducing cycle time and cost, and achieving 100% compliance. Each chapter is based on practical, proven guidelines and examples from a "real life" case study to provide new insights and show you how to make better decisions.

> Build the framework, measure it, make improvements, achieve comprehension and compliance, and help your organization evolve into a proactive organization!

►This book is a <u>must-read</u> and is an <u>ADDITION</u> to my book, *"Establishing a System of Policies and Procedures,"* that focuses on building a framework. This new book focuses on metrics, quality tools, audits, continuous improvements, communications, training, mentoring, and cost benefit analyses. These are areas often overlooked by procedures analysts. This book has been written to help the procedures analyst improve his core competencies and skills in these areas.

TERMS FREQUENTLY USED IN THIS BOOK (refer to Glossary of Terms)

<u>Business Process</u>. A process is a structured, measured set of activities designed to produce a specified output for a particular customer or market. A process places a strong emphasis on *how* work is done within an organization. A business process does not always result in a written policy or procedure. There are hundreds of "unwritten" business processes like contacting a computer help desk, using a FAX machine, contacting the benefits or payroll department for assistance, or making complaints to a healthcare provider, that have yet to be converted to procedures.

<u>Policy</u>. A policy is a general strategy or guideline and a predetermined course of action established as a guide toward accepted business strategies and objectives. Policies create expectations and guides for action. In most organizations, the policy document will provide the general guidelines for procedures and work instructions.

<u>Procedure</u>. A procedure is a plan of action for achieving a policy; it provides the instructions needed to carry out a policy statement. Procedures provide the means by which the actions (provided by a policy) can be carried out by management and by employees. A procedure is always the result of one or more business processes.

<u>Continuous Improvement Tools</u> (also quality tools). Continuous improvement tools refer to charts, diagrams, matrixes, presentation techniques, or other methods used to measure the compliance of policies and procedures. These tools help the procedures analyst to begin or sustain any quality improvement effort.

<u>Procedures Analyst</u>. The term *procedures analyst* is used to represent that person or group of persons responsible either for coordinating the efforts needed to establish a policies and procedures infrastructure or for researching, writing, coordination, publishing, implementing, communications, training, doing compliance activities, auditing, and conducting continuous improvement activities. In some cases, the term, "Policies and Procedures Department," will be used to refer to the functional area where the procedures analyst works.

<u>He</u>. The traditional, "He," will be used because it is generally accepted in literature. Every attempt will be made to use gender-free terms, instead of a gender term. Rather than using, "He fills in the purchase requisition . . . ," a sentence with a gender-free term could read, "Employees complete purchase requisitions . . ." While I prefer, "He or She," the traditional "He," will be used instead.

Policies and Procedures Infrastructure. A framework that refers to a system of resources, people, facilities, documents, equipment, hardware, software, training, forms, reports, tools, and anything needed to ensure the successful operation of a policies and procedures system in an organization.

Compliance. Compliance is defined as conforming or adapting to a rule. From this definition, compliance is assumed to be 100% of an effort. Total compliance is defined as 100% of an activity; in other words when compliance is 100%, each individual identified in a target audience complies with an activity. Compliance can also be loosely defined as achieving a "comfort level," or a stable process, within a predefined margin of error.

Variation. Variation is the extent to which things vary from one to the next. A primary goal of statistical process control (SPC) is to reduce variation in inputs, methods, and outputs. The measurement of variation is a critical component of control charts.

Target Audiences. Loosely defined as the users of a system. Users could be defined as employees, customers, suppliers, or any group which uses a process, policy, or procedure or is impacted by these documents. The word *target* is used because the term *audiences* could refer to one, two, or more groups of employees, or all employees. If users of a new purchasing system were only buyers within a Purchasing Department, then they would be considered a target audience. If a procedure can be used by all employees, then a specific audience would not be targeted, rather the audience in the policy or procedure would be referred to as, "All employees affected."

Life Cycle. Life cycle is a term used to describe how long a policy or procedure remains active and in use by audiences. The cycle extends from initiation to approval to publication to communication, training, measurement, improvement, revision, and so on, until the policy or procedure becomes obsolete. This means that the job of the procedures analyst does not stop after the policies and procedures are published and implemented. The procedures analyst must continue to monitor all business processes, policies, and procedures until they are permanently removed from the policies or procedures infrastructure.

ACKNOWLEDGMENTS

This book could never have been written without the experience I gained from the many multinational companies for which I have worked during the past 30 years, both in a full-time capacity and in a consulting role. I have held managerial and non-managerial positions and have been involved with all phases of researching, coordinating, writing, publishing, communicating, training, measuring, auditing, and improving business processes and policies and procedures. I also had the pleasure of helping other teams, departments, and divisions incorporate new or revised business processes and policies and procedures. As this experience of developing and designing policies and procedures infrastructures was repeated, my techniques became more refined. I have used this knowledge of policies and procedures in writing this book. In looking back at my career, I think that the varied assignments (e.g., projects, company initiatives, implementing new systems) I worked on helped me write this book. In addition to my policies and procedures experience, some of these projects included Total Quality Management (TQM), ISO 9000 Quality Standards, Capability Maturity Model (CMM), the Malcolm Baldrige Award, Six Sigma, Statistical Process Control (SPC), Value Engineering, Software Life Cycle, Quality Circles, and the study material used to achieve certification in one quality association, one records association, and one forms association.

The two jobs that contributed most to my career and to the writing of this book included a position of ten years as Policy Development Manager at Datatape, a division of Eastman Kodak, in Pasadena, California and a position as a Quality Analyst at Qwest Communications in Dublin, Ohio. I had excellent managers for both of these jobs. They permitted me to participate in various associations, attend seminars, read books to improve my job skills, and transfer my knowledge to other employees and departments, through training and mentoring roles.

I wish to thank James Maxwell, Supplier Manager - Systems Purchasing, of Mettler Toledo, Inc., in Worthington, Ohio for his advice and expertise on purchasing matters. This company is the world's largest Marketer of weighing instruments of use in laboratory, industrial, and food retailing applications. James has more than 39 years of experience in the purchasing field. The case study selected for this book is about purchasing activities and James was gracious to help edit the two flow charts and two procedures in Chapters 3 and 11.

He spent many hours of his own time editing the procedures and he permitted me to conduct several interviews with him and his staff. He helped me find alternate solutions to the labor, intensive *Purchasing System* process selected for the first case study. The solution selected to significantly improve this *Purchasing System* was a *Purchase Card System*, i.e., second cast study. You will find that this solution is the correct choice after you read this book as the first case study is transformed into this choice in Chapter 11, *"Conducting Profitable Continuous Improvement Activities."*

James provided the actual procedure used at Mettler Toledo for "Purchase Cards"(the primary exception was the dollar amount for the purchase cards: *Mettler Toledo used $25,000 and I used $500.00*). Most of the content of the Mettler Toledo "Purchase Card" procedure was incorporated into the *Purchase Card System* procedure referenced in Chapter 11, *"Conducting Profitable Continuous Improvement Activities."*

I owe special thanks to my daughter, Lisa, for editing this book. She took time away from her busy schedule to read my book. She also assisted me with the design of the book cover.

I sincerely thank my wife and family for allowing me to spend countless days, nights, and weekends to write, publish, and advertise this book.

Part One

Developing a Policies and Procedures Infrastructure

Part One contains six chapters which start with an overview of continuous quality improvement and continue with guidelines for writing effective policies and procedures that can be measured. A case study is presented which will be used as a major example in most of the chapters in the book. Effective methods for communicating and training published policies and procedures are presented. The last chapter introduces a method by which the procedures analyst can monitor potential changes in an organization to anticipate changes to business processes, policies, and procedures.

Chapter 1

Introducing the Policies and Procedures Improvement Cycle

Continuous quality improvement is a major principle and theme of this book. Change is continuous, and as shown in Figure 1-1 below, the process to achieve continuous quality improvement is iterative, or repetitive. Achieving 100% compliance of policies and procedures does not happen the first time a policy or procedure is published; it takes a plan of action to coordinate the processes and activities necessary to set the stage for achieving the ambitious goal of achieving 100% compliance. Major changes are possible with re-engineering projects, but incremental changes are the norm. Ideally, each change is added to the previous change with the goal of improving the business process, policy, or procedure. This change process begins when a problem, issue, or concern is identified. The problem is analyzed and researched. The solution is selected and transformed into a draft policy or procedure that is coordinated, approved, published, and communicated. The published policy or procedure is measured and audited and the findings are reviewed, reported, and any improvements are incorporated in the business process, policy, or procedure.

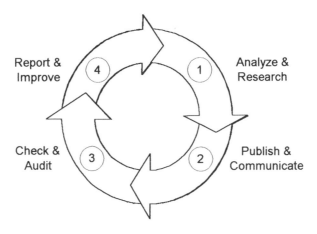

FIGURE 1-1: *Policies and Procedures Improvement Cycle (PPIC)*

This iterative process as illustrated in Figure 1-1 above, is referred to as the "Policies and Procedures Improvement Cycle" (PPIC). The PPIC is a four-phase process that takes you from Phase 1, "Analyze & Research," through Phase 4, "Report & Improve" each time a change is considered. This cycle is the basis for this book and is founded on solid quality principles. The "Policies and Procedures Improvement Cycle" (PPIC) is tailored after quality expert, Dr. W. Edwards Deming's "Plan-Do-Check-Act (PDCA)" Cycle. Both cycles have four phases, run clockwise, and are iterative. The PDCA Cycle was originally developed in the 1930s by quality expert, Walter Shewart. The cycle was later pioneered by Deming where the PDCA Cycle became known as the "Deming Wheel" as illustrated Figure 1-2.

Figure 1-2: *Deming Wheel*

The *Deming Wheel* was designed to be used in a team environment to tackle problems and find solutions. This cycle has traditionally been used as a systematic method for solving problems and improving business processes that can be repeated on different problems or opportunities. Deming emphasized that changing systems alone do not assure continuing improvements unless there is continuous training and education commitment to all employees. The PDCA problem-solving technique has been used by hundreds of thousands of companies when planning, implementing, checking compliance, and making improvements to problems, issues, or concerns.

> The PDCA Cycle can be used by a team to find a solution to a problem.
> The PPIC can be used to turn a solution into a policy or procedure.

The PDCA Cycle was selected as the underlying framework for the PPIC because the phases are similar in content and goals. The primary difference is the resulting application of the cycle. The PDCA Cycle is used in team problem-solving sessions and the PPIC can be applied to any business process, policy, and procedure regardless of size or complexity. Both the PDCA Cycle and the PPIC start from some kind of problem, issue, or concern. In Table 1-1, the four phases of both PDCA and PPIC are compared.

TABLE 1-1: *Phase Comparison of PDCA and PPIC*

PHASE	PDCA CYCLE	PPIC
1	PLAN	Analyze and Research
2	DO	Publish and Communicate
3	CHECK	Check and Audit
4	ACT	Report and Improve

Writing effective policies and procedures requires solid problem-solving skills. Problems are turned into solutions; solutions are transformed into policies and procedures; policies and procedures are published, communicated, trained, measured, and improved, and the process begins again, hence the cycle. The comparison of the two cycles becomes clear when you review the details of each cycle in Table 1-2.

TABLE 1-2: *Detailed Comparison of PDCA and PPIC*

PDCA	PPIC	
	Analyze & Research	
PLAN Identify and Analyze Problem	1	Identify the business processes that impact the problem and select one or more processes for analysis and research.
	2	Define the problem and develop objectives.
	3	List the steps in the processes as they now exist.
	4	Identify possible causes of the problems or issues.
	5	Collect and analyze data related to the problems or issues.
	6	Review current flow charts, or create new flow charts of the work flow.
	7	Verify or revise the original problem statement.
	8	Identify root causes of the problem using a cause-and-effect diagram or a Pareto analysis.

		Publish & Communicate
DO Develop Solutions and Implement Plan	9	Set measurable goals for the problem solving effort.
	10	Establish a process for coordinating with and gaining the approval of senior management.
	11	Establish criteria for selecting a solution.
	12	Generate possible solutions that will address the root causes of the problem.
	13	Do cost benefit analyses of the possible solutions.
	14	Select a solution based on the results of the cost benefit analyses.
	15	Gain approval and support for the selected solution.
	16	Plan and implement the solution through published policies and procedures.
	17	Communicate and train the information contained in the published policies and procedures.

		Check & Audit
CHECK Evaluate the Results	18	Design appropriate metrics to measure the compliance of published policies and procedures.
	19	Gather data from logs, forms, reports, and other documents used to implement and monitor published policies and procedures.
	20	Analyze the data using continuous improvement tools to analyze a business process before and after a solution is selected.
	21	Continuously monitor the performance of the business process after the improvement is in place.
	22	Check progress frequently with customers.
	23	Prepare findings in a formal report for submission to management.

Was your Goal achieved?

If Yes, go to the ACT (Report & Improve) phase

If No, return to the PLAN (Analyze & Research) phase

		Report & Improve
ACT Use Feedback to Improve and to Replan	24	Conduct cost benefit analyses and prepare findings in a report.
	25	Submit reports to management and obtain approvals for incorporation of changes.
	26	Adopt a solution, implement changes to business processes, policies, or procedures, and execute communication and training strategies.
	27	Plan ongoing monitoring of the published policies and procedures and continue to look for incremental improvements.

PPIC: A GLOBAL USE OF PDCA

The four phases of the PPIC are a global use of the PDCA Cycle. In the *"PLAN"* (Analyze & Research) phase, the scope and objectives are defined. The new process (or revision of a current process) is thoroughly analyzed and researched and a Pareto analysis is used to prioritize the main solutions to the problem or new process. In the *"DO"* (Publish & Communicate) phase, the business processes are transformed into published policies and procedures using a standardized writing format. The policies and procedures are communicated and trained as they are deployed. In the *"CHECK"* (Check & Audit) phase, data is gathered for self-assessment checklists, continuous improvement tools, and systems audits. In the *"ACT"* (Report & Improve) phase, the results of the "CHECK" phase are coordinated with policy and procedure teams that are focused on making improvements to current business processes, policies, and procedures. The approved changes are incorporated into the policies and procedures infrastructure as new or revised policies and procedures. The cycle continues clockwise to the first phase again. Both the PDCA Cycle and the PPIC are continuous processes and should be viewed as continuous or cyclical. For the PDCA Cycle, the team needs to set goals to measure success; otherwise, the team may feel like the problem is not being solved. For the PPIC, the process is truly iterative. Management must set strategic goals to improve business processes continuously, policies, and procedures for an organization to remain competitive. Each phase of the PPIC is listed and compared to chapter titles in Table 1-3 below.

TABLE 1-3: *Chapter Titles and PPIC Phases*

PPIC PHASE	CH.	CHAPTER TITLE
ANALYZE & RESEARCH	2	Writing Effective Policies and Procedures
	3	Focusing on a Case Study to Apply the Principles of this Book
PUBLISH & COMMUNICATE	4	Establishing a Communication Strategy
	5	Developing an Effective Training Strategy
CHECK & AUDIT	6	Creating a Review and Communication Control Plan
	7	Establishing a Compliance Plan
	8	Developing Self-Assessment Checklists
	9	Using Continuous Improvement Tools to Measure Compliance
	10	Conducting Systems Audits
REPORT & IMPROVE	11	Conducting Profitable Continuous Improvement Activities
	12	Saving $1 Million with Cost Benefit Analyses
	13	Preparing an Organization to be Receptive to Change
	14	Looking to the Future

The "Introduction" provided important information about achieving 100% compliance, change processes, resistance to change, and the value of an organization that is receptive to change. Each chapter in this book brings you one step closer to achieving 100% compliance to policies and procedures. You can think of each chapter topic as adding one building block to the strategic plan of achieving 100% compliance to published policies and procedures.

CHECKLIST FOR CHANGE:

✓ The concept of a "Policies and Procedures Improvement Cycle" (PPIC) is introduced for the continuous improvement of business processes and published policies and procedures.

✓ The "Plan-Do-Check-Act" (PDCA) Cycle is a problem solving technique that is generally used to resolve problems, issues, or concerns. The PDCA Cycle can also be used as the first step of the PPIC.

✓ The "Policies and Procedures Improvement Cycle" (PPIC) is a global use of the PDCA Cycle as it is applied to writing effective policies and procedures for a policies and procedures infrastructure. The PDCA Cycle can be viewed as the first phase of the PPIC, "Analyze & Research."

✓ The PDCA Cycle can be viewed as a part of the "Analyze & Research" Phase of the PPIC. The PDCA Cycle helps to find solutions to problems, issues, or concerns. The PPIC applies the concepts of the PDCA Cycle on a much larger scale than was originally intended by quality experts' Shewhart and Deming.

✓ The PPIC will help you transform business processes into policies and procedures and achieve 100% compliance of published policies and procedures through the continuous cycling of the four phases of the PPIC.

APPLYING WHAT YOU HAVE LEARNED:

Use the "Plan-Do-Check-Act" (PDCA) Cycle for solving problems in a team environment and for evaluating business processes related to the specific problem.

Use the "Policies and Procedures Improvement Cycle" (PPIC) for developing an effective policies and procedures infrastructure which includes published policies and procedures that are continuously being improved and communicated, to move closer to the goal of 100% compliance.

Review your business processes, prioritize them, and start the process of transforming them into approved policies and procedures using the PPIC method.

ACHIEVE 100% COMPLIANCE:

In this first chapter, you have been introduced to the "Policies and Procedures Improvement Cycle" (PPIC) that will help you achieve 100% compliance of published policies and procedures. Through the iterative nature of the PPIC process, each change should build on the previous change. In the ideal world, each change will be an incremental improvement, and eventually, 100% compliance can be reached.

REFERENCES:

Bemowski, Karen and Straton, Brad, *101 Good Ideas - How to Improve Just About Any Process*, ASQ Quality Press, Milwaukee, Wisconsin, 1998.

Berry, Thomas H, *Managing the Total Quality Transformation*, McGraw-Hill, Inc., New York, New York, 1991.

Edosomwan, Dr. Johnson A., *Organizational Transformation and Process Reengineering*, St. Lucie Press, Delray Beach, Florida, 1996.

Harrington, H. James, *Business Process Improvement*, McGraw-Hill, Inc., New York, New York, 1991.

Harrington, H. James; Esseling, Erik K.C., Van Nimwegen, harm, *Business Process Improvement Workbook*, McGraw-Hill, Inc., New York, New York, 1997.

Nadler, David A; Gerstein, Marc S; and Shaw, Robert B. and Associates, *Organizational Architecture*, Jossey-Bass Publishers, San Francisco, California, 1992.

Page, Stephen B, *Establishing a System of Policies and Procedures*, BookMasters, Inc., Mansfield, Ohio, 1998.

Poirier, Charles, C. and Houser, William, F., *Business Partnering for Continuous Improvement*, Berrett-Koehler Publications, San Francisco, California, 1993.

Scherkenbach, William W. *The Deming Route to Quality and Productivity*, CEEPress Books, Washington, D.C., 1991.

Senge, Peter; Kleiner, Art; Roberts, Charlotte; Ross, Richard; Roth, George, Smith, Bryan, *The Dance of Change*, Doubleday, New York, New York, 1999.

Shewhart, Walter A., *Statistical Method from the Viewpoint of Quality Control*, Dover Publications, Inc., New York, New York, 1986.

Chapter 2

Writing Effective Policies and Procedures

Understandably, achieving 100% compliance of policies and procedures is an ambitious goal! Reaching 100% compliance is a possibility but it is unlikely to occur the first time policies and procedures are published and measured. In fact, 100% compliance may <u>never</u> be achieved but at least you can get close and make significant improvements along the way. When policies and procedures are measured for the first time, the likely compliance percentage will range from as low as 5% to as high as 75% (these figures may vary depending on your organization or industry). A figure higher than 75% is possible but unlikely <u>except</u> in the case of policies and procedures that significantly affect the well being of the target audiences. Employees tend to read and apply any process, policy, procedure, standard, or form that affects their quality of life. For instance, compensation or benefit policies often receive high acceptance because they directly affect the pocketbook of the employee! Compare this kind of policy to an engineering procedure. Which one would you read first?

The purpose of this chapter is to provide the reader with methods and guidelines for achieving the highest degree of success the first time the policies and procedures are published and communicated. The 40-step plan of action used to write effective policies and procedures is used during the first phase (i.e., Analyze & Research) of the "Policies and Procedures Improvement Cycle" (PPIC) a concept that was introduced in Chapter 1, "*Introducing the Policies and Procedures Improvement Cycle.*" The last few steps of the 40-step plan overlap into the second phase (i.e., Publish & Communicate) of the PPIC. Five important areas for writing effective policies and procedures are addressed below:

1. Management commitment is crucial to setting up a policies and procedures function

2. Importance of the key word, "effective," to writing policies and procedures and building a policies and procedures infrastructure

3. Plan of action for writing effective policies and procedures and monitoring their life cycle from publication, communications, training, measurement, and improvement

4. Usefulness of a flow chart to illustrate business processes for the purpose of analyzing graphically, researching, and improving business processes

5. Necessity of using a standard, structured writing format for policies and procedures

The concept of a *baseline* is introduced as a means of setting a standard, or goal, to measure progress or change to a policy or procedure.

MANAGEMENT COMMITMENT - A KEY TO SUCCESS or FAILURE

The commitment of senior management and the effectiveness of their communication to their staff is pivotal to the success of the policies and procedures system. While the procedures analyst can still implement a policies and procedures infrastructure without total management commitment, the system will ultimately fail without full support and sponsorship. Support can start with one senior manager becoming a sponsor for the efforts of the procedures analyst. This senior manager can promote the efforts and the importance of writing effective policies and procedures and achieving 100% compliance to the rest of the senior managers.

> Without management commitment, the policies and procedures infrastructure will eventually fail.

Employees need to feel comfortable that their management supports continuous improvement efforts. Without this comfort "zone," employees become fearful of making improvement suggestions or participating on improvement teams. Management can show their support through continual communications and corporate strategic goals and objectives. Management can use every opportunity (e.g., staff meetings, company meetings, newsletters, personal letters, or attendance to meetings conducted by procedures analysts) to show their sponsorship of continuous improvement programs and the policies and procedures infrastructure. They can also promote the Policies and Procedures Department as being the individuals who will publish and implement the policies and procedures infrastructure for the organization.

IMPORTANCE OF WRITING "EFFECTIVE" POLICIES AND PROCEDURES

The key word in this section heading is "effective." The word has different meanings to people and can give a different impression, subject to individual perceptions based on each person's own experiences. The term *effective* is defined as producing a decided, decisive, or desired effect. Synonyms to *effective* are well-coordinated, competent, impressive, powerful, convincing, and proficient. Applying this definition and synonyms to writing policies and procedures, these descriptive words focus on quality, productivity, efficiency, user buy-in and acceptance, structured writing format, easy-to-read content, and thorough research and analysis.

The benefits of writing well-coordinated, convincing, proficient, and competent policies and procedures include:

1. <u>Well-coordinated</u> policies and procedures imply that a problem, issue, or concern has been discussed with process owners, management, users, and other individuals that may have a direct impact on or may be impacted by a forthcoming policy or procedure. A flow chart is often used as a visual representation of a business process and an excellent "talking" tool for the procedures analyst when discussing new or revised business processes, policies, or procedures with users and management. The more involved the users are in the early stages of the analysis and research phase of writing effective policies and procedures, the more likely they will ready accept a policy or procedure when it is implemented, communicated, and trained.

2. <u>Convincing</u> policies and procedures suggest that the published policies and procedures contain benefits to the reader, are easy to train, easy to understand, and easy to apply to the work environment. Policies and procedures that are easy to read and understand implies that a structured writing format is used. A standard, structured writing format is introduced later in this chapter.

3. <u>Proficient</u> and <u>competent</u> policies and procedures suggest that the best solution was selected by those individuals that assisted with the coordination of the draft policies and procedures. This also suggests that the appropriate quality tools (e.g., brainstorming, affinity diagrams, Pareto charts, cause-and-effect diagrams, or flow charts) may have been

used in the evaluation process. The endorsement of senior management can add to policies and procedures being viewed as proficient and competent.

After writing well-coordinated, convincing, proficient, and competent policies and procedures, the resulting approved and published policies and procedures should be easy to communicate, train, review, measure, audit, and improve. A structured writing format lends itself to writing clear and logical sentences that can be easily measured. Measurement is important because without it, your policies and procedures may fall victim to the phrase, *"Data that is not measured is only an opinion."* This phrase will be discussed in more detail in Chapter 9, *"Using Continuous Improvement Tools to Measure Compliance."*

If your policies and procedures are written in the most effective and efficient manner the first time they are published, and a continuous communication and training strategy is deployed, then there is a good possibility that when these published policies and procedures are measured the compliance percentage will be <u>higher</u> than if the policies and procedures were hastily written and implemented without coordination and research. The higher the compliance percentage is at the onset, the time necessary to achieve acceptable compliance levels should be less. The initial compliance figures are likely to be quite low if the policies and procedures are written and published quickly with little regard for the users of the system and how they might receive information that is being forced upon them.

Personal Example

> *When I worked at Qwest Communications in Dublin, Ohio, the Product Assurance Department developed and implemented an automated software configuration management system without considering the primary users of the system. The system was implemented quickly because of a management deadline. The configuration management system (and processes, policies, and procedures) received unfavorable response and it took more than nine months for the Product Assurance Department to backtrack, work with users, and publish the system properly. Compliance of this system was about 5% when published. When coordinated and published correctly, the compliance percentage jumped to 80%. The users were pleased that they were involved with the coordination of*

the new system — this resulted in early buy-in. I have since left Qwest
and I do not know if the compliance levels have gone up or down.

Another unfortunate situation is when an individual assigned to write a policy or procedure thinks he is the "subject matter expert" and does not consult anyone when doing the research and writing the policy or procedure. The result is a policy or procedure that often does not consider the impact it may have on other policies and procedures, different functional areas, or customers. The effect of these hastily written, and poorly researched and coordinated policies and procedures, is that few people follow these published policies and procedures or even know that they were disseminated for general use. Achieving any reasonable level of compliance is improbable.

PLAN OF ACTION FOR WRITING EFFECTIVE POLICIES AND PROCEDURES

This plan of action contains 40 steps for writing policies and procedures that are well-coordinated, convincing, proficient, and competent. Details behind many of these steps are found in my earlier book, *"Establishing a System of Policies and Procedures."* This earlier book is especially useful for setting up the framework, or system, of policies and procedures. In this plan of action, emphasis has been placed on assuring that any person reading these 40 steps for the first time will gain a clear understanding about what has to be accomplished from start to finish. The steps are not explained in any detail because it is expected that the procedures analyst already has a system of policies and procedure in place or in the process of developing one.

PLAN OF ACTION

Management Function

1. Show commitment to the Policies and Procedures Department by including statements in their vision, mission, strategic goals, and objectives about writing effective business processes, policies, and procedures, communicating, training, mentoring, measuring, improving, and achieving 100% compliance.

2. Assign a person or group to manage a policies and procedures function who will be accountable for the policies and procedures infrastructure from analysis to implementation and from compliance to improvement.

3. Review the mission, vision, and business strategic goals of the organization. Compare these statements with those of the Policies and Procedures Department.

4. Identify a process, problem, issue, or concern that needs to be improved or documented. Some of these problems or issues might include high cost, long cycle times, errors, rework, or delays.

5. Start identifying process owners, management sponsors, and primary user contacts.

6. Define the high level process, scope, mission, objective(s), and boundaries of the process.

7. Establish a cross-functional team to study the process and find several alternate solutions. Establish a team charter, ground rules, and guidelines for the operation of the cross functional team. Set goals to know when you are successful and when the team has completed its objectives.

8. Select a team leader — the team leader is normally the procedures analyst. If the team leader is not the procedures analyst, the role of facilitator should be assigned to him so he can remain accountable for the business processes, policies, and procedures. The team leader can also serve as the facilitator.

9. Provide team training (e.g., problem-solving, listening skills, and interviewing skills, as well as the use of continuous improvement tools like affinity charts, brainstorming, flow charts, Pareto analysis, control charts, run charts, scatter diagrams, histograms, and flow charts).

10. Discuss a high level overview of the process, issues, concerns, and challenges, and brainstorm with the team members.

11. Challenge current assumptions and accepted business processes, policies, and procedures.

12. Define internal interfaces and responsibilities.

13. Diagram the process flow using a flow chart format to depict the relationships of all the activities in the process.

14. Identify problem areas, discuss, and verify key causes; document and rank the causes using the Pareto analysis quality tool.

15. Collect cost, time, and value data for future measurement purposes.

16. Observe the process first-hand by "walking through" the various departments. Identify any new problems, or shortcomings, of the process. Interview additional people as needed. Document any new findings and redraw your flow chart.

17. Identify short-term improvements to the process.

18. Concentrate on streamlining the process and resolving differences.

19. Update flow chart and write a summary of the tasks and activities from the flow chart.

20. Generate a list of possible solutions.

21. Prioritize the solutions using the Pareto analysis quality tool and select the most significant solution.

22. Test the solution with the process owners, management sponsors, and primary users; identify any new issues and refine the solution. Redraw the flow chart and revise the detailed process flow as necessary.

23. Transform process documentation and flow charts into a draft policy or procedure using a standard writing format for policies and procedures.

24. Obtain approvals of the draft policy or procedure from the cross-functional team, users, and other affected parties like customers or suppliers. Obtain final approval from senior management following the user approvals.

25. Establish a communication strategy (Chapter 4, *"Establishing a Communication Strategy"*), training campaign (Chapter 5, *"Developing an Effective Training Strategy"*), and review plan (Chapter 6, *"Creating a Review and Communication Control Plan"*).

26. Publish the approved policy or procedure.

27. Begin the communication campaign (Chapter 4).

28. Conduct formal and informal training in accordance with the master communication strategy and the training strategy (Chapter 5).

29. Create a review and communication control plan (Chapter 6).

30. Establish a compliance plan (Chapter 7).

31. Conduct continuous improvement activities using tools like checklists (Chapter 8), control charts, histograms, or scatter diagrams to evaluate the effectiveness of the published policies and procedures (Chapter 9).

32. Conduct systems audits to supplement the continuous improvement activities (Chapter 10).

33. Conduct improvement activities and cost benefit analyses (Chapters 11 and 12).

34. Collect process data to verify that changes (from improvement activities) were effective and that they achieved the desired results.

35. Decide whether the changes were positive, or negative, and take the appropriate action(s).

36. Create file folders (physical and/or electronic) to maintain the collected data, flow charts, and procedures for process improvement efforts.

37. Re-evaluate the compliance plan, change any compliance methods as appropriate, and make preparations for continuing with the current compliance methods and/or start using the new list of compliance

methods for the current business processes and published policies, and procedures.

38. Communicate progress, throughout all of the above steps, to process owners, sponsors, management, or users. Broadcast progress about new or revised policies and procedures to the company through media described in the communication strategy.

39. Promote the activities of the policies and procedure group through the use of a "Policies and Procedures" newsletter or other communication method available.

40. Add the policy or procedure to the review plan (refer to Chapter 6, *"Creating a Review and Communication Control Plan"*) to monitor.

Each of these steps could be accomplished by one or more persons depending on the size of the company. In a small company, the procedures analyst might be responsible for all the steps. In larger companies, these steps could be accomplished by the procedures group along with the quality assurance and audit functions. The organizational layout is up to you; I do recommend that the policies and procedures group remain accountable for the entire policies and procedures infrastructure. The 40 steps of the plan of action relate to the "Policies and Procedures Improvement Cycle" (PPIC) in Table 2-1:

TABLE 2-1: *Plan of Action and the Policies and Procedures Improvement Cycle*

STEPS	PPIC PHASES
1-24	1 - Analyze &Research
25-29, 38-39	2 - Publish & Communicate
30-32	3 - Check & Audit
33-37, 40	4 - Report & Improve

FLOW CHART

A flow chart is defined as a method of graphically describing a current process, or a proposed new process, by using symbols, lines, and words to display pictorially the activities and sequences in the process. The flow chart is a universal method for analyzing, improving, and understanding business processes. Well designed and coordinated flow charts highlight the areas in which "fuzzy" processes and procedures disrupt quality and productivity. These flow charts can also help you establish clear accountability for the total process performance by defining the boundaries of the work required to produce a specific output independent of how many functions or departments the work flow crosses to reach its ultimate destination.

Every flow chart presents unique opportunities. Many opportunities show up in these process flows. Using a pictorial flow of activities, it becomes an easier task to identify opportunities for improvement and measurements. When time, cycle time, and cost information are added to these process flows during the improvement phase, it becomes possible to do a cost benefit analysis to determine the length of time it takes to do the steps, the duration between steps, and what it will cost to perform each task. Flow charts do an excellent job highlighting confusing business processes and procedures; this point becomes obvious when the cross-functional team is forced continually to redraw the flow chart to get it right. This normally means that the business processes and/or procedures are unclear or have never been properly defined or documented. While "getting it right" is an ongoing effort, any improvement is a step in the right direction. Flow charts enhance the full value of the process

The use of a well-thought out a flow chart will provide the basis for meetings and brainstorming sessions. Team members can use this process flow as a discussion tool. The flow chart helps them to recognize redundancies and gaps in the current process flow. Flow charts consistently hook people on quality management because the flow chart shows a clear picture of the true process that could not have otherwise been envisioned.

The flow charting process prepares employees for the productive changes ahead because employees who participate in developing flow charts recognize their own competence and influence and they gain an understanding of each other's jobs, resulting in increased cooperation in the work environment. Building flow charts builds teamwork. At the same time, individual accountability blooms. The analysis of the flow chart process triggers improvement efforts, adherence to standards of quality, and commitment to reduce process variations.

In the next chapter, a flow chart technique called a *block diagram* is used to illustrate a *Purchasing System* that is the basis for the case study used throughout this book.

This flow chart technique uses only blocks, or rectangle boxes, to describe business processes. The block diagram is the simplest kind of flow charting tool and it eliminates the frustrating task of trying to find the "right" symbol to represent an activity, decision, delay or storage device (Harrington, 1991). This diagram is then transformed into a procedure using the standard writing format or template described in the next section. A detailed flow chart can be easily transformed into a draft procedure. Often a flow chart parallels the "Procedures" section of the writing format.

There are two excellent books by H. James Harrington (1991) and Robert Damelio (1996) that provide step-by-step instructions for diagraming a business process. The Damelio book is very good and if you have a choice between the two books, I would recommend this book first. H. James Harrington's book is another good choice because it provides worthwhile supplemental material about business processes.

WRITING FORMAT

A writing format is a method of expressing words in an outline format. All policies and procedures should use the same format or template. The writing format is the heart of a policies and procedures system: *it provides a structure for information collected during the research and analysis phases of writing.* This logical, structured format is a basic requirement for any policy or procedure. Readers can easily be frustrated if the content in a policy or procedure is not presented in a logical order from paragraph to paragraph and from section to section.

Policies and procedures written with few, or no headings, or with headings that change from procedure to procedure, are frustrating. This kind of inconsistency can make it difficult to read a policy or procedure. For instance, if a procedure is written in a different format each time, the reader does not know what to expect. I have seen policies and procedures written in outline form one time and in paragraph form the next.

Most readers need to find information quickly. Research suggests that the way many unformatted policies and procedures are written inhibits easy reading. Poorly written policies and procedures do not support fast reading because major ideas are buried, headings are ambiguous or uninformative to the reader, important details are hard to locate, and instructions are either nonexistent or difficult to find or understand. Consistency saves time because readers can find the information they need quickly and focus on content rather than format.

The writing format recommended in this book is called the *Basic Writing Format*; this is a technique borrowed from my earlier book, *"Establishing a System of Policies and Procedures."* For policies and procedures, the structure remains the same, only the content changes. This writing format enables the reader to understand the main objectives, methods, business processes, target audiences, tie to business strategic goals, definitions, and responsibilities in the first two or three pages of a policy or procedure. This writing format is the easiest method available for readers who want to skim a document; the reason behind that claim resides in the fact that the reader can understand the basis of the entire policy or procedure within the first few pages of a policy or procedure. This is a benefit to the reader because he is more inclined to read something that appears structured and orderly and easy to understand..

BASIC WRITING FORMAT

There are seven principal headings to the basic writing format. These headings will always appear in the sequence presented on the next page for both policies and procedures. The only difference in content between from a policy and a procedure is that the policy usually does not contain content in the 7th heading, *"Procedures."*

Recall from the "Introduction" that a *policy* is a general guideline and often does not contain process steps. A *procedure* is a plan of action to carry out a policy and/or a series of routine steps to accomplish an action. While a policy contains the 7 headings, the words, "Not Applicable," are normally written under the 7th heading. This, seventh heading remains a part of the format, and the format maintains its consistency. In the case of a *procedure*, the process flow that describes the activities of the procedure is written in this section. They are typically laid out in a linear fashion in which the first step in this section starts the process and the last step ends the process. I often refer to this section as the place where you outline the entire process from "A to Z."

If you have completed an accurate flow chart and wrote out your sequence steps in detail, transforming your information to a writing format should be straightforward. This transformation process is illustrated in Chapter 3, *"Focusing on a Case Study to Apply the Principles of this Book,"* when the flow chart in the case study is transformed into a draft procedure. The first flow chart and written procedure are presented in Chapter 3, *"Focusing on a Case Study to Apply the Principles of this Book."* After improvements are made to this case study, a new flow chart and procedure are presented in Chapter 11, *"Conducting Profitable Continuous Improvement Activities."*

1.0	<u>Purpose</u>. Explain objectives for writing a policy or procedure. Two or three sentences are adequate for this introductory paragraph. Do not include acronyms or technical terms that have yet to be defined in this heading.
2.0	<u>Revision History</u>. Provides history of document changes whether they are minor typographical errors, major improvements, or re-engineering projects.
3.0	<u>Persons Affected</u>. Provides a list of those persons or groups that might be impacted by the policy or procedure (i.e., target audiences or users). When all employees are affected, simply write, "All Employees." External groups like customers or suppliers should also be listed.
4.0	<u>Policy</u>. Provides general organizational attitude of an organization; it reflects the basic objectives, goals, or vision. This is a good place to show the tie to business strategic goals. (*The inclusion of this statement within a procedure makes the procedure easier to understand without having to refer to another source for policy information.*)
5.0	<u>Definitions</u>. Provides explanations of abbreviations, acronyms, forms, words infrequently used, words not consistently understood, and technical terms. This is an important heading and should contain an explanation of the title, keywords, forms, references, and any exhibits. (*References can be placed in an exhibit and defined in this section.*)
6.0	<u>Responsibilities</u>. Provides a short summary of the responsibilities of the individuals involved with a procedure. The specific title is generally used (e.g., Benefits Manager, CEO, or Buyer; the generic term, "Employee," can be used when necessary). This section should be written in the same sequence of events that occurs under the "Procedures" section.
7.0	<u>Procedures</u>. Defines and outlines the rules, regulations, methods, timing, place, and personnel responsible for accomplishing the policy as stated in Section 4.0. This section should follow the process flow as described in the flow chart. The process is described from start to finish, including all the inputs, outputs, and value-added activities.

The title, policy or procedure number, effective date, revision number, revision date, number of pages, and approvals can be included in a header if this is a printed document. If the output is on a network or Intranet, then this information can be referenced at the top of the screen or as a hyperlink or pop up window. The choice is yours — however, try to be consistent if you produce both printed and electronic policies and procedures.

BASELINES

Each time a policy or procedure is approved and published, a "baseline" is established. The term *baseline* is used to describe the foundation created when a policy or procedure is approved, published, and implemented. A *baseline* can also be described as a snapshot in time of a published policy or procedure: *The content of the policy or procedure is frozen.* When improvements are made, a new snapshot is taken of the published policy or procedure. A new revision or version number is assigned to the document. Throughout this book, when the term *baseline* is used, think of foundation, snapshot in time, or a starting point. A baseline model is illustrated in Figure 2-1 below. The model is ideal in the sense that all measurements result in increased compliance percentages. In the real world, the percentages could go up or down depending on the change incorporated and the receptivity of the users to the change.

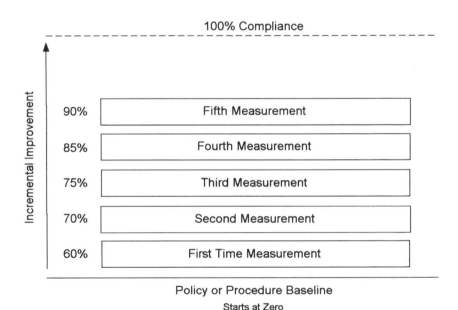

FIGURE 2-1: *Baseline for a Policy or a Procedure*

CHECKLIST FOR CHANGE:

✓   Write well-coordinated, convincing, proficient, and competent policies and procedures to produce effective policies and procedures that will have a good probability of achieving the highest possible compliance percentage the first time the published policies and procedures are measured.

✓   A detailed plan of action (40-step process) has been introduced for writing effective policies and procedures and for monitoring them from idea to publication, communication to compliance, and then to improvement.

✓   The 40-step process for writing effective policies and procedures is accomplished during the first phase of the PPIC.

✓   A comparison between the plan of action for writing effective policies and procedures and the PPIC is presented.

✓   The flow chart has been identified as an important tool for diagraming a process flow and identifying process gaps and opportunities for improvement.

✓   A standard writing format has been introduced for writing policies and procedures.

✓   Baselines are discussed as a convenient way to identify a starting point when conducting measurement studies of published policies and procedures. An ideal diagram has been illustrated to show the effects of incremental changes on a policy or procedure.

APPLYING WHAT YOU HAVE LEARNED:

The best starting point for applying the information in this chapter is to read my earlier book, *"Establishing a System of Policies and Procedures."* This book contains detailed information on conducting research and analysis, using a writing format, coordinating and publishing a policy or procedure, communications, training, and converting printed policies and procedures to a network or an Intranet environment. With this background information, adhere to the 40-step plan of action in this chapter when writing a policy or procedure. Use a flow chart tool to diagram the process during the research and analysis phase. Use the standard writing format to write draft policies and procedures consistently. Publish the final policy or procedure. Start plans for communication and training strategies.

ACHIEVE 100% COMPLIANCE:

In this chapter, you have developed effective policies and procedures using various techniques to achieve well-coordinated and structured policies and procedures. If you have followed these guidelines and those presented in my earlier book, "*Establishing a System of Policies and Procedures*," you should have written policies and procedures that will have the highest probability of being accepted when implemented. These policies and procedures become the baseline to measure against as you enhance the policies and procedures infrastructure through a communication strategy, training campaign, and review plan. These effective policies and procedures will move you closer to 100% compliance.

If you did not use the techniques presented in this chapter to write your policies and procedures, your current policies and procedures will become your baseline. If you did not coordinate (completely or partially) the design and research of the flow charts and draft policies and procedures with the process owners, users, management, and any other impacted group, the result will be less than "effective" policies and procedures and your baseline will probably be subject to frequent improvements and change.

REFERENCES:

Bemowski, Karen and Stratton, Brad, *101 Good Ideas - How to Improve Just About Any Process*, ASQ Quality Press, Milwaukee, Wisconsin, 1998.

Chapman, Robert L, *Roget's International Thesaurus*, Harper & Row, New York, New York, 1977.

Damelio, Robert, *The Basics of Process Mapping*, Quality Resources, New York, New York, 1996.

Davenport, Thomas H., *Process Innovation*, Harvard Business School Press, Boston, Massachusetts, 1993.

Edosomwan, Dr. Johnson A., *Organizational Transformation and Process Reengineering*, St. Lucie Press, Delray Beach, Florida, 1996.

Hammer, Michael and Champy, James, *Reengineering the Corporation*, HarperBusiness, New York, New York, 1993.

Harrington, H. James, *Business Process Improvement*, McGraw-Hill, Inc., New York, New York, 1991.

Harvard Business Review Paperwork, *Harvard Business Review on Knowledge Management*, Boston, Massachusetts, 1998.

Hultman, Ken, *Making Change Irresistible*, Davies-Black Publishing, Palo Alto, California,1998.

Johansson, Henry J., McHugh, Patrick, Pendlebury, A. John, and Wheeler, William A., III, *Business Process Reengineering*, John Wiley & Sons, New York, New York, 1993.

Katzenbach, Jon R., *Teams at the Top*, Harvard Business School Press, Boston, Massachusetts, 1998.

Milas, Gene H., *Teambuilding and Total Quality*, Engineering and Management Press, Atlanta, Georgia, 1997.

Page, Stephen B. *Establishing a System of Policies and Procedures*, BookMasters, Inc., Mansfield, Ohio, 1998.

Parker, Glenn M., *Cross-Functional Teams*, Jossey-Bass Publishers, San Francisco, California, 1994.

Parker, Glenn M., *Team Players and Teamwork*, Jossey-Bass Publishers, San Francisco, California. 1990.

Pasmore, William A,. *Creating Strategic Change*, John Wiley & Sons, Inc., New York, New York, 1994.

Peters, Tom, *The Circle of Innovation*, Alfred A. Knopf, New York, New York, 1997.

Poirier, Charles, C. and Houser, William, F., *Business Partnering for Continuous Improvement*, Berrett-Koehler Publications, San Francisco, California, 1993.

Princeton Language Institute, edited by Kipfer, Barbara Ann, Ph.D., *Roget's 21st Century Thesaurus*, Delta Tradebacks, New York, New York, 1999.

Sandy, William, *Forging the Productivity Partnership*, McGraw-Hill, New York, New York, 1990.

Sashkin, Marshall and Kiser, Kenneth J., *Putting Total Quality Management to Work*, Berret-Koehler Publishers, San Francisco, California, 1993.

Scherkenbach, William W., *The Deming Route to Quality and Productivity*, CEEPress Books, Washington, D.C., 1991.

Shewhart, Walter A., *Statistical Method from the Viewpoint of Quality Control*, Dover Publications, Inc., New York, New York, 1986.

Chapter Three

Focusing on a Case Study to Apply the Principles of this Book

The premise of this book is to show you how to measure business processes and published policies and procedures to ensure variation is minimized, quality is improved, cycle time is shortened, and material and labor dollars are reduced. I am using a case study of a "Purchasing System" business process that I was accountable for when I was a purchasing supervisor at a company in California to illustrate the principles of this book. The use of this case study is important because the results are not theoretical, rather they are based on activities that actually happened as far I can remember the details. Each chapter is based upon practical, proven guidelines and examples from this case study to provide new insights and show you how to make better decisions.

In Chapter 11, *"Conducting Profitable Continuous Improvement Activities,"* the flow chart and procedure from this chapter will be rewritten and improved based on the information collected from relevant chapters. The book has been set up with the case study as its focal point.

> The *Purchasing System* case study is based on a real situation, real people, real meetings, and real results. The case study is not based on theory. The flow charts and procedures presented in this chapter were actually used in a Purchasing Department at Dataproducts, in Woodland Hills, California.

➤We start with a flow chart and procedure, do a communication and training plan, write a compliance plan, execute five quality tools, do a systems audit, establish an improvement plan, and select a solution that results in a major improvement. In Chapter 12, *"Saving $1 Million with Cost Benefit Analyses,"* a cost benefit analysis is conducted to illustrate why the selected solution, *Purchase Card System*, is the best solution for the manual, labor intensive *Purchasing System* presented in Chapter 3,

"Focusing on a Case Study to Apply the Principles of this Book." This book is unique because it addresses the activities and steps necessary to reach this solution, achieve a high compliance level, and achieve customer satisfaction.

SELECTION CRITERIA FOR CASE STUDY

A case study on a *Purchasing System* was selected because every reader should have some familiarity with purchasing functions both in a business and personal sense. In our personal world, we typically follow many of the same activities accomplished by a purchasing department (i.e., searching out sources, negotiating, making a payment, and receiving the order). For instance, if you buy a car, you probably researched several sources and tried to negotiate the best possible price. When you buy something on the Internet, you probably researched several sites and products, selected one, paid by credit card, and the rest was out of your hands.

In a business environment, purchasing functions are typically handled by a Purchasing Department if the number of employees warrants a separate department; in smaller company, the purchasing functions may be handled by an Administrative Manager or an Administrative Assistant. There are many possibilities for making purchases in companies depending on the size of a company and the philosophy of its management. Regardless of how purchases are made, there are normally documents for requesting purchases (e.g., purchase requisitions), purchase orders, receivers, and invoices.

CASE STUDY DEFINED

I selected a manual, paperwork intensive *Purchasing System* as the original case study because I am familiar with the business processes, analysis, and research that took place to diagram the process and develop policies, procedures, and forms for the *Purchasing System* business process. The case study represents an actual business process used at Dataproducts, a company in Woodland Hills, California.

After using the *Purchasing System* process for nearly two years, we formed a new cross-functional team and re-engineered the process. We combined four manual forms into one form (i.e., the form was called a *"Modified Purchase Order"*) and saved more than $1 million annually in material costs alone. When I first started writing this book, I had this solution (i.e., "Modified Purchase Order") in mind, but the actual results from the analysis in Chapters 8 to 12 pointed to a *Purchase Card System* as being a better and more efficient solution to the combination form.

30

The use of this case study is important to the reader because the principles of this book are explained through practical examples of the case study. In every example, the case study will be referenced as the *Purchasing System*. The case study starts with an overview of a purchasing process. A high level summary of a generic purchasing system is illustrated to give you a "ten thousand foot" view of the purchasing process. A detailed flow chart is illustrated to show the actual steps in the purchasing process. A procedure is then written based on this detailed flow chart.

"PURCHASING PROCESS" OVERVIEW

In a general sense, purchasing describes a buying process. In a broader context, purchasing involves determining the need, selecting a supplier, arriving at an appropriate price, terms, and conditions, issuing a contract or order, following up to ensure delivery and material inspection, and paying an invoice. A purchasing system typically covers the purchase of all items from supplies to major capital investments. The purchasing system process describes the many sub-processes, policies, procedures, and forms for acquiring items and services for the organization. The purchasing process varies depending on the type and size of an organization, company policies and procedures, management attitudes, company culture, and computer technology. A purchasing process could be as simple as a single person responsible for all buying functions to hundreds of managers, buyers, purchasing assistants, and purchasing clerks.

> A case study about a Purchasing System was selected as the case study because every reader can identify with purchasing functions from both a business and a personal sense.

For this case study, I narrowed my focus to the purchase of supply and office-type items that are <u>not</u> for resale or used for production purposes. These types of items are referred to as "MRO" items, or <u>M</u>aintenance, <u>R</u>epair, and <u>O</u>perating items. In a manufacturing environment, MRO orders can account for 80% of the volume of paperwork while administrative time accounts for the remaining 20%. In service industries like insurance, banking, and health care, MRO purchases may account for 100% of the activity within a Purchasing Department (Grieco, 1997). A high level overview of a purchasing system is included in Table 3-1. A detailed flow chart is illustrated for the *Purchasing System* in Figure 3-1. A 16-step task list is derived from the flow chart and a procedure is written based on the flow chart and task list.

TABLE 3-1: *High Level Purchasing System Overview*

FLOW	DESCRIPTION OF ACTIVITIES
Recognition of Need	Employee recognizes a need to purchase office or supply-type items and prepares a Purchase Requisition.
Supplier Selection	Buyer determines best method for purchasing the requested items.
Purchase Order Awarded	Buyer awards a Purchase Order to a selected supplier.
Supplier Fills Order	Supplier fills order and ships requested order to the receiving department.
Receipt and Inspection of Order	A receiving department receives and inspects order from a supplier. Discrepancies are noted on the receiving documents.
Order Sent to Requester	A receiving department forwards items to the requester of the order.
Invoice Paid Order Closed	Requester receives order. The Accounting Department pays the invoice upon receipt of documentation. Purchasing closes order.

CASE STUDY EXPLAINED

This case study is tailored after a business process in Dataproducts Corporation, a manufacturing company in Woodland Hills, California. There were 3600 employees worldwide. The corporate Purchasing Department was located in Woodland Hills, California, and they had 40 employees. There were 10 Buyers, 2 of which were MRO Buyers responsible for small tools, maintenance items, and office supplies. There were 3 Purchasing Managers responsible for different commodities, 3 Purchasing Agents that supported the Managers, 2 Purchasing Assistants for the 3 managers and 1 Purchasing Supervisor. The rest of the employees were expediters, purchasing analysts, and administrative support. There were three ways to request purchases:

1. A standard Purchase Requisition was used for purchases made for single a purpose. Requisitions could be used multiple times to order the same

item but generally the standard Purchase Requisition was used to order MRO items on an "as needed" basis. These requisitions were 3-part, landscape format, legal sized, carbon-interleaved forms.

2. A "traveling requisition" was used for items purchased on a regular basis (like tools or low-cost items used for production), a special form made of card stock was used for these purchases.

3. A computerized Bill of Material (BOM) and Material Requirements Planning (MRP) Schedule were used for ordering production items.

The case study starts with an employee preparing a manual Purchase Requisition.

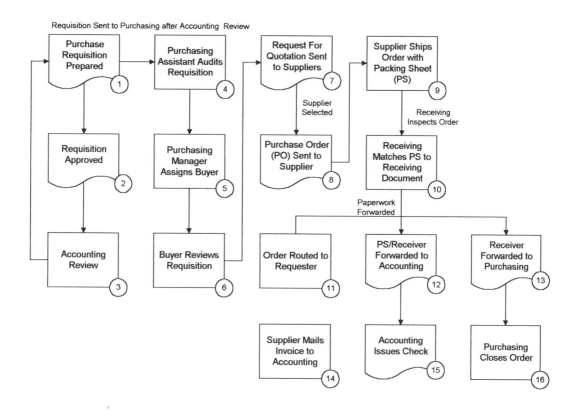

FIGURE 3-1: *Flow Chart of Purchasing System*

The flow chart is drawn and redrawn until the cross-functional team is satisfied that all steps have been identified. Additional interviews and discussions with process owners could be necessary to ensure the process flow is adequately defined.

SUMMARY OF FLOW CHART

1 <u>Purchase Requisition Prepared</u>. The requester prepares a three-part Purchase Requisition form and sends it to his supervisor for approval.

2 <u>Requisition Approval</u>. The requester's supervisor makes the decision to approve or disapprove the requisition if the value of the requisition exceeds $250 and is less than $500.00, a second signature is needed. The supervisor sends the requisition to his manager for approval.

3 <u>Accounting Review</u>. The requester's supervisor sends the approved Requisition to the Accounting Department for budget, charge (or account) number, and signature authorization review.

<u>The Accounting Department returns the Purchase Requisition to the Requester. The Requester removes the last copy and sends the Purchase Requisition (original and copy) to the Purchasing Department for processing</u>

4 <u>Purchasing Assistant Audits Requisition</u>. The first point of contact for incoming Purchase Requisitions is the Purchasing Assistant. He reviews the requisition to ensure it is completed in accordance with the current procedure. The Purchasing Assistant initials the requisition if it passes his review and forwards it to a Purchasing Manager.

5 <u>Purchasing Manager Assigns Buyer</u>. The Purchasing Manager reviews the requisition, notes the appropriate Buyer on the requisition, initials it, and forwards it to the Buyer for order placement.

6 <u>Buyer Reviews Requisition</u>. The Buyer reviews the requisition and determines his course of action for selecting a supplier including reviewing published lists, blanket order contracts, purchase history, and new suppliers.

7 <u>Request for Quotation (RFQ) Sent to Suppliers</u>. The Buyer sends a three-part Request For Quotation form to at least three suppliers to obtain competitive bids. The Buyer selects one supplier based on the returned bids.

8 <u>Purchase Order (PO) Sent to Supplier</u>. The Buyer prepares a five-part Purchase Order form and separates it by mailing two copies to the supplier,

the third copy to Purchasing, the fourth copy to the Accounting Department, and the fifth copy to the Receiving Department.

The Receiving Department reproduces a "Receiver Set" on a photocopier using a four-part pre-collated, colored, paper set (*Color set typically consists of four distinct colors: white, canary, green, and pink*).

9 Supplier Ships Order with Packing Sheet (PS). The supplier fills the order in accordance with the terms and conditions of the Purchase Order; the order is packaged, and shipped to the requester's Shipping Department, along with a two-part Packing Sheet.

10 Receiving Matches PS to Receiver. The Receiving Department counts the quantity of the received order and matches the order quantity on both the Packing Sheet and the Receiver.

Depending on the type of item ordered, an Inspection Department may inspect the order before it is forwarded to the Requester.

11 Order Routed to Requester of Items. The Receiving Department completes the Receiver and forwards the order to the requester.

12 PS/Receiver Forwarded to the Accounting Department. The Receiving Department forwards both the packing sheet and the receiving document to the Accounting Department for payment.

13 Receiver Forwarded to the Purchasing Department. The Receiving Department forwards a copy of the receiving document to the Purchasing Department to follow up on the order and to close the order when it is confirmed the order has been received, inspected, and paid.

14 Supplier Mails Invoice to the Accounting Department. The supplier mails the invoice to the organization's Accounting Department for payment.

15 The Accounting Department Issues Check. The Accounting Department matches the packing sheet with the receiving document and/or Purchase Order and keeps the two documents together until the invoice is matched; a check will then be created and mailed to the supplier.

16 <u>Purchasing Closes the Order</u>. The Purchasing Department closes the order and files it for reference purposes after the Buyer receives notification that the parts have been received and there were no discrepancies.

After the flow chart has been completed and the cross-functional team is satisfied with the flow chart, the cross-functional team should perform a walk through (the team literally "walks through" a department and observes activities and asks questions about the process) to ensure that the process in the flow chart and summary description matches the real situation as seen through the eyes of those doing the work. Any missing information can be added to the flow chart and any gaps in the flow can be further researched through interviews with the users and process owners of the task being performed.

Time permitting, the team could research books on the subject and they could benchmark with other companies to study their purchasing system. Once the cross-functional team is assured that the flow chart represents the best solution, a procedure draft can be written using the flow chart and summary description using the standard writing format referenced in Chapter 2. The information from the flow chart and summary description can be translated into the 7th heading of the "Procedures" section.

A sample procedure based on the flow chart in Figure 3-1 is documented in the next few pages. This is a real procedure that Dataproducts, Woodland Hills, California, actually used.

WRITTEN PROCEDURE — "PURCHASING SYSTEM"

| Purchasing System Maintenance, Repair, and Operation (MRO) Supplies *(abbreviated as "Purchasing System")* | Procedure No. | Date |
| | Revision No. | Page__ Of__ |

1.0   <u>Purpose</u>

This procedure establishes guidelines for the business process by which employees can request the purchase of items that have a total cost of $500.00 or less and is not-for-resale. The process will begin with a Purchase Requisition and end with the payment of an invoice.

2.0   Revision History

DATE	DESCRIPTION	AUTHOR INITIALS
1/10/2000	Original Document	SBP

3.0   Persons Affected

All employees, suppliers, and customers.

4.0   Policy

The policy of this company is to ensure:

4.1   All expenditures of company funds for goods and services are properly reviewed and approved prior to commitment.

4.2   The Purchasing Department is the only department that is authorized to engage suppliers through Purchase Orders, contracts, and to obligate funds.

4.3   The Purchasing Department follows published guidelines for obtaining the best "purchase value" for requested items or services.

4.4   The Purchasing Department establishes and maintains a supplier base to ensure that adequate capacity and quality are available and that the level of service and price are optimal.

4.5   Personal items (e.g., flowers, refreshments, personal subscriptions or items, gifts, etc.) are not procured or received by the company either through the Receiving Department or any door of the company.

4.6   The Purchase Requisition is the only document used by employees when requesting "one-time" goods and services ordered by the Purchasing Department.

4.7   The Accounting Department only pays funds to a supplier when the paperwork has been processed and approved.

5.0 Definitions

5.1 Maintenance, Repair, and Operating Supplies (MRO). Expense materials that are used by employees to help them perform their jobs. These materials can include, but are not limited to small tools, cleaning supplies, office supplies, and a variety of other consumable items.

5.2 Purchase Requisition (PR). Three-part, pre-numbered, form used to request the purchase of materials or services by the Purchasing Department. The Purchase Requisition is the prime document authorizing the purchasing department to buy specific materials, parts, supplies, equipment, and services. The requisition describes what is to be purchased, provides a record of the Purchase Requisition, and approves the commitment of funds. A requisition is a request to order, not an order itself. Completion of the requisition alone does not constitute placing the order. The requisition used for MRO items is a single-use requisition and is appropriate in situations where users are requesting items on a one-time basis.

5.3 Request for Quotation (RFQ). Three-part, pre-numbered, form used by the Purchasing Department to request bids from suppliers. A request for quotation is a means of inviting bids from prospective suppliers. The request for quote is the Buyer's first official contact with possible suppliers. The quality and content of the RFQ can determine the outcome of the bidding process because it sets the stage for discussions and negotiations.

5.4 Purchase Order (PO). Five-part form used by the Purchasing Department to establish a legal contract between the company and a supplier. The Purchase Order is written evidence of a contract between the Buyer and the supplier for the purchase of goods and services at an agreed price and delivery date. The issuance of the Purchase Order is based on formal or informal bids and proposals. The document should contain general instructions, standard terms and conditions, space to describe the agreement fully, and the signature of a duly authorized agent for the company. The PO is the only document that can be used in transactions for the purchase of equipment, materials, supplies, and services.

5.5 Receiver. A four-part, pre-collated, four-color set of blank paper that is used to create a receiving document from an issued Purchase Order. The receiver serves as proof of delivery and the document that records the inspection, acceptance of goods and services, and payment approval.

5.6 Packing Sheet (PS). Normally a two-part, pre-numbered, form issued by a supplier when filling the terms and conditions of a Purchase Order. This form, or similar document, should accompany any items being shipped to the company from a supplier. All packing sheets must make reference to an authorized and issued Purchase Order number.

6.0 Responsibilities

6.1 The Purchasing Department Executive (*manager, vice president, or senior person in the Purchasing Department*) is responsible for ensuring that the personnel within his department adhere to the guidelines outlined in this procedure.

6.2 Employees are expected to select the most current Purchase Requisition form and adhere to the guidelines of this procedure when requesting MRO items. Employees will obtain needed approvals from their management and from the Accounting Department.

6.3 A person in the Purchasing Department, designated as a Purchasing Assistant, shall review all incoming Purchase Requisitions to ensure that the requisitions are completed in accordance with this *Purchasing System* procedure. The Purchasing Assistant will return any incomplete requisition to the requester with an explanation of non-conformance.

6.4 A Purchasing Manager shall review all incoming Purchase Requisitions before they are forwarded onto a Buyer; he will assign a Buyer to negotiate and place the order. (*For the purposes of this procedure, I have not listed all of the functions of a Purchasing Manager, only those that refer to the main functions outlined in this case study.*)

6.5 The Buyer shall review the requisition, select at least three sources, solicit bids, review bid packages, select a supplier, issue a Purchase Order, and monitor the receipt of the items.

6.6 The Receiving Department shall monitor the receipt of the order, inspect the order, report any discrepancies, and process the paperwork to the appropriate departments to ensure timely payment.

6.7 The Accounting Department shall process the receiving documentation and generate the paperwork to authorize payment to the supplier.

7.0 Procedures

7.1 Establishing Need

7.1.1 Any employee can create a Purchase Requisition to purchase MRO supply items in accordance with the requirements referenced in this procedure. The employee should normally review several catalogues or past department orders to get an estimate of the total order value of the Purchase Requisition; this research will aid the employee and his manager in determining if the Purchase Requisition is a useful purchase for the department.

7.1.2 The employee will complete the Purchase Requisition and obtain signatures for the estimated value of the order. If the estimated value is lower than the value of the order, the requisition will be returned by the Buyer for added signatures, as necessary.

Signature Levels
for the Total Value of the PR

Up to $250.00	$251.00 to $500.00
Requester Supervisor	Requester Supervisor Manager

7.1.3 Upon receipt of the appropriate approvals, the employee will forward the Purchase Requisition to the Accounting Department for review of the budget, charge number, and authorized signatures. The Accounting Department will return the Purchase Requisition to the requester with an approval decision.

7.1.4 Once approved, the employee will remove the last copy of the Purchase Requisition for his records and forward the original requisition and first copy to the Purchasing Department for review and processing.

7.2 Purchasing Department Activities

7.2.1 A Purchasing Assistant will review all incoming manual Purchase Requisitions to ensure compliance with this procedure. He will ensure that the signatures are correct and that all fields (*the charge number is most important field*) have been properly completed in accordance with the form instructions outlined for the Purchase Requisition at the back of this procedure (*the form is not shown in this example*). He will initial the requisition at the lower bottom right corner of the requisition and then forward the requisition to a Purchasing Manager for review.

7.2.2 A Purchasing Manager will review the Purchase Requisition and assign it to the appropriate Buyer responsible for the purchase of the MRO items. The Purchasing Manager will initial the assignment of the Buyer. The Purchasing Manager will forward the Purchase Requisition to the selected Buyer.

(*In a small company, the MRO Buyer might be known in advance. In larger companies, there can be several MRO Buyers and the Purchasing Manager will select one.*)

7.2.3 The Buyer will review the Purchase Requisition and begin the necessary negotiations with selected suppliers to find the most competitive bid. The Buyer may contact the requester to ask for further clarification if the request is not clear and/or if the information is inadequate or does follow the current *Purchasing System* procedure. The Buyer will determine if this is a one-time buy or if it is anticipated that this item might be purchased again in the near future. In this latter case, the Buyer can make arrangements for volume pricing if the items being procured will be repetitive. For the purposes of this procedure, the Buyer is required to contact at least three suppliers for bids.

7.2.3.1   At least three suppliers are selected either from published lists, Purchase Order history, blanket orders, or from new suppliers. The information from the Purchase Order is normally transferred to a Request For Quotation (RFQ) Form, including a preferred schedule and delivery times. Two copies of the RFQ are mailed to each supplier, the third copy is retained in a Buyer's open status file. The Buyer should allow at least two to three weeks for the supplier to return a bid package if the requester's deadline permits adequate bidding time.

7.2.3.2   The Buyer reviews the returned bid packages and makes a selection; in some cases, the suppliers will be contacted for further discussions about the price and service offered.

7.2.3.3   The Buyer then selects the best bidder in accordance with internal purchasing guidelines. The best bidder is not always the bidder with the lowest price.

7.2.3.4   If prepayment is needed, the Buyer will generate the necessary paperwork to obtain a check, money order, or cash (C.O.D. - Cash On Delivery) for the order.

7.2.3.5   A Purchase Order is awarded to the selected supplier and an order is generated.

   •   The original Purchase Order and first copy are forwarded to the supplier. The supplier should review and return the acknowledgment copy indicating that the Purchase Order has been received. The Buyer needs to review any changes in terms and conditions before accepting the acknowledgment copy. If the returned copy appears satisfactory, the copy is added to the open status file. The order is not closed until the Receiving Department notifies the Buyer that the items have been received and forwarded to the Requester.

- Copy 3 is forwarded to the Buyer's open-order follow-up file, Copy 4 is forwarded to the Accounting Department, Copy 5 is forwarded to the Receiving Department.

7.3   Receiving Department Process

7.3.1   Upon receipt of the Purchase Order, the Receiving Department will use a pre-collated, four-part set of colored paper, to photocopy a Receiving document based on the Purchase Order. This four-part set is now called a "Receiver."

7.3.2   Upon receipt of the material, the Receiving Department matches the order received to the Packing Sheet provided and to the Receiver. The receiving information is recorded on the Receiver and any discrepancies are noted. The Receiver is distributed as follows:

7.3.2.1   Copy 1 is forwarded to the appropriate Buyer. The Buyer closes the file.

7.3.2.2   Copies 2 and 3 are forwarded to the Accounting Department.

7.3.2.3   Copy 4 is retained by the Receiving Department for 60 days before it is discarded.

7.4   Accounting Department Process

7.4.1   The Accounting Department files the two copies of the Receiver with the current copy of the Purchase Order received from the Purchasing Department.

7.4.2   Upon receipt of the invoice demanding payment for the order, the Accounting department will verify that all the documents match and will initiate the process to pay the supplier in accordance with the terms and conditions of the Purchase Order.

7.4.3   The payment is sent to the supplier of the order in accordance with the terms and conditions of the Purchase Order. A copy of the check is filed with the original order previously filed in the Accounting records.

END OF PROCEDURE---

WHAT'S NEXT — THE POWER OF THE CASE STUDY

The *Purchasing System* case study is referenced in Chapters 3 through 12 as the primary example to illustrate the principles and themes of this book. The power of this book is in these examples. You will be able to trace a business process from idea to analysis, research, coordination, approval, publication, communication, training, compliance, metrics, auditing, improvement, and cost savings. No other book can make this claim. You are presented with a scenario and the original flow chart used in a manufacturing company in California. You are shown how a procedure is written from a flow chart. You will be then taken through communication, training, review, compliance (quality tools and metrics), and improvement plans. The result is a revised flow chart and written procedure. Significant cost savings are shown through the calculation of labor and material savings using a cost benefit analysis.

> This book has been written using a major case study to illustrate the principles and themes of this book. No other book can make this claim.

CHECKLIST FOR CHANGE:

✓   A *Purchasing System* for MRO items is presented as the case study that is referenced as the primary example to apply the principles of this book.

✓   A flow chart is drawn (and presented) that is based on a paperwork, labor intensive *Purchasing System* procedure.

✓   A method is presented for translating a flow chart into a summary of tasks for the *Purchasing System* business process.

✓   A procedure is written from the flow chart and summary of tasks using the standard writing format that is introduced in Chapter 2, *"Writing Effective Policies and Procedures."*

✓   The power of the case study is examined. You are asked to pay attention to these examples as they will help you to understand and appreciate how well this system of policies and procedures works. With this understanding, you will be able to apply the principles and themes to your business processes, policies, and procedures.

APPLYING WHAT YOU HAVE LEARNED:

Use a flow chart tool to diagram your own business processes. Translate the flow chart into a summary task list. Write a draft policy or procedure from the flow chart and task list. Use the standard writing format to write a policy or procedure. Obtain approvals and publish the policy or procedure based on the methods and techniques presented in my earlier book, *"Establishing a System of Policies and Procedures."*

ACHIEVE 100% COMPLIANCE:

In this chapter, a case study was introduced which will be referenced throughout the book. Even though the case study does not bring you any closer to 100% compliance, you were taught skills that could help you with writing effective policies and procedures that can be measured and improved.

REFERENCES:

Bemowski, Karen and Stratton, Brad, *101 Good Ideas*, ASQ Quality Press, Milwaukee, Wisconsin, 1998.

Damelio, Robert, *The Basics of Process Mapping*, Quality Resources, New York, New York, 1996.

Dataproducts Corporation, Woodland Hills, California: *Company where case study originated while I was a Purchasing Administration Supervisor. In addition to my duties of supporting the administrative activities of the Purchasing Department, I was responsible for developing the Purchasing Manual for the corporation and its divisions.*

Fearon, Harold E., Dobler, Donald W., Killen, Kenneth, H., *The Purchasing Handbook*, McGraw-Hills, Inc., New York, New York, 1993.

Grieco, Peter L., Gozzo, Michael W., Claunch, Jerry W., *Just-In-Time Purchasing*, PT Publications, Plantsville, Connecticut, 1989.

Grieco, Peter L. Jr., *MRO Purchasing*, PT Publications, Inc., West Palm Beach, Florida, 1997.

Harding, Michael and Harding, Mary Lu, *Purchasing* (Barron's Business Library), Barron's Educational Series, Inc., Hauppauge, New York, 1991.

Harrington, H. James, *Business Process Improvement*, McGraw-Hill, Inc., New York, New York, 1991.

Harrington, H. James; Esseling, Erik K.C., Van Nimwegen, harm, *Business Process Improvement Workbook* ,McGraw-Hill, Inc., New York, New York, 1997.

Johansson, Henry J., McHugh, Patrick, Pendlebury, A. John, and Wheeler, William A., III, *Business Process Reengineering*, John Wiley & Sons, New York, New York, 1993.

Maxwell, James, *Interview with James Maxwell*, Manager of Purchasing at Mettler-Toledo Scales for Purchasing System in this Case Study, Worthington, Ohio, 9/1999 and 1/2000.

Mettler Toledo, Inc., Worthington, Ohio: *James Maxwell, Supplier Manager - Systems Purchasing, assisted with the editing of the sections of this book involving purchasing matters.*

Page, Stephen B., *Establishing a System of Policies and Procedures, BookMasters, Inc.*, Mansfield, Ohio, 1998.

Poirier, Charles, C. and Houser, William, F., *Business Partnering for Continuous Improvement*, Berrett-Koehler Publications, San Francisco, California, 1993.

Chapter Four

Establishing a Communication Strategy

The success of individuals, teams, and companies is becoming increasingly dependent on effective business communications as a result of the growing complexity of business transactions, products, and services. The need for improved business communications is being driven by the fast demands of business, global, and technological revolution, as well as stiff competition. Organizations are finding that they need to adapt more quickly to changing environmental conditions and to competitive initiatives. If change does not happen quickly and effectively, organizations might not be able to keep up with the competition and will be left behind, wondering, "*What happened?*"

Many companies today are losing business because their operations are not running as smoothly as their competitors according to the standards of such organizations as the International Organization of Standards (ISO), Software Engineering Institute (SEI), or external auditing groups. Organizations have to use every tool at their disposal to create and maintain organizational effectiveness to remain competitive. Effective learning, sharing of information, and knowledge is rapidly becoming requirements for organizations. Change is inevitable and business communications will be one of the vehicles for making change happen. Organizations are discovering that the establishment of an effective communication strategy for policies and procedures is a useful tool not only for the policies and procedures infrastructure but also for the communication of other important company programs like Total Quality Management, ISO Quality Standards, Capability Maturity Model (CMM), Six Sigma, or Continuous Improvement Programs.

The primary objective of improving business communications is for the business (or company) to learn faster and smarter. Being *smarter* means receiving and assimilating information the first time rather than taking time to interpret it, digest it, and ask questions for clarification. If it takes time to understand information, then it was either poorly documented or poorly presented. Communication must convey information and motivate the audiences. Without this motivational element, the audiences might not fully understand the message. There have been many books written on communication and its importance. Some of the factors affecting how a message is received include:

1. The receiver hearing what he wants to hear

2. The sender and receiver having different perceptions

3. The receiver evaluating the message before accepting it

4. Words meaning different things to different people

Communications are virtually useless unless they are effective for the sender and the receiver of the information. An important goal of a communication strategy is to convey information in as many different methods as possible. When you consider that people do not always understand the same message in the same way, the solution lies in using communication media in different ways because you never know which one will be most effective for a particular individual. Precision in selecting the most effective media is as important as accuracy in the content of the message.

For instance, when learning a software program, some learn quickly from online tutorials or videos while others learn better from printed text. In this example, there were three communication methods identified: *Printed text, video, and online tutorial.* You never really know which communication method will be the most effective until you try it and measure its effectiveness. No one medium is right for every purpose or person. Each has a distinct advantage. If one method were superior in any way, then the other methods would not be needed. Fortunately, there are many communication methods from which to select. For the purposes of this book, the term *communication methods* will be used when referring to communication media.

COMMUNICATION DEFINED

The term *communication* can be defined as a process of providing information with the aim of achieving a shared meaning. Typical literary definitions of communication include:

1. An exchange of information

2. An act or instance of transforming information

3. A verbal or written message

4. A technique for expressing ideas effectively

There are two types of communications found in organizations. The first is external communication and the second is internal communication. The term *external* is defined as outside, and in this case, it means communicating to audiences outside of the company as in annual reports or press releases. The term *internal* is defined as inside and applies to communication to audiences within an organization like newsletters, meetings, bulletin boards, posters, email, voice mail, or training. These communication methods become mechanisms for sending content or messages to target audiences.

> A communication strategy for a policies and procedures infrastructure is an important tool for the dissemination of policies and procedures over their life cycle.

When these various communication methods are combined in a plan of action, it is called a "communication strategy." In the context of this book, the term *communication strategy* refers to a well-organized, logical plan for using appropriate media to communicate the content of policies and procedures to target audiences. A communication strategy is used in three ways. First, you could develop a plan for the policies and procedures infrastructure. Second, you could develop a plan for each policy and procedure within this infrastructure. Third, you could develop a master communication strategy with sub-plans for the policies and procedures of each functional area. The choice is yours. A communication strategy generally includes, but is not limited, to:

1. Scope statement and audience selection

2. Appropriate communication methods for the content being disseminated

3. Schedule and time line for ensuring the communication strategy is applied continually over the life of the business processes, policies, and procedures

COMMUNICATION STRATEGY EXPLAINED

Establishing a communication strategy for a policies and procedures infrastructure seems, at first glance, to be a simple task. Nothing is further from the truth. Communications can originate from almost anywhere in the company and almost anywhere in the world using a variety of media including the printed word, audio, video, and electronic data. With all of these variables, it becomes important to offer a diversified mix of media to reach as many people as possible. Unfortunately, procedures analysts tend to send out communications only once and do not consider them an ongoing activity. They often do not consider any kind of continuing plan for communicating information about policies and procedures that have already been disseminated! This is the wrong attitude. Procedures analysts are accountable for policies and procedures over their life cycle, from initiation to revision, and ultimately, to their replacement or obsolescence.

> Communications for policies and procedures must be rolled out in planned phases over the life of policies and procedures!

WHO DEVELOPS COMMUNICATION STRATEGIES?

In many organizations, there is normally a Communication Department that handles internal communications and/or a Public Relations Department that handles external communications. These functions typically have names like Communications, Corporate Communications, Business Communications, Public Relations, Human Resources, Personnel, Administrative Services, or Office Services. In some cases, the Communications and Public Relations Departments are combined in one department; in other cases, the role of company communications might rest with a single person within a department like Human Resources, Administration, or the Office of the President. The reporting structure for the communication function is often dependent on budget, time constraints, and resources.

Communications are everywhere and it is common to find departments writing their own newsletters, doing department-specific training, or posting departmental events on bulletin boards within their work area. If there is a Total Quality Management (TQM) department, then they probably have their own version of communication that can include award ceremonies for approved suggestions, recognition letters, certificates of appreciation, or training classes.

The procedures analyst should develop a communication strategy for the policies and procedures infrastructure. This enables him to retain control and accountability over the dissemination of business processes, policies, and procedures over the life cycle of these processes and documents. This communication strategy should be a combination of traditional communication media and new, innovative, communication methods.

The procedures analyst should make a concentrated effort to determine what other departments within the company are doing in communications. There can be an overlap and there might be areas where the timing of the communications could be coordinated to ensure that the largest audience is being reached with the same, or similar, kinds of information. The procedures analyst must ensure, if possible, that conflicting information is not being disseminated by other departments.

COMMUNICATION METHODS

There are a number of different communication methods that could be used by the procedures analyst; a brief description of each method is summarized in Table 4-1 below. These communication methods will form a communication strategy for the policies and procedures department. The schedule and time line for this strategy is discussed in Chapter 6, *"Creating a Review and Communication Control Plan."*

TABLE 4-1: *Communication Methods for Policies and Procedures*

COMMUNICATION METHOD	FORMAT	COMMUNICATION METHOD USED FOR:
1. Policies and Procedures	Printed or Electronic	Distribution of policies and procedures to printed and/or electronic (i.e., local area network (LAN) or Intranet) company manuals. Printed only, electronic only, or both printed and electronic formats are possible.
2. Letters	Printed or Electronic	Significant business process releases, e.g., an Accounting System and its new processes, policies and procedures, can be announced with a personal or companywide letter.

3. Newsletters	Printed or Electronic	A paragraph in a newsletter could be used to announce new or revised policies, procedures, forms, or other changes.
4. Magazines	Printed or Electronic	Magazines can be used to announce major events like a new policies and procedures infrastructure, a major business process, or a re-engineering effort.
5. Paycheck Stub or Inserts	Printed	Short one-sentence announcements can be printed on a paycheck stub, e.g., it could read, "New medical form, see Human Resources," or an announcement could be placed inside the Payroll check envelope.
6. Posters	Printed	Campaigns for the roll-out of a TQM program or motivational information to supplement a policy or procedure could be illustrated with bright colors and words.
7. Bulletin Boards	Printed	Focused flyers or announcements can be placed on bulletin boards to supplement the release of policies and procedures.
8. Brochures or Pamphlets	Printed	Brochures or pamphlets can be distributed along with a policy or procedure for important topics like business ethics or sexual harassment.
9. Training	Printed, Oral, or Electronic	Training is the chief method used to disseminate information about policies and procedures to target audiences. Learning is achieved when information is applied to work areas with the assistance of mentors, coaches, or managers.
10. Team Meetings	Oral	Team meetings can be used by supervisors to share policy and procedure information with their subordinates. Other topics can include process improvement efforts within their work areas, and so on.

11. Town Meetings	Oral	Senior management can hold companywide meetings to discuss policy and procedure topics. The term *town meeting* is defined as a meeting of all the inhabitants, or employees, of the town, or company.
12. Voice Mail	Audio	Policies and procedures information can be broadcasted over a telephone to all recipients within a target audience using voice mail, a feature normally found on telephones in a place of business.
13. Conference Calls	Audio	Policy and procedure team meetings can use a telephone to speak with several people at the same time; this feature of a telephone is especially useful when team members are geographically dispersed.
14. Video Conferencing	Video, Audio	Video conferencing is an excellent tool for conducting policy and procedure meetings because both video and audio signals can be sent over a telephone or satellite to compatible receiving equipment.
15. Electronic Mail (Email)	Electronic	Email can be used to broadcast information about policies and procedures to anywhere that can accept email transmissions. Email can now be converted and received as a FAX transmission through special services offered by FAX services over the Internet like Efax, located at http://www.efax.com. Faxes can also be converted to email.
16. World Wide Web (www)	Electronic	The Internet (i.e., an electronic communication network that connects computer networks around the world) provides procedures analysts an opportunity to set up web sites that can provide timely dissemination of information to users.

17. Videotape	Video, Audio	Videotapes (i.e., a recording of visual images and sound) are typically used for the dissemination of major business processes, policies, or procedures to employees, or large target audiences. The recipient must have videotape viewing equipment.
18. CD-ROM	Disk	CD-ROMs (i.e., compact disks containing data that can be ready by a computer) can be used to disseminate large amounts of information to individuals who have compatible playback equipment. The CD-ROM can be used to store complete policy and procedure manuals, training material, catalogues, or other large documents.
19. Facsimile (FAX)	FAX, Printed, Electronic	FAXes can be used to send policy or procedure messages to offices with compatible FAX machines as a supplement to other communication methods.
20. Telephone	Oral	The telephone is so commonplace that we take it for granted. The telephone is used in various ways to send policy and procedure information to target audiences including two-way conversation, conferencing, video conferencing, facsimile, or voice mail.

Each of these communication methods will be explained in more detail in the next few pages. Each method will be related to policies and procedures and how the method could be useful to the procedures analyst. The procedures analyst needs to keep abreast of new technologies, attend seminars, trade shows, and be alert to new ways to communicate policies and procedures. The procedures analyst should experiment with various methods to determine which method works best for him.

COMMUNICATION METHODS EXPLAINED

1. Policies or Procedures. Policies and procedures are distributed by a variety of formats including printed manuals, online networks, Intranets,

videotapes, CD-ROMs, or diskettes. The distribution of policies and procedures to a printed company manual on subjects of a similar topic (e.g., finance or marketing manual) has been and still is the traditional method for the dissemination of policies and procedures for immediate use. Depending on the organization's environment, policies and procedures might be distributed through an internal company mail system, through email as an attachment, placed in a file on the network to be accessed at a later date, or hyperlinked from a web page. There are many possibilities depending on the organization's current practice for handling these kinds of documents.

2.   Letters. Letters written and addressed to supervisors and employees are the backbone of internal and external organizational communication. With the aid of a computer, individualized letters are being used more frequently to establish direct, speedy communication with employees and target audiences. The advantages of using letters are economy, individualized format, impact, and speed. A major disadvantage is that you cannot know if the letter has been read.

Letters supplement magazines and newsletters. Letters offer an opportunity for senior management to communicate policies and procedures directly to a target audience and their families. The procedures analyst can coordinate a communication campaign with the CEO or President to send out a personal letter describing important new processes, policies, or procedures after internal communications have been used for disseminate important information.

3.   Newsletters. Newsletters are the most formal of periodical publications. They are relatively easy, fast, and inexpensive to produce. Newsletters have the advantage of speed and are quick to read. Like a letter, the newsletter lacks feedback and you cannot be sure if the message was read or received as intended. This kind of communication works well if the information is aimed at the employees' local work areas.

Many large organizations still use newsletters to disseminate timely policy and procedure information to all employees. Unfortunately, newsletters often do not change the behavior for large numbers of employees. The newsletter can, however, be used as a supplement to other media used. The newsletter is a good vehicle for supplementing information after the frontline supervisors have had a chance to communicate the information to their employees.

The procedures analyst can write a column in a newsletter and ask for feedback or he can place a short paragraph in the newsletter to announce a forthcoming change or new process, policy, or procedure that is being published. A chief problem with the placement of policies and procedures information in a newsletter is the editor often has his own deadlines. If a deadline is tight or if the newsletter has lots of stories and advertisements, then information about policies and procedures is often dropped. The procedures analyst can combat this deadline problem by designing and issuing his own newsletter.

4. Magazines. Magazines are an internal publication that most often have the largest impact because they can be comprehensive, entertaining, and dynamic. Magazines take a long time to produce and they can be expensive. Magazines can be useful when announcing a forthcoming new business process or a policy. One disadvantage is the procedures analyst cannot publish timely material in magazines because each issue can take up to three months, or longer, to produce.

5. Paycheck Stubs or Inserts. Anyone who has received bills from utilities, credit card companies, or cable companies know about inserts and enclosures. Short, one-line, messages about business processes, policies, and procedures can be an excellent use of white space on the lower portion of a check.

6. Posters. Posters are often large, colorful cardboard pictorial or decorative displays that are hung on walls or doors in work areas. The themes of such posters are usually safety, health, housekeeping, productivity, teamwork, and security. Campaigns for TQM, team building, or employee referral contests are often done through a series of posters over a period of time. Themes on posters can also be used in conjunction with the roll-out of policies and procedures. For instance, at a division of Eastman Kodak where I worked in the 1980's, we published a procedure on team building and meetings. We coordinated this roll-out with the TQM committee that was a similar campaign.

7. Bulletin Boards. The use of bulletin boards might seem like a thing of the past but they are widespread in companies and are here to stay. Bulletin boards can be open and hung on a wall or enclosed in a glass case with a locking door. Bulletin boards offer a good place to display information that can corroborate policy and procedure information. The messages should be brief and easy to read from ten or twenty feet.

    The procedures analyst could take it upon himself to research and draft a procedure on bulletin boards. There are a variety of bulletin boards in a company and are often controlled by departments like Human Resources or Administration and are frequently employee-generated postings. Information about new business processes being evaluated or new policies or procedures being published can be displayed, and using brightly colored paper for easy visibility for passing employees. When I worked in a manufacturing company in the 70's, I remember placing a bulletin board near the Human Resources lobby to display the most current table of contents for published policies and procedures.

    When I worked for a division of Eastman Kodak, we had a Bulletin Board procedure that specified that all information to be posted would be forwarded to the Human Resources department for review, posting, and maintenance. This information would be maintained on the bulletin board for no longer than five business days.

8. Brochures or Pamphlets. Brochures and pamphlets are typically produced as 5½" x 8½" booklets. These booklets are often used to supplement a major program like policies and procedures, TQM, or Business Ethics. Brochures or pamphlets are an excellent reference source and can be distributed to all employees quickly. These publications can be used as supplemental reference material to published business processes, policies, or procedures.

    For instance, business ethics, sexual harassment, or timekeeping are good examples of topics for pamphlets. Separate policies and procedures are written and disseminated to all employees but these pamphlets can also be written for employees for easy reference at their work stations. Pamphlets can be distributed with paychecks or handed to the employees as they exit their place of work.

9. Training. Training is the topic of the next chapter but this subject has been referenced because it is also considered to be a communication method. This communication method is almost universally selected as a part of a communication strategy as it is the method traditionally used to share information with employees. Training can come in many different formats; for the purposes of this book, I will address the traditional formal training in classrooms, computer-based training, or informal training by supervisors or professional trainers.

    The purpose of any training program is to deliver results. The goal is for individuals to be more effective after training than before. Training is an excellent communication tool for teaching the importance of using a new policy or procedure. The repetition and reinforcement of ideas presented during training is what enables employees to assimilate the information more quickly than learning by trial and error. Mentoring and coaching will also be introduced as a method to help employees reinforce the learning process. Training must be combined with as many tools as possible to ensure the information received during training is assimilated quickly into the workplace.

10. Team Meetings. Team meetings bring people together, providing opportunities to speak and listen: *Two-way communication is established.* People come together in a meeting setting for many reasons including to discuss a process, review the activities of the week, or discuss the next holiday party. These meetings can be formal or informal. The procedures analyst can use a meeting in three ways:

    a. Conduct cross-functional team meetings.

    b. Develop sponsors and champions for the purpose of promoting policy and procedure topics in their work areas.

    c. Conduct one-on-one interview meetings when doing research and coordination at just about any phase of writing effective policies and procedures.

    The more ways the procedures analyst can find to share information about policies and procedures, the better chance that these policies and procedures will be followed and applied. The compliance level will also be raised with more employee involvement in writing effective policies and procedures.

11. <u>Town Meetings</u>. In the corporate world, the term, *town meeting*, refers to an informal meeting whereby the CEO, President, or member of senior management will speak to a large crowd about major events or news. Town meetings can also be used to relay information about business processes, policies, and procedures. This is a perfect opportunity for a procedures analyst to ask a senior manager presenting at a town meeting to speak about an important subject that might be troubling the policies and procedures department. For instance, let's suppose that a new process or procedure has been rolled out regarding a documentation method which has not received the attention it deserves. The senior manager can explain the importance of the documentation method and ask for the support of those attending the town meeting. The procedures analyst can follow up reinforcing messages presented in several communication methods.

12. <u>Voice Mail</u>. Voice mail (i.e., an electronic communication system in which spoken messages are recorded or digitized for later playback to the intended recipient) is a voice messaging system normally offered by a local telephone carrier. This technology offers such features as broadcasting capability, immediate message delivery, answering services, paging notification, or directory search. When voice mail is used for "group broadcasting," it will save time and money when sending information to all of the users of voice mail technology. In the case of the dissemination of policies and procedures, it works well to broadcast a short policy statement along with a brief overview of the communication strategy that will be used to communicate a process, policy, or procedure.

13. <u>Conference Calls</u>. A conference call is a feature offered by a local telephone carrier on a telephone whereby three or more conversations can be connected into a single call. A conference call has two primary uses, though it does serve other purposes as well. First, meetings can be conducted when the attendees are geographically dispersed, and second, conference calling often supplements video conferencing when

compatible video conferencing equipment is not available. This method is especially useful when a CEO makes an announcement and haves everyone to be present.

14.   Video Conferencing. Video conferencing is a relatively new and innovative method of communication for sharing information between two or more geographically separated individuals or groups in which audio and video images of the participants are transmitted between locations. The video images might be sent either in one direction or in both directions and can be both audio and video or just audio or video in either direction.

Technological advances in satellite communication have expanded the range of possibilities for meetings and speeches. Senior management can use satellite video to reach employees in a global organization. Video conferencing is an excellent media for working with business processes, policies, and procedures especially when team members are geographically separated by buildings, states, or even other countries.

15.   Electronic Mail (Email). Email (i.e., messages sent and received electronically as between terminals linked to telephone lines or microwave relays) has revolutionized the sending and receiving of mail. This form of communication has caught on so fast and is so popular that it cannot be ignored as an excellent form of inexpensive, fast, efficient form of communication. Email has almost become transparent, requiring no knowledge of how it works, to use it effectively. Presentations, video and audio files, word processing documents, and graphic files can be attached to an email message and forwarded to anyone in the world with an email address and compatible hardware and/or software. Also, there are services which can convert email to a FAX for almost the same costs as for email, which is virtually nonexistent. Thus, if the recipient does not have an email address or compatible equipment, the information can still reach him, using these FAX services that are seamless to the sender and receiver. Email makes it easy to send policy and procedure updates and forms that are a part of a business process, policy, or procedure.

16.   World Wide Web (www). The web is a global hypertext system for locating and displaying Internet resources. Web characteristics include

graphics, easy navigation, cross platforms, and dynamic interactions. The World Wide Web (www) has made it possible to transfer data between computers on the Internet to virtually anywhere in the world where there is receiving equipment capable of accepting this data, e.g., personal computer, cellular phone, pager, palm pilot, or other wireless instruments. The procedures analyst can promote policies and procedures through a web site dedicated to a policies and procedures infrastructure. I like the use of a web site for policies and procedures because so much information can be placed on a web site that can be searched and updated within minutes of a change being approved. Decision makers are able to analyze business processes, business opportunities, and business goals much faster, when information can be retrieved quickly.

17. <u>Videotape</u>. The videotape has been used for many years but it is not as popular as it used to be because of its cost and reproduction concerns. Videos are effective under two conditions: *First, communicating technical information with immediate application and, second, senior management responding to a dramatic event of concern to all employees*. Videotape has little chance of changing the behavior of employees because: (1) Videos are generally not targeting frontline supervisors; (2) Videos do not provide for one-one-one conversations; and (3) Videos do not focus on the performance of the local work area.

18. <u>CD-ROM</u>. The CD-ROM has been revolutionizing the storage industry. CD technology has been one of the most important developments in the history of the personal computer. Until recently, CD-ROMs have been expensive to reproduce and they have only been used for large catalogues or databases. With the recent technological advances, many personal computers have CD-ROM readers/writers and information can be quickly written to a CD-ROM for less than a dollar for 650 Mb of information, or the equivalency of 450 diskettes of 1.44 MB each. The CD-ROM is becoming a more viable option for sending out complete policies and procedures manuals on a single CD. Changes can be almost immediate because the CD-ROM can be quickly updated, duplicated, and mailed. The CD-ROM is an excellent media for transporting large quantities of information such as company manuals, reference material, or catalogues of information. While the CD-ROM has not been

61

traditionally used as a communication method by the procedures analyst, I believe the CD-ROM format will become a major communication method for procedures analysts in the future.

19.   Facsimile (FAX). The acronym "FAX" is a commonly used term for the word, "facsimile," which means exact copy. The FAX is a method for transmitting graphic images over a telecommunications facility. Messages can be broadcast to many locations all over the world at the same time using a FAX machine. The FAX is a quick way to send out one or two page announcements to supplement the dissemination of policies and procedures to other locations with compatible FAX units.

The FAX serves another important purpose: *There are some parts of the world where email equipment is not available — in this case, email can be converted to a FAX format.*

20.   Telephone. The telephone is one of the most important communication tools ever invented because it provides the ability to speak to another party from almost anywhere in the world. With the advent of cellular and satellite phones, people can be reached almost everywhere. This portability feature has brought new dimensions to communications. The Internet and email are now accessible to cellular phones. Cellular telephones provide some interesting potential as employees will be able to access policies and procedures from anywhere in the world depending on the coverage areas for cellular phones.

COMMUNICATING TO EMPLOYEES — THE RIGHT WAY

Communication has two goals: *Sharing information and improving performance.* Communication is supposed to help employees do their jobs better, but does it always? Management often believes that after an employee receives a training course, reads an article in a newsletter, receives a voice mail message from senior management, or listens to a CEO call for changes and requests that they return to their work areas, that they will perform their jobs better than before. The employee, however, does not learn this way. For many years, CEOs and senior management have always thought that the most effective way to reach employees is through communications intended directly for the employee, like letters addressed personally to each employee.

Let's take an example of a CEO who conducts a company meeting and invites all of the employees to the meeting. He proceeds to give a motivating speech about the deployment of a Total Quality Management (TQM) program and tells employees how business will improve almost immediately if they improve their attitude and strive for the highest quality in everything they do. He ends the speech asking for total support starting immediately. Following the speech, a communication campaign begins. Videos are sent to every company location. Three video conferencing rooms are set up and a toll-free number is provided for answering questions. The entire first page of the company newsletter is dedicated to the benefits of total quality management. Posters are hung in every hallway showing the TQM way. A contest is announced for the best quality improvement idea. Wallet-sized cards with the TQM mission and vision statement printed on them are given to every employee. The campaign continues.

➤You can guess what happens. Senior management is happy with their success; they think they have done everything right, quality will improve, and the company will reap the benefits of better products and service. The underlying assumption of this communication campaign is that the employees are likely to change just because the message came from the office of the CEO! Wrong!

> All of this glitter is just that, glitter. Senior management assumes that the CEO is a reliable source and that anything he says should be immediately followed because, after all, he is the leader of the company! Unfortunately, most employees do not even know the name of their CEO and have no reason to trust what he says. They will listen to the CEO, return to their jobs, and continue as usual as if nothing was said. Worse, management is not aware of this attitude!

COMMUNICATING TO FRONTLINE SUPERVISORS FIRST, NOT EMPLOYEES

Ask any employee whom they want their information from and the answer is almost always the same, from their immediate supervisor. The CEO is a stranger to most employees. This is not the credible source that they can trust and believe in. Management knows the CEO, but often few others have heard his name or seen him. Even if employees have heard his name, this is not enough when it comes to trusting him for buy-in and acceptance of important information. This is an important lesson for managers who need to understand just how important trust is to the dissemination of a message. Moreover, if senior management goes directly to the employee, they could be weakening the supervisors' ability to communicate information and changes, and consequently weakening the supervisor's ties to their subordinates. If you weaken the direct lines to the employee and to the supervisor, then going forward with a communication strategy might be a waste of time and money. Employees prefer to hear changes directly from their supervisor first. When the employees hear the CEO speak the same message at a later time, not only will they be informed, but they are more likely to put more trust in the message.

> Employees learn best from their supervisors! Management makes the assumption that employees listen to senior management. Employees trust their immediate management, not senior executives they do not know or have never even seen!

Employees have to believe in the source that is providing them information. If they believe that their supervisor is trustworthy, honest, and fair, then they will put their faith in him and turn to him to answer questions in a timely manner. The worst thing that can happen is for the employee to ask his supervisor a question and get an answer like, *"I don't know,"* or *"Where did you hear that?"* This is not the answer the employee was expecting. The supervisor is showing disinterest in the company and/or poor communications with his senior management. This is not what the employee wants to hear. The supervisor is the first line (or frontline) of management that needs to know information before the employee does. The supervisor needs to understand this information so he can relay it back to his employees with confidence and answer questions intelligently.

Few employees will find value in these communication methods unless the information came to them through their supervisors first. In other words, if new business processes and procedures are introduced all of a sudden, then the employee is unlikely to pay attention. But if senior management had sent the information to all supervisors at least a week (longer if time permits) prior to the communication strategy rolling out, then the published information will be supplemental to what they have already heard from their supervisors. The employees will be more receptive to information if they are already familiar with the information as received from a familiar source, i.e., their supervisor (Larkin, 1994).

I have one more example that will help to explain this point about the targeting the frontline supervisors first. When consultants are brought into a company to present a new concept, they will often target the employees and will conduct meetings for large groups of people. They are making the same mistake the CEO made in the previous pages, i.e., targeting the employees will not be effective unless the frontline supervisors are notified first and they have adequate time to communicate to their subordinates before a companywide campaign is launched. The consultants lacked credibility and trust just as the CEO did. These same consultants often do not consult the correct process owners, users, or subject matter experts. Management often directs them to several individuals who may or may not have the knowledge or expertise to answer all the questions of the consultants.

ESTABLISHING A COMMUNICATION STRATEGY — A COMBINATION APPROACH

The secret of establishing a communication strategy for a policies and procedures infrastructure is using a combination approach of (1) Targeting the frontline supervisor first, and (2) Using appropriate communication methods as referenced in Table 4-1. There are four steps to developing a combination approach to a communication strategy for business processes, policies, and procedures:

1. Determine what will be communicated, its frequency, the urgency of the message, and to which audiences. These choices will become more evident with the three textual and graphical examples that follow later in the chapter.

2. Determine the names of the frontline supervisors within the target audiences for which the process, policy, or procedure is going to be directed. While it is not always easy to learn the current names of supervisors, you might first go to the department responsible for hiring employees and ask for a complete listing. If this method is not successful, you might be able to obtain organization charts of the various target areas to find the names of the current supervisors. The last way is to contact the department heads of the target audiences and ask for a listing of supervisors (while this seems like the most logical way, in large companies, department heads may not have the most current information about the "supervisory" status of their employees).

    Depending on how large the organization is and how many supervisors have been identified, a strategy could be developed for reaching these individuals. When I worked at Litton Data Command Systems in

Agoura Hills, California, I asked the Information Technology Department (or data processing department) to generate a list for me of all current employees, supervisors, and managers weekly. Thus, I was assured of having the most current information at all times. The other methods cannot be trusted for complete and accurate information as organization charts are often not kept up-to-date.

3. Identify several effective communication methods to disseminate the content of business processes, policies, and procedures to the frontline supervisors: *There is no need to use all possible communication methods for this first communication to supervisors.* Once the front supervisors have received the information and disseminated it to their subordinates, select as many communication methods as feasible to disseminate the content of business processes, policies, and procedures to the target audiences. When the frontline employees receive the information a second time, it is more likely to be favorable received.

4. Begin the communication campaign by disseminating information directly to the identified supervisors with information on how to deliver this documentation to their subordinates. Commence the roll-out of the full version of the communication strategy to the target audiences. Coordinate these communication plans with any Company department that is responsible for communications, if one exists.

Separate communication strategies should be developed for disseminating communication methods to the frontline supervisors and for the supervisors to disseminate similar information to their subordinates. The methods for achieving these two strategies will be discussed in the next few pages.

STRATEGY FOR REACHING FRONTLINE SUPERVISORS

The fastest and easiest way to reach the frontline supervisors is through face-to-face meetings, voice mail broadcast, email broadcast, video conferences, or telephone conferences. The communication methods selected will depend on the size of the audience, their geographical locations, technology in place, and budget planned for the communication of this information. The message should contain the content of the business processes, policies, and procedures that is being disseminated as well as the game plan for disseminating this information to all users within the target audiences.

A combination of these communication methods would be an excellent way to reach all supervisors. Where the technology permits it, you can request an autoreply when a message is delivered, read, and even deleted without being read. In every case, you should ask for feedback within a few days after the information is sent. With face-to-face meetings are used, feedback can be immediate. The feedback will prove valuable in developing future communication strategies for new or revised policies and procedures. The procedures analyst could prepare a meeting notice as follows:

> *"The Policies and Procedures Department (or it could read the title of the senior manager requesting the meeting) invites each of the supervisors to attend a meeting (or listen to a conference call or video conference) one week from today (give exact location, date, and time). This meeting will explain the roll-out of a new method (business process, policy, or procedure) which will be deployed to the organization (or just name the functional areas impacted) one week (or specified time period) after you have had a chance to digest the new information and have presented it to your subordinates. As a frontline supervisor, you are required to attend this meeting. If you are unable to attend, you can call the following number (list number) for a replay of the message. If there are any questions, please call this number (list name and number)."*

The procedures analyst will often conduct these initial meetings to communicate the content of business processes, policies, or procedures to the frontline supervisors. He may invite other subject matter experts, or even the President or CEO, depending on the importance of the new or revised business process, policy, or procedure. For instance, the CEO may wish to be invited to a meeting that addresses business ethics, while he may not wish to attend a meeting that discusses new per diem rates to a travel policy. The meeting will address how the new or revised business process, policy, or procedure will be deployed. The meeting will also address how the supervisors should disseminate this information to their subordinates. Special training classes can be prepared for those supervisors who are uncomfortable with presenting this information to their subordinates. Briefing cards (8" x 5-1/2") could be prepared to help the supervisor with this presentation. Two paragraphs should be adequate. An example of a briefing card will follow in the next few pages (Larkin, 1994).

Supervisors must be given the opportunity to ask questions either in the meeting or after the meeting. Even after the supervisors present this information to their subordinates, they might have feedback that will be valuable when the information is rolled out to the target audiences. These written presentations can be altered many times depending on the feedback of the audience as they are presented. If feasible, the procedures analyst should plan on contacting each supervisor following the transmission of the messages being conveyed to determine if the message were understood. The procedures analyst could also attach a short questionnaire to any message being sent out to supervisors. The feedback from the answers can be helpful when rolling-out the business processes, policies, and procedures to the rest of the target audiences. Any feedback from the dissemination of policies and procedures will be useful in the continuous communication campaign. In summary, the procedures analyst could disseminate information to frontline supervisors as follows:

1	Determine the content that will be disseminated to the organization or selected audiences.
2	Request a meeting of all supervisors within the selected target audiences. Conference calls and video conferencing meetings can also be used depending on the size of the audience.
3	Conduct the meeting, or calls, and explain the information being deployed, its benefits, background, timing, and support.
4	Instruct the supervisors how to disseminate the information to their subordinates and to give feedback on how the information is received.

STRATEGY FOR SUPERVISORS TO SPEAK WITH SUBORDINATES

The supervisors should make every attempt possible to communicate the new information to their subordinates as soon as possible in a meeting setting and/or in face-to-face conversations. If this is not feasible, email or voice mail will suffice. More importantly, the supervisors need to explain this information to their subordinates in terms that they will understand. Research has shown that the supervisors can be most efficient if they can explain the information in terms related to the employee's local work area. Employees understand their own work environment and it is easier for them to relate to these changes if they are explained in terms of making their jobs easier and more efficient (Larkin, 1994). Information has less meaning if employees hear examples about the organization as a whole and/or about other departments. The supervisor needs to learn how to relate new information to the performance of their

68

subordinates' own work area to achieve the highest probability of acceptance to the new business process, policy, or procedure being deployed. The supervisors should ask for feedback so that this information can be returned to those managing the communication strategy. The feedback can be important because there could be subtle issues that have been overlooked which should be corrected before disseminating the content to the entire audience.

If feedback is not readily returned, the supervisor should discuss the importance of feedback during meetings or one-one-one interviews. Informal data gathering can be a lot less intimidating than a group of 200 members in a room. There are four steps supervisors can use to disseminate new information to their subordinates:

1	Speak to the employees in person through meetings or one-on-one conversations.
2	Give the information meaning by providing examples of the process, policy, or procedure as it relates to their local work area.
3	Ask for feedback to the information presented.
4	Follow up on a regular basis.

PRACTICAL EXAMPLE FOR SUPERVISORS

Let us take a scenario where the supervisors have been provided information about a new business process and now it is their turn to share the information with their subordinates in a way that the subordinates will be able to understand the information and apply it to their work environment. The scenario is one based on a real example that occurred to Litton Industries, a large defense company, in the 1980's. This example is recalled from memory: *I worked as a Policies and Procedures Manager at a division of Litton I..dustries from 1981 to 1984.*

This defense company conducted part of its business with the government and their purchasing practices were audited at a division somewhere in the southeast for compliance with governmental standards. A major audit revealed that this division did not have well-documented policies and procedures. Also, it was discovered that many purchases did not even go through purchasing. Requesters were doing their own research and negotiations with suppliers. Items were ordered without any kind of supporting documentation and when received they were not even inspected. The audit resulted in the entire company being requested to do something about their purchasing system or give up governmental contracts. The company decided to comply. The Policies and Procedures Department of each division became involved and developed new business processes, policies, and procedures to tighten the purchasing process and to satisfy the government's concerns.

With the completed business processes, policies, procedures, and new purchasing forms, the procedures analyst knew that his first step was to distribute the information to the frontline supervisors and then deploy a communication campaign to the rest of the company. Working with the Communication Department and the CEO, a summary statement was written; the CEO was asked to personally deliver the message to frontline supervisors through town meetings, letters, and pamphlets. The CEO granted the procedures analyst the necessary authority to continue with the roll-out of the new purchasing system.

The procedures analyst set up meetings with the supervisors. Multiple communication methods were used including employee and staff meetings, newsletters, pamphlets, and video conferencing. The procedures analyst indicated the importance of following the new purchasing system and asked for their cooperation in communicating this information to their subordinates in ways that would make sense. The key change was the Purchase Requisition form; it was important that when items were requested that a Purchase Requisition form be prepared and forwarded to the Purchasing Department for placement. The buyers would document the placement steps, award a Purchase Order to a supplier, and set up inspection instructions for receiving the items when they arrived at the receiving dock. The important point about this new purchasing system was that it was documented and that only authorized buyers could contact suppliers and negotiate orders with them.

The procedures analyst communicated first to the frontline supervisors and provided briefing cards and asked that they tailor the information to fit the work environment so the subordinators can relate and comply with the new business processes, policies, procedures, and forms. Below is an example of the "briefing card" we used:

BRIEFING CARD EXAMPLE

> *"We have been informed that our purchasing system is inadequate and that if we do not clean up our act, we'll lose our governmental business; losing that business could result in a major downsizing*

initiative. We do not want this to happen, thus, I am asking you to pay attention to me now."

"I have copies of the new purchasing system on my desk. These documents include business processes, policies, procedures, and forms. While it is not necessary for each of you to read this information, it is important that you no longer call suppliers to ask about items you want to buy. Rather you need to complete a Purchase Requisition form with the information you want, come find me to sign it, and then send it to the Accounting Department for budget approval and then to the Purchasing Department for processing. You will get your requested items in accordance with your urgency. The Purchasing Department will work with us; they will make mistakes in the beginning, as we will. Please use this new system. You have a chance to control your own future by helping out, so let's do something about it, and show the other departments that we are the best."

"In about a week or two, the company will start a communication campaign to reach all of the employees in the company. Look for newsletter articles, posters on the wall, pamphlets, and FAX reminders. Please ask me any questions that you might have now or in the future. We want to get this right; we do not want to be losing any business. Thank you for your cooperation."

THREE EXAMPLES — SELECTING COMMUNICATION METHODS

I have added three examples to this chapter to illustrate how different communication methods might be used when publishing new or revised policies and procedures. The selection process of communication methods for the target audiences is often done in parallel as information is being disseminated in advance to the frontline supervisors. The procedures analyst will be ready to roll-out the communication campaign to the rest of the target audiences after the frontline supervisors have had a chance to ask questions and to communicate the changes to their subordinates, and possibly return feedback to the procedures analyst. The procedures analyst may have to adjust his communication strategy to the rest of the target audiences if major concerns are voiced by the frontline employees. Each example will contain a scenario, a visual selection of methods, and an explanation of each selection. The supervisors will have already received the information and will have communicated it to their subordinates. The key aspect to remember is to select as many communication methods as possible within your schedule, timing, and budget. The selection process will vary depending on the content, make up of target audiences, and the commitment of management.

FIRST EXAMPLE
New Purchasing System

In this example, a new purchasing system (Chapter 3, *"Focusing on a Case Study to Apply the Principles of this Book"*) has been completely documented including all of the business processes, policies, procedures, and forms, additionally, the new system has been approved by senior management and the President and CEO. A procedures analyst and a cross-functional team has researched, analyzed, coordinated, and published the documentation necessary to implement the purchasing system. The purchasing system is ready to be deployed to the organization. Refer to Figure 4-1 for a sample communication strategy for a new purchasing system and to Table 4-2 for an explanation of the communication methods.

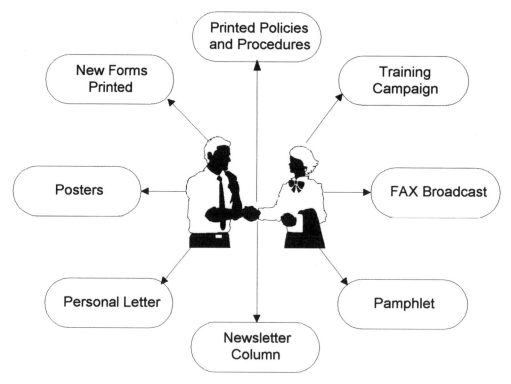

FIGURE 4-1: *New Purchasing System — Communication Methods*

During the first review and coordination of the new purchasing system, the procedures analyst has already identified many supervisors and each of them is ready to move forward. The early coordination with the supervisors makes implementation easier and compliance will be higher than had this coordination <u>not</u> taken place.

The new business process, policies, procedures, and forms have been printed and are ready for distribution. Training classes will be conducted, letters will be mailed out, and a FAX broadcast will be used to announce that the new system is effective immediately. A newsletter column will be run throughout the year with emphasis being placed on the first several issues. The newsletter article will describe the importance of the new system to the company and why everyone should discard their old ways of doing things, and follow the guidelines of the new system. Posters will be hung on the walls and displays will be placed in strategic places (like in the cafeteria, vending machines, or near the exit doors) to stress the benefits of the new purchasing system and the importance of employees adhering to the business processes, policies, procedures, and forms generated from the new system.

TABLE 4-2: *Explanation of Communication Methods — New Purchasing System*

NO	COMMUNICATION METHOD	USE OF COMMUNICATION METHOD
1	Business Processes, Policies, and Procedures	Policies and procedures are printed and formatted for distribution to the system of company manuals.
2	Forms	Purchase Requisition forms are printed and stocked in a forms stockroom. The old forms are discarded.
3	Training Campaign	Training classes and mentor programs are used to assist employees with the assimilation of information into their work place.
4	FAX Broadcast	CEO sends out a FAX broadcast about the importance and benefits to using the new purchasing system. This FAX could be directed to sales offices and other remote areas.

5	Pamphlet	The pamphlet, signed by the CEO, is printed with a list of the guidelines of the purchasing system. The pamphlet is distributed to each employee.
6	Newsletter	Articles about the benefits of using purchasing system are printed in the weekly newsletter.
7	Posters	Posters are printed with colorful, visual displays of the process flow of the new purchasing system. These posters are posted in hallways. Posters can also be hung on bulletin boards within each department.
8	Personal Letter	The CEO could send out a letter first to the frontline supervisors; a week later, a letter could be sent to employees explaining the benefits of the new purchasing system.

The communication campaign can be coordinated to repeat messages, provide ongoing newsletter articles, and change posters and displays. Checklists, continuous improvement tools, audits, and surveys can be used to determine satisfaction with the purchasing system and the way the new business processes, policies, and procedures were rolled out. The information gathered can be used to improve the communication campaign. The communication campaign of any new or revised policies and procedures should be continual until there is a revision to the specific business process, policy, or procedure. When the revision is communicated, a new communication campaign is developed for the revised policy or procedure.

EXAMPLE TWO
Revision to a Travel Policy
Updated Travel Guidelines

In this example, the procedures analyst has revised a policy for travel guidelines. He has learned about two tax law changes that might impact the Company's travel policies and procedures, from the Controller of the Company:

1.   The Internal Revenue System (IRS) has simplified the way meal and lodging expenses are claimed and reimbursed. Less documentation is required to prove the nature of these expenses. This is good news for both the company and employee.

2.   The mileage rate for driving a personal automobile while on business travel has been increased.

     This change will also cause several other policies and procedures to be changed that reference these rates. Examples include:

     a.   Local Business Travel Policy; and

     b.   Accounting Policy for processing travel expense reports.

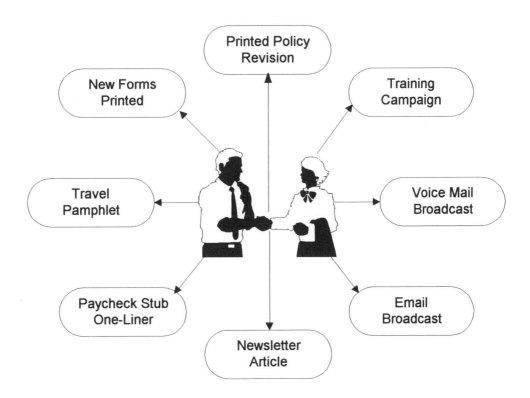

FIGURE 4-2: *Updated Travel Guidelines — Communication Methods*

Other changes to the policy include a revised printed expense report to accommodate these changes and an alternate electronic version.

TABLE 4-3: *Explanation of Communication Methods — New Travel Guidelines*

NO	COMMUNICATION METHOD	USE OF COMMUNICATION METHOD
1	Revised Policy	A new policy has been researched, coordinated, and approved by the CEO and his staff. The policy will be distributed to all manual holders. Policies will also be available upon request from authorized travelers.
2	New Expense Report Forms	New forms have been printed and are available in the stockroom. The procedures analyst will broadcast the location of the electronic version of the new expense report form.
3	Training Campaign	Frontline supervisors are responsible for setting up training times for those employees who travel on company business. Training is essential for new or revised policies, procedures, and forms. Training will be repeated every three months, or as requested.
4	Voice Mail	Summary message of the updated travel policy is broadcast to the target audiences through the telephone.
5	Email	Summary message of the updated travel policy is broadcast to authorized travelers through electronic mail. Samples of new expense report forms can be attached to email messages.
6	Newsletter Article	Two paragraphs have been written explaining new travel guidelines; articles will be run every other issue. The importance of the changes to the company and employee should be discussed. The location of the new forms should be identified.
7	Paycheck Stub	One line message is printed on stub announcing that a new expense report form has been designed and printed.

8	Travel Pamphlet	Four-page pamphlet is printed; as travelers request authorization to travel, they will be handed this travel pamphlet which is a summary version of the new policy.

The communication campaign can be coordinated in such a way to repeat messages, provide ongoing newsletter articles, and to send out periodic voice and email messages to all potential travelers. Checklists, continuous improvement tools, audits, and surveys are used to determine satisfaction with the travel changes.

THIRD EXAMPLE
Revision to the Travel Policy
Increase in per Diem Rates

For this third example, I have selected another revision to the Travel Policy but in this case, I have used a small change to illustrate how this kind of policy change could be executed. In this case, the only change is an increase of the meal rates from $40.00 per day to $60.00 per day for Washington, D.C., New York, and Los Angeles. Because many employees travel to these cities, this change needs to be communicated quickly. The first round of communication directed to supervisors can be bypassed because of the urgency of transmitting the message to authorized travelers. This type of policy change will be readily accepted and applied because it is a benefit to the traveler.

As the roll-out of this change must be quick, re-issuance of the policy does not make sense for a minor change like this one. Disseminating information directly to the supervisors does not make sense in this case. The change should be made in the file but held until there is another change that affects functionality. If policies and procedures are issued for every little change, it will create extra work for you and the distribution of multiple revisions of policies and procedures might not have the same impact as a revision that is released less frequent. Training classes are not needed for this small change; this change could be communicated with future training on travel guidelines.

Voice mail and FAX broadcast, email, and paycheck one-liners would make the most sense as they could easily be sent to all potential travelers. A new FAX broadcast could be distributed to all company administrators who assist employees who request authorization to travel. The broadcast message can be posted in strategic locations within their work area, e.g., near coffee services, copiers, fax machines, restrooms, conference rooms, or exit doors. The paycheck "one-liner" could be used indicating the rate change. A summary letter could be written by the Chief Financial Officer (CFO), or the Controller, that could be strategically placed within the Accounting and Payroll Departments. The letter could also be posted on bulletin boards. Short newsletter articles could be written in the next two issues. Refer to Table Figure 4-3 above and Table 4-4 below:

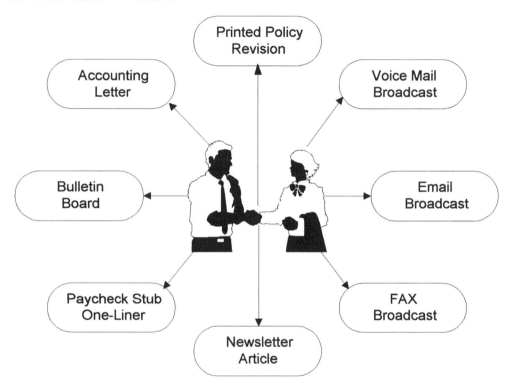

FIGURE 4-3: *Increase in Per Diem Rates — Communication Methods*

TABLE 4-4: *Explanation of Communication Methods — Increase in Per Diem Rates*

NO	COMMUNICATION METHOD	USE OF COMMUNICATION METHOD
1	Revised Policy	A revision is made to the policy but not printed until a more significant change occurs. The revision is held in a file with other revisions until there are a significant number to release.

2	Accounting Letter	Chief Financial Officer (CFO) or controller posts letter in Accounting and Payroll areas for administrative support personnel and for employees considering traveling to see.
3	Voice Mail	Procedures analyst or CFO broadcasts summary statement about the per diem changes to authorized travelers and administrative support personnel.
4	Email	Procedures analyst or CFO sends a summary statement about the per diem changes to authorized travelers and to administrative support personnel.
5	FAX	Procedures analyst or CFO mails or emails an Accounting letter to all authorized travelers and to administrative support personnel.
6	Paycheck Stub	A "one-liner" is printed on the paycheck stub announcing an increase in per diem rates.
7	Newsletter Article	Short articles are published in the next two issues of a company newsletter.
8	Bulletin Boards	Accounting letter signed by CFO or Controller announcing the per diem changes is posted on all available bulletin boards in company.

The communication campaign can be coordinated in such a way as to repeat messages, provide ongoing newsletter articles, and to send out periodic voice and email messages to all travelers. Checklists, continuous improvement tools, audits, and surveys can be used to determine satisfaction with the travel changes and the way in which the policy revision was rolled out.

If the procedures analyst or his management decides to use other compliance methods like questionnaires or feedback forms, the procedures analyst would adjust his communication strategy to reflect these new methods. He should also add the new methods to a review plan that is used to track external and internal changes. The concept of the review plan will be discussed in Chapter 6, *"Creating a Review and Communication Control Plan."*

SUMMARY OF THREE EXAMPLES

These three examples were used to illustrate how policies and procedures of different complexities and different audiences could be disseminated quickly and efficiently. I used a combination technique for these communication strategies. Using multiple communication methods is important because procedures analysts often believe that after they distribute a policy or procedure that it will be automatically followed. This is just an illusion on part of the procedures analyst to think that policies and procedures are read and applied just because they were approved by the CEO and distributed. While we can be assured that well-coordinated written policies and procedures will be accepted quicker than those that are hastily written without much coordination, we have no way of knowing if all of the users within the target audiences know about and use these policies and procedures. The purpose of this chapter has been to point out multiple ways to communicate published policies and procedures to target audiences. In the next chapter, we will address a training campaign coupled with a mentoring and coaching plan.

CHECKLIST FOR CHANGE:

✓   Create a communication strategy and decide who should coordinate the dissemination of business processes, policies, and procedures.

✓   Select communication methods for the dissemination of business processes, policies, and procedures to both supervisors and the target audiences. Decide which communication methods will be used for the target audiences.

✓   Understand the importance of communicating to the frontline supervisors before communicating to the employees.

✓   Understand how to decide if a revision should be held for a future release.

✓   Use the three examples that are presented to get an idea of how communication methods could be selected for different situations.

APPLYING WHAT YOU HAVE LEARNED:

Plan to study the communication methods presented in this chapter and find out which methods your organization has and which methods you can use. Work closely with your Communication Department and your Public Relations Department, if they exist, to identify what you can do for each other. Find out if your Communication Department has ownership of their communication methods, and if so, identify who to work with so you can have access to as many communication methods as possible. Build a strong relationship with these departments and with senior management so that when you have an important policy or procedure to publish and communicate, you can go to them for assistance.

Develop your own communication strategy. Pick applicable communication methods for the dissemination of business processes, policies, and procedures to both frontline supervisors and to target audiences. Establish a policies and procedures newsletter. Start "tooting your own horn" by advertising your department and the benefits that your department provides to the company. Assist supervisors and employees whenever possible with the interpretation of business processes, policies, and procedures.

ACHIEVE 100% COMPLIANCE:

In this chapter, the communication strategy has brought you one step closer to ensuring that the target audiences are complying with the implemented policies and procedures. With the combination technique of disseminating first to frontline supervisors (and supervisors to their frontline employees) and then to the rest of the target audiences through a communication campaign using a number of communication methods, there is a higher probability that the published and communicated policies and procedures will be more readily accepted. As acceptance rises, the compliance level should also rise.

REFERENCES:

Alessandra, Tony, Ph.D. and Hunsaker, Phil, Ph.D., *Communicating at Work*, Fireside Book, Prentice-Hall, Inc., Englewood Cliffs, New Jersey, 1993.

Carr, Clay, *New Manager's Survival Manual*, John Wiley & Sons, Inc., New York, New York, 1989.

Cohen, William A., *The Art of the Leader*, Prentice-Hall, Inc., Englewood Cliffs, New Jersey, 1990.

Cutlip, Scott M; Center, Allen H; Broom, Glen M., *Effective Public Relations,* Prentice-Hall, Inc., Englewood Cliffs, New Jersey, 1985.

Dilenschneider, Robert L. and Forrestal, Dan J., *The Dartnell Public Relations Handbook*, The Dartnell Corporation, Chicago, Illinois, 1987.

Floyd, Elaine, *Quick and Easy Newsletters*, Newsletter Resources, New York, New York, 1998.

Hall, Brandon, *Web-Based Training*, John Wiley & Sons, Inc., New York, New York, 1997.

Hendricks, Dr. William; Bartlett, Sam; Gilliam, Joe; Grant, Kit; Mackey, Jack; Norton, Bob; Siress, Jim; Stanley, Jim, and Wright, Randall, *Coaching, Mentoring, and Managing*, Career Press, Franklin Lakes, New Jersey, 1996.

Litton Industries, Inc., located in Beverly Hills, California: *In the 1980's, there was an incident in the Southeast whereby one of Litton's divisions had a severe fallout from an audit that caused headquarters to re-examine the purchasing business processes of all its divisions worldwide. I have recalled this incident from memory and while some of the details may be incorrect, the purpose for using this example is clear.*

Svenson, Get and Riderer, M.J., *The Training and Development Strategic Plan Workbook*, New York, New York, 1992.

Swindle, Robert E. and Swindle, Elizabeth M., *The Business Communicator*. Prentice-Hall, Inc., Englewood Cliffs, New Jersey, 1989.

Vicker, Lauren and Hein, Ron, *The Fast Forward MBA in Business Communication*, John Wiley & Sons, Inc., New York, New York, 1999.

Chapter Five

Developing an Effective Training Strategy

The demands of our new economy have made employee know-how or expertise a strategic necessity because of the increasing flexibility needed in production and service delivery, the customer's increasing requirements for service and quality, and the need for advanced technologies. High-performing and successful organizations depend on employees who can perform complex tasks like problem-solving and decision making. As tasks have become increasingly complex, they have also been subject to constant change. The demand for employee expertise and the accompanying need to meet changing expertise requirements have placed greater emphasis on training programs that meet the business needs of an organization.

Training is the primary means in which organizations develop employee expertise. Expertise is what the most capable employees know and can do on the job, while training is the means used to communicate that knowledge and skill to others. Training alone cannot make an employee an expert. Training can only help an employee achieve a level of mastery; the employee must make an effort over time to develop expertise.

Training strategy is a subset of the communication strategy as described in Chapter 4, *"Establishing a Communication Strategy."* Training has its own chapter because it is the only communication method that could have a substantial plan of action. Training is often selected as a communication method as a part of the communication strategy. The training strategy, in addition to presenting nine training methods, will introduce the important role of a mentor and coach for transforming information obtained during training into learning and subsequently into knowledge and wisdom.

Training is defined as to make prepared, to teach to be proficient, to undergo instruction, or to practice. In business, training is the formal process used to develop in an employee the attitudes, knowledge, and skills an employee needs to make him capable of efficient performance (i.e., needs less time to carry out assignments).

Formal business training can include the traditional classroom, computer-based training, web-based training, and team meetings. Informal business training includes learning from others in one-on-one discussions, from manuals, or lesson books.

Training is not new to us. We have been involved in some form of training all of our lives. We have experienced formal training in school and informal training like advice from friends and parents. We could not have grown as individuals without this training. Training started with our upbringing as children. Our parents, or care givers, brought us in this world. They taught us to laugh, play, sit up, crawl, eat, talk, use the toilet, and walk. Later, we entered school and we were taught how to live in society. When we entered the workplace, we were taught our jobs in a variety of ways including learning by trial and error, in classrooms, from others, or through manuals, books, or tutorials.

The training strategy is one of the components of the second phase (i.e., Publish & Communicate) of the "Policies and Procedures Improvement Cycle" (PPIC). Other components of the second phase include the communication strategy (Chapter 4, *"Establishing a Communication Strategy"*) and the publication of policies and procedures (Chapter 2, *"Writing Effective Policies and Procedures"*).

TOILET TRAINING — AN ANALOGY TO BUSINESS TRAINING & LEARNING

Toilet, or potty, training is perhaps the first important training event in our early life; it is a combination of training methods including on-the-spot training, just-in-time training, mentoring, and coaching. All of these methods are important to training in the business environment. I use this example of toilet training for two reasons: (1) We should all be able to identify with toilet training, and (2) The methods and techniques used in toilet training provide insight to how training could be executed in business.

Our care givers taught us how to use the toilet four ways including telling, showing, doing, and assisting. Toilet training is not a self-taught or a self-motivated task like learning to walk. Some children do learn toilet training on their own but this learning follows some kind of observation: *Using a toilet is not a natural act.* Children need the assistance of care givers in learning what is expected of them and how to perform the many small activities that are a part of becoming responsible for their own toileting. Toilet training is like any ideal business training situation — first you are taught and shown how to do something by training instructors, then mentors and coaches (these individuals could be the same training instructors) enter the picture and watch as you practice an exercise. The training is completed as your care givers watch as you try it solo when it is believed you are proficient.

Toilet training should be slow and deliberate. The goal of toilet training is to become independent and responsible for attending to toilet matters. The objective is to turn this information gained from the care givers into knowledge that can used to improve the situation; in this case, the goal is to go from messy diapers and accidents to a responsible child who uses the toilet without added assistance. (*I need to add that toilet training is no easy task. There are many variables that can slow the training process; this example is meant to be a simple analogy. There will be some children that never really learn.*) No matter how long it takes and by what techniques, the results are always the same: *The child learns to use a toilet through the guidance of his care givers and through the regular repetition of practice sessions in the child's "living" environment.* The care givers also give the child encouragement and praise for making advancement toward the goal of becoming proficient and independent in the use of a toilet.

> The child learned how to use a toilet because he applied his training to his environment. Learning can be accomplished when training is applied to the child's personal (or work) area.

The most important lesson learned in this toilet training activity is that the child was given the opportunity to learn what he was taught immediately following training and each day thereafter until he was able to do it without guidance from a care giver. The child is the student who has taken the instructions and used them in his everyday routine. The care givers became the child's mentors or coaches when they were reinforcing his learning. Typically, training deepens the knowledge a person has about a subject, in this case, it was about using the toilet.

The process used to toilet-train children is very similar to the ideal way an employee should be trained. Following training, the employee needs a mentor to help him with the application of the new information to his work place. He then uses this knowledge and wisdom to make improvements to his work environment. In the section above on toilet training, the primary lesson learned was that a child could be taught to use a toilet over time through repeated instruction, encouragement, and mentoring. If an instructor could use real life props (a potty chair) and a realistic goal (to become proficient using a potty chair or toilet), learning could be achieved. With learning comes knowledge and wisdom to apply this new information to achieve improvement to the process. In the business world, we learn from this lesson that knowledge and wisdom can be attained by:

1. Receiving training in a formal or informal setting

2. Receiving motivation, praise, and regular reinforcement from mentors, coaches, or managers

3. Repeatedly applying new information to a work environment

4. Receiving feedback from continual, incremental successes

Just as in business, the trainee will occasionally make a mistake and revert back to his old ways. The mentors and coaches must be prepared for these events and immediately give the necessary training and reinforcement to ensure the information is never lost.

TRAINING VERSUS LEARNING

Training teaches people to do things differently, which results in attitude changes. These changed attitudes are needed to modify the culture of an organization. Many people in business think that learning means training. They seem to think that after you are trained you have also learned something. The term *learning* means to gain knowledge or skill acquired by instruction or study. Knowledge or skills acquired by learning are by no means the same as undergoing instruction. Listening to a lecture, reading a book, or completing a computer-based training class has no bearing on your understanding or skill level of the subject matter taught. If you equate training to learning, you lose the ability to learn daily in your local work setting.

> If you equate training to learning, you lose the ability to learn daily in your local work setting.

People learn in two basic ways. First, they learn from experience, from using their five senses to observe and read, listen, feel, smell, and hear. Sometimes the learning activity is deliberate as with attending a class, reading a book, and listening to an audiotape. Second, people also learn from less deliberate methods like watching their own manager and other managers, and learning what we like and do not like. People also learn from discovery and trial and error. Sometimes we use scientific methods or critical thinking to make discoveries. We also discover by accident. We learn from other people by listening to people who have knowledge that we would like to develop in ourselves, brainstorming with other individuals who are facing or have faced problems or situations similar to ours, or observing how other people react to and deal with such situations. Knowledge is developed in its application to the job, people are only repositories of knowledge. Therefore, when we seek knowledge, we must learn from other people (Senge, 1999).

Learning occurs over time and in real life contexts, not in classrooms or training sessions. Learning in a real life context can be difficult to control, but it generates knowledge that lasts. The goal of organizations is for their employees to learn faster and smarter. The key is to see learning as inseparable from everyday work. Training, by contrast, is often one-time and detached from the context in which results are produced. Training is frequently viewed as something done apart from a job setting, perhaps in a classroom or lab area. You learn in training settings and you work in job settings. However, the line between the two is becoming more fuzzy. Learning can be supported both on the job and in formal training settings.

Most organizations think that training is critical to their survival in this century but as we shall see, they do not understand how it should be applied to gain its full value. Management thinks it is their duty to provide employees time for the "sake of training" to attend seminars, workshops, and local association meetings. They think that the trained employee makes their workforce more valuable and consequently, more competitive. Again, this perspective is wrong. Many training programs take place in some retreat, far away from a work setting, or business context. Even when people love the material, they find it hard to relate to the current work environment. Trained people may feel elated and motivated for a few days or weeks but this dissipates and work returns to normal in a few weeks or months without receiving support and reinforcement of what they learned from sources outside of the training environment.

TRAINING DEPARTMENTS

Many organizations make the mistake of setting up training departments and giving them total responsibility for employees' training needs. By placing the focus and responsibility for learning on a training group, company leaders and managers at all

87

levels give up their own responsibility for ensuring that employees gain the knowledge and develop the skills they need to succeed as individuals, as departments, and as a company. This shift of training responsibility to a training department can lead to undesirable consequences.

> Training can be an occasional activity but employees must learn continuously.

No matter how large or good, a training group cannot hope to understand the company's business as well as the employees and managers who run the company. Without the participation of frontline management, the training group can only examine generic training skills. By separating training from day-to-day business functions and goals, the company almost guarantees that training programs will have limited relevance back on the job. By equating learning with training, the company is ignoring, not fostering, the daily learning all employees must participate in if the company is to succeed. The biggest mistake the organization can make is taking the responsibility for employee-learning away from frontline management. This gives management a chance to ignore their own responsibility to reinforce the integration of learning activities in an employee's job.

> Training is not learning unless it can be practically applied and repeated.

Management must take responsibility for their employee's learning activities, provide continuous learning opportunities, and reinforce learning as employees try out new skills. When an individual uses training on the job, it becomes knowledge. When he applies this knowledge to his work place and makes improvements, he is using the wisdom he gained from training and learning (Senge, 1999).

> The issues of "training versus learning" are addressed in more detail in two books by Peter Senge, "*Fifth Discipline*," and "*The Dance of Change*." Both books are excellent because their primary focus is on change. I recommend that you read both books.

We have learned that training is not learning unless it can be practically applied and repeated. If an employee can return from training and be held accountable for incorporating the new information in their local work environment, then effective training might occur. For instance, if an employee returns from a seminar on using control charts for measuring policies and procedures, then the manager must insist that the employee start using control charts for measuring tasks, business processes, policies, and procedures. If the employee is uncertain how to apply the new information, he must feel that it is appropriate (in the company culture) to seek assistance from his management or other subject matter experts, and/or request a mentor to work with him to understand the information obtained from the training class or session.

> The objective of training is to teach information; when this information is applied to effective work settings, learning has occurred. The objective of learning is to generate knowledge and wisdom that lasts (Senge, 1999).

TRAINING MEANS MANY THINGS TO PEOPLE

The kind of training that we receive in our place of business will vary tremendously depending on the company's culture and management's commitment to training. Management's beliefs, definitions, and goals of training have a direct bearing on how people learn. They think that the ultimate purpose of training is to teach a person to be proficient. These proficient students are <u>supposed</u> to be able to go back to the work place and make improvements that will help the company become more competitive. This perspective is incorrect: *Management really thinks that training leads to learning (This is a major misnomer)*.

Think back on your career and ask yourself how many managers have said, "Okay, Steve, training is over, so let's get back to work. There is a pile of papers on your desk and you must have hundreds of email messages." The manager does not ask about training nor does he assist you with the application of the new information you heard. Too many managers treat training as a benefit rather than something of practical use to his department. They let their employees attend training sessions but have no intention of using that information in their department. They do not have time. Management often sees training as <u>separate</u> from the workplace. This problem of not taking training seriously is why we need to address an effective training strategy for policies and procedures. Processes, policies, and procedures are used in everyday life at work and training cannot be separated from their work environment!

AVOIDING THE "TRAINING TRAP"

Many companies are "trapped" by their tendency to offer training as a benefit and not as a "learning experience" that can be applied to the work environment. The *trap* is taking training for granted and taking training classes for any reason without an obvious or time-relevant relationship to an employee's work environment or personal goals. A shift needs to occur in business practices — employers should provide training close to the time when it can be applied to a problem, issue, project, or task. This has been called *just-in-time-training*. Providing training when it is most needed makes more sense than providing training as a benefit.

For instance, if an organization wants to train their employees in statistical methods or continuous improvement tools, they should provide training very close to the time when the employees will start applying this information to their work environment. Without this immediacy of using the information soon after it is received, the information will be quickly lost. Training fails when there are unrealistic expectations, courses which are not tailored to the audience, training which is irrelevant to the work place, when management does not support the subject matter, or when there is a lack of follow up on the part of the trainer and management.

With so much negativity about training, the procedures analyst has to be careful not to get in this "training trap" of teaching information about policies and procedures that is never used, or used improperly. Organizations that insist that their employees take a specific number of hours of training each year are not approaching the problem correctly.

For instance, many organizations require that, "Each employee shall take 40 hours of training each year." In this case, the training content is not specified, though it is assumed that the employee will take training that will help his job and his career. If an employee is a Purchasing Assistant and wants to take courses involved with the Purchasing function like supplier selection, negotiations, make or buy decisions, and purchasing performance measurements, his manager would likely approve these courses because they involve purchasing.

A VICTIM OF THE TRAINING TRAP

If you remember in Chapter 3, *"Focusing on a Case Study to Apply the Principles of this Book,"* the Purchasing Assistant provided administrative support to the

Purchasing Manager when reviewing incoming Purchase Requisitions forms for accuracy and consistency. While the above selected courses would be appropriate for a Buyer or Purchasing Manager, they would not be immediately useful for the Purchasing Assistant. You might argue that the career goal of the Purchasing Assistant might be to become a Buyer and eventually a Purchasing Manager and that these courses are appropriate. I do agree with that argument but I feel that the timing is wrong. If these courses are taken by the Purchasing Assistant, they will not be applied to his work place in the near future and this information will be forgotten. This training would not become knowledge and the Purchasing Assistant would not help the company make any improvements. Therefore, the Purchasing Assistant becomes a victim of the "training trap."

This "training trap" can be avoided in several ways. First, the Purchasing Assistant should select courses that would be applicable to his work area and beneficial to the Purchasing Department and the organization. Second, the Purchasing Assistant's management needs to become a part of the solution: *They need to become a mentor or coach to the Purchasing Assistant once he completes training courses.* Management needs to work closely with the Purchasing Assistant and develop a plan for incorporating the information that is gained in the training courses. Management should also help the Purchasing Assistant set up career goals and courses to help him achieve his business and personal goals over a specified time. Additionally, if management can provide a mentor to help the employee, it will reinforce his learning and the information will not be forgotten.

Establishing an effective training strategy for policies and procedures can be achieved if properly controlled by the procedures analyst. Not only can the procedures analyst ensure that the target audiences are trained using the most effective media for the situation but he can also coordinate a mentoring and feedback system with his management. In some cases, the procedures analyst can volunteer to be a mentor or coach for an employee.

BEST ENVIRONMENT FOR TRAINING

The best environment for training occurs when a company develops a culture that facilitates and encourages learning and open sharing of knowledge and ideas. The company should offer opportunities and the means for a wide variety of learning activities, sharing of knowledge and ideas, and coaching and reinforcement of newly acquired knowledge and skills. Employees must recognize the need for continual learning to improve their own performance and that of the company. The company becomes knowledge-enabled when it permits the employee to receive training, apply it to their work areas, and develop wisdom. Companies must endorse a culture that nurtures learning. This concept will be further explained in Chapter 13, *"Preparing an Organization to be Receptive to Change."* The procedures analyst is shown how he can assist the senior management of his organization to be receptive to change.

DEVELOPING A TRAINING STRATEGY FOR POLICIES AND PROCEDURES

A training strategy is a part of the communication strategy discussed in the previous chapter. The procedures analyst should ensure that any training program implemented as a part of a training strategy be interwoven with the communication strategy developed in Chapter 4, *"Establishing a Communication Strategy."* The communication strategy is planned before the training strategy. There is no sense in rolling-out a training strategy before the complete communication strategy is laid out.

A training strategy for policies and procedures is made up of two parts: (1) The selection of one or more training methods and (2) The coordination of the most appropriate method to ensure that the information obtained during training is integrated by the students in their work environment. The selection of training methods is dependent on the kind of material being presented and the impact it will have on the organization. For instance, if a major process is being rolled-out to the entire organization, then the procedures analyst will want to incorporate several training methods at the same time. If a new procedure is being disseminated that affects several departments, then one training method can be adequate if the appropriate methods of support are used. Methods of support can include the involvement of a mentor, coach, or manager to ensure that the material heard during training is applied to the employee's work environment. The procedures analyst can play a supportive role by assisting management in the mentoring role as needed. The procedures analyst is often the subject matter expert for policies and procedures and can make an excellent mentor.

SELECTION OF TRAINING METHODS

There are a variety of training methods available today from the traditional training room setting to multimedia, computer-based training. Training must be designed to give hands-on practice to bridge the gap between knowing how to do something and being able to do it. In the context of this chapter, the most popular methods will be presented, though there are many others available to the person doing the training. Methods for training have come a long way with the use of the computer and other multimedia capabilities. Computers have opened our minds to video conferencing training, web-based training, shared network meetings, and pre-taped audio training. The opportunities seem endless. Nine popular training methods are included below:

1. Lecture. This is the traditional method of training and is still used by most organizations worldwide. The lecture is conducted in the classroom where a topic is presented, handouts are distributed, and visual aids like an overhead machine, flip charts, white boards, or computer graphic displays, are used. Lectures can be used for hundreds, if not thousands, of people at one time depending on the size of the room or auditorium used. With the varied computer technologies available today, it is possible to employ video conferencing and audio telephone conferencing to broaden the scope of these training classes. Toll-free numbers can be offered for callers to call anytime to hear about new training material. There are many possibilities for the trainer. He should investigate different alternatives to ensure that he is presenting the material in the best possible way and reaching the most people at one time. While the lecture is the most common method for training policies and procedures, this method often results in poor learning unless a mentoring program accompanies the training process.

2. Workshops. This presentation method is best used for small groups of people (usually no more than 20). Workshops are used for short discussions or training topics and when the expected duration is an hour or less. The leader can be the supervisor or manager or sometimes the procedures analyst. The participants are the employees in the department. With small-sized groups, the leader can facilitate more than lead. Discussions and greater sharing of information are more likely when there are open dialogues rather than domination by one person.

The workshop is personal and is normally used within the employee's work environment. In this case, a process, policy, procedure, or form could be the topic of discussion. Workshops offer good interaction and feedback in a work setting and can be held without much preparation and notice. They could be set up by the employee's management or be requested by the employees within a department.

3. <u>Department Meetings</u>. Employees' supervisors should make it a habit to hold regularly scheduled meetings in their department to discuss issues and to conduct training. The leader is the supervisor or manager. The participants are the employees that report to the supervisor or manager. Department meetings provide an excellent opportunity to talk about new or revised business processes, policies, and procedures. These meetings could be held weekly, monthly, or even daily depending on the size of the department. The supervisor could request a procedures analyst to attend departmental meetings to support the presentation of a business process, policy, or procedure.

4. <u>Structured On-The-Job Training (OJT)</u>. On-the-job training is a process in which a supervisor or manager passes job knowledge and skills onto another employee. OJT is usually done at the work location or as near to the work as possible. In lieu of formalized training, OJT is an excellent way for a supervisor or manager to train employees in doing policies and procedures. OJT can be conducted in a team environment immediately following training. OJT can be a very effective method when several employees from one work area attend the same training course. There are seven steps to on-the-job training: (1) Showing an employee how to do a task; (2) Explaining the key points; (3) Letting the employee watch as you do the task; (4) Letting the employee do the simple parts of the task while you watch; (5) Helping the employee do the whole task; (6) Letting the employee do the whole task while you watch him; and (7) Letting the employee perform the job solo (Jacoba, 1995).

5. <u>Multimedia Training</u>. Multimedia training is computer-based training that uses two or more media, including text, graphics, animation, audio, and video. In practice, multimedia uses as many of these media as is practical to produce a colorful, engaging program delivered via the computer. A computer program will lead the student through the program at their own progress and pace. The multimedia training category often includes CD-ROM training, computer-based training (CBT), and web-based training (WBT).

6. <u>CD-ROM Training</u>. CD-ROM training is interactive multimedia training with audio and video files, stored on a portable disk, and presented on

a computer screen without the wait times cause by the Internet. CD-ROM training is good for remote sites or for employees who travel frequently where access to other means of training is not readily accessible. The CD-ROM format is quickly becoming popular for disseminating policies and procedures' manuals to employees all over the world.

My personal favorites in CD-ROM training include the *"Step-by-Step Microsoft Office"* series of books. They take each software program within Microsoft Office, add exercise files on CD-ROMs or floppy diskettes, and use a textbook to walk you through the exercises. These books are excellent and perhaps the best training tools I have ever used. My conclusion is that CD-ROM training can and does work if used properly.

7. Computer-Based Training (CBT). This is an all-encompassing term used to describe a computer delivered training class including CD-ROM and the web. CBT is also called Computer-based Instruction (CBI). Computer-assisted Instruction (CAI) is a subset of CBT. CAI refers to a computer program coded to display prompts and instructions to a student plus information and interactive exercises on a subject or topic. Moreover, the program is coded to keep track of the student's path and to offer immediate response to the student's input. CBT, CBI, or CAI would be an excellent use for policies and procedures training.

8. Web-Based Training (WBT). Web-based training is a type of instruction that is delivered over the Internet or over a company's Intranet. Advantages include cross-platform, readily available, flexibility, accessibility, convenience, cost and time savings, inexpensive worldwide distribution, and ease of updates. Training is accessed using a web browser over a company's Intranet. Web-based training is making a difference in organizations today by providing a way of delivering training that is often less expensive and more convenient than the alternatives. There are three types of web training:

    a. Text and graphics web-based training programs. These programs are text documents that are converted to HTML and then turn like pages in a book. Web viewing is easier than flipping paper documents. Displays can be enlarged and documents can be quickly accessed.

b.   Interactive web-based training program. This program is an interactive computer training program; at a minimum, it can include application exercises, drag and drop, column matching, testing, text entry, and even programming code entry. This goes beyond simple text and graphics and brings the trainee closer to the program with the content and practice exercises.

c.   Interactive multimedia web-based training (WBT) program. This kind of training allows the user to manipulate graphic objects in real time, sometimes taking on the quality of a game playing exercise. WBT is an inexpensive way to train employees to use various policies and procedures. WBT could also be a way to incorporate just-in-time training by offering training almost immediately after policies and procedures are updated online. A lecture could be delivered on specific policies and procedures; at the end of the class, a special URL address could be given to the student to continue practicing and eventual learning through an Intranet or the Internet.

9.   Computer-Assisted Network Discussion Groups. With the current technology, software companies are offering programs whereby employees can sit at a computer anywhere in the world and network with other computers through Internet meeting software. Presentations, spreadsheets, databases, or word processing files can be shared during this meeting. This is just another possibility that could be addressed for communicating policies and procedures.

TRAINING STRATEGY EXPLAINED - USING AN EXAMPLE

To explain a training strategy further, I have elected to use the *Purchasing System* case study described in Chapter 3, "*Focusing on a Case Study to Apply the Principles of this Book*." I have listed possible training topics for the *Purchasing System* in Table 5-1 below. I have kept the information simple and provided little detail as each organization has different organizational structures and training strategies for their purchasing functions.

TABLE 5-1: *Purchasing Training Topics — High Level*

PURCHASING SYSTEM	TRAINING CONTENT	TRAINING METHODS
Purchasing System (This course is a prerequisite to all other purchasing courses)	This course could be a systems overview course of the *Purchasing System*. The purpose, benefits, and importance of the system could be presented. Sample flow charts, policies, procedures, and examples can be used as handouts.	• Lecture • Department Meetings • CBT • WBT
Purchase Requisition Procedure	This course can be a follow up course to the *Purchasing System*. The purchasing procedure would be reviewed in detail with a focus on the supporting procedures and forms.	• Lecture • Workshops • Department Meetings • CBT • WBT • Mentors
Purchase Requisition Form Instructions	This course can be a detailed, hands-on course for understanding and using the purchase requisition form. There could be several relevant examples to the student's work environment. Self-assessment checklists can be used for the students to check their work.	• Lecture • Workshops • CBT • WBT • Mentors
MRO Buying Basics	This course could be developed for Buyers only within the Purchasing Department. Methods, techniques, and guidelines would be provided for understanding the importance of MRO items and how to negotiate with suppliers. Training can focus on every step from supplier contact, to ordering, and delivery.	• Lecture • Workshops • Department Meetings • CBT • Coaches

The involvement of mentors, coaches, and managers is important to ensure that the information obtained from these courses is applied to the trainee's work environment.

SELECTION OF TRAINER

The trainer for business processes, policies, and procedures should be the subject matter expert for the business process, policy, or procedure being released. This could be the process owner or department expert. In most cases, though, the better choice for the trainer is the procedures analyst. There are two reasons for this choice. First, the process owner may not be available to follow through on all the steps needed to roll out successful communication and training strategies. Second, the procedures analyst is normally the one held accountable for ensuring that effective policies and procedures are written, deployed, communicated, and trained. He has often been closely involved with research and analysis and understands the subject from a systems viewpoint.

MENTORING, COACHING, AND MANAGING

This is the time management has to do something for the employees. Their employees may have just returned from a lecture, a workshop, department meeting, or some kind of multimedia training. The manager has to do something to ensure the training his employee just received is worthwhile for the employee and for the manager's department. The information your employees gained during training will be lost unless the manager can do something to ensure that the employee is able to apply his training to his work environment. The next three sections on mentoring, coaching, and managing are for the supervisor or manager. Management can use these business processes to make a difference and help the employee with the application of his training to his work environment. A manager can be a mentor or coach, or both.

MENTORING

A *mentor* is a trusted guide. The definition of a mentor is someone who excels in a particular subject or skill and takes an interest in guiding and instructing a less experienced, usually younger person. While the mentoring role is often reserved for managing a person whose performance is standard or average, in business, a mentor can be used to assist other employees with their career development. A mentor can give feedback, help, suggest, advise, instruct, and use influence as he oversees life choices for another person.

When you mentor, it is your job to teach new skills. Mentoring is defined as hands-on instruction. In short, mentors teach their students. They also supply feedback on tactics for handling people and solutions to problems. They give support and help build self-confidence by encouraging their students with pep talks. Mentors will guide their student, help them take on more responsibility, gain promotions, and often risking their own reputation in the process. While the supervisor or manager is often the mentor for his employee, the mentor could also be an experienced person in another department, or even the procedures analyst, as he is often a subject matter expert for most company business processes, policies, and procedures.

There are three phases of mentoring (Hendricks, 1996):

1. <u>Observing</u>. In this phase, the employee observes you doing the job. As he watches you do the job, the employee should be answering questions. The supervisor needs to answer the following questions even if not asked, *"Why this job is important, what are the key components of the job, what are the cautions, what timing issues are crucial, and what's in this for me?"*

2. <u>Participating</u>. After you have demonstrated the job, the next phase is to have the employee do the job with you. Together you can determine how the job can be shared and determine how you can be confident that your employee understands the process. Allow plenty of time for the employee to learn.

3. <u>Doing It Alone</u>. Once you have done the task with the employee, it is time for him to do it alone. There are four questions to resolve: *How can the student show competency, what level of competency should be addressed, how much inaccuracy will be allowed, and when will the student be allowed to do unsupervised work.*

The primary focus of mentors is on helping individuals and teams engage in continual learning to identify what they can do, what they want to do, and what they must do to make the optimal contribution to their organization. A mentor cannot make change happen. A mentor helps people make changes. Besides teaching the employee how to apply the information learned from the application of training information to his work place, the mentor often helps the employee with other parts of his job like social interaction, problem resolution, general guidance, and rules of business etiquette. The mentoring process is one of the best ways to ensure trained material is applied to the employee's work area. Employees can learn business processes, policies, and procedures the fastest through training coupled with a strong mentoring program backed by management.

COACHING

Coaching is a process in which a manager gives employees feedback on how well they are doing particular duties and teaches them how to do better. The term *coach* is defined as to train intensively by instruction, practice, and demonstration. An effective coach is one who plays a supportive role all the time, not just once in a while. The greatest coaches are those who know how to motivate others to succeed, stay focused, believe in themselves, and overcome disappointments. Coaches inspire others to aim higher, work harder — and enjoy doing it. Coaches must be flexible, helpful, have empathy, be understanding, value the employee, be a good listener, have a proactive mind set, offer effective feedback, be enthusiastic and optimistic, and have a good sense of humor. When you look at football or soccer, there is almost always a coach on the sidelines. He inspires his team to play harder. The players must treat him as their leader and they must have total trust in him, or his support role as a coach will crumble (Hendricks, 1996).

When you apply coaching to policies and procedures, you can think of the coach as a manager that cares. Tom Peters came up with the concept called "Management By Walking Around (MBWA)." This means simply being with the members of your team. The manager needs to get out and be among his people and be available for questions and assistance. The more involved the manager gets with his team members, the more they will become involved with his goals and those of the organization. When you choose to get involved with team members, you are saying you care. You are saying each member is valuable to you and the organization.

Think for a moment about all those managers that made an impact on your life, how did they support and inspire you? The coach helps you clarify expectations and verify understanding. In a team meeting, the coach may be the leader or the facilitator and he will ensure that the team members work together with one another and stay focused on the topic.

When the employee returns from training ready to take on the world, you can be there for him. You can discuss what he has learned and answer questions. You can give him the go-ahead to put the training in practice. The coach role, in this instance, is to support and motivate his employees to use this new information. The coach will watch an employee doing his job and will ask questions about what he is doing and how he is doing it, in a non-threatening manner. He might say, "This is pretty complicated, please do not hesitate to ask me to make something more clear."

Relating to the Purchase Requisition form from the case study in Chapter 3, "*Focusing on a Case Study to Apply the Principles of this Book,*" the manager (coach) might be watching an employee completing a purchase requisition and he might observe some hesitation in completing the fields on the requisition form. Rather than show the employee how to complete the requisition as a mentor would, the coach could say, "Let's stop for a moment and deal with questions you have about this process. I had many questions myself when I first used one of these new forms." One of the most crucial things a manager can do as a coach is to offer feedback that can be easily understood and applied.

Some of the most common errors when coaching includes detached leadership, a failure to be specific, a failure to secure commitment, taking the course of least resistance, a failure to identify results, and impatience. Detached leadership, for example, is a serious offense for a manager because this person does not want to get involved with his employees. The manager would rather stay in his office and not communicate unless he has to, with this kind of coach, employees do not often make improvements. Another major error is when the manager tries to generalize instead of being specific in his comments or directions to his employees. This causes confusion on the part of the employees and often employees do not know what to do.

MANAGING

The term *managing* is getting things done through others. Your job as a leader is to work through the people who work for you. This is how you will get results from your team. Management cannot escape the responsibility for training. The responsibility for carrying out the intent of policies and procedures is shared by management. A truly good manager is really like a coach. The greatest coaches are those who know how to motivate others to succeed, stay focused, believe in themselves, and overcome disappointments (Hendricks, 1996).

Managers are coming to the painful realization that there is no "one-minute" solution to today's complex problems. Managerial mentors must think "out of the box" to become learning leaders. They must replace their traditional control-based practices with new working collaborations designed to meet customer needs in a changing marketplace. Their focus is on helping individuals and teams engage in continual learning to identify what they can do, what they want to do, and what they must do to make the optimum contribution to their organizations.

ROLE OF TRAINEE

Up to now we have addressed the trainer and not the trainee. The trainee (also called pupil or student) is often an employee. He may have been sent to a training class or has been asked to learn all he can about a subject by attending a lecture or seminar, or by participating in a CBT or WBT. The trainee may also have requested training on his own. The trainee has an obligation to his department and organization for which he works. When the trainee returns to his work environment, he must make an effort to use what he has been taught. If there is a mentoring or coaching program in place, he can ask his management about this program. If a program does not exist, he should make this information known to the trainer sometime before the training class starts. This way, the trainer can make an effort to contact the employee's management to ensure that they know what is expected of them when the trainee returns with new information to share.

CHECKLIST FOR CHANGE:

✓ Develop a training strategy for business processes, policies, or procedures. Coordinate the roll out of a training plan with the communications strategy.

✓ Select appropriate training methods based on their differing levels of complexity for business processes, policies, and procedures.

✓ Select a trainer for training classes.

✓ Apply training to the employee's work environment with the intent of turning training into learning, learning into knowledge, and knowledge into wisdom. Use this wisdom to make better decisions.

✓ Assign a mentor, coach, or manager to an employee returning from a training course to assist him with the integration of the training into his work environment.

APPLYING WHAT YOU HAVE LEARNED:

Set up a training strategy as early as it is known that a business process, policy, or procedure is going to be published and implemented. Work with process owners and subject matter experts to determine the best topics to receive training in to ensure that the correct information about a process, policy, or procedure is being taught to the target audiences. Keep abreast of changing technologies in training and utilize new techniques. Use the latest technologies available to your company.

ACHIEVE 100% COMPLIANCE:

The use of a training campaign as a part of a communication strategy is good practice. While there are many excellent methods to disseminate information like email, video conferencing, voice and fax broadcasting, or CD-ROMs, the training strategy is what holds it together. In the next chapter, *"Creating a Review and Communication Control Plan,"* a plan will be established to incorporate methods for ensuring that communication and training strategies are ongoing and not just one-time events. Deploying a training strategy with any, all, or part of the nine training methods coupled with a mentor and/or coach, will improve understanding by users within the target audiences. Process variation should be minimized, quality improved, cycle time reduced, and productivity increased — the result should be an increased compliance level when the business processes, policies, and procedures are measured.

REFERENCES:

Carr, Clay, *New Manager's Survival Manual,* John Wiley & Sons, New York, New York, 1989.

Carr, Clay, *Smart Training*, McGraw-Hill, Inc., New York, New York, 1992.

Cutlip, Scott M; Center, Allen H.; and Broom, Glen, *Effective Public Relations*, Prentice-Hall, Inc., Englewood Cliffs, New Jersey, 1985.

Deeprose, Donna, *The Team Coach*, American Management Association, New York, New York, 1995.

Eitington, Julius E., *The Winning Trainer*, Gulf Publishing Company, New York, New York, 1996.

Grieco, Peter L., Jr., *MRO Purchasing*, PT Publications, West Palm Beach, Florida, 1997.

Hall, Brandon, *Web-Based Training,* John Wiley & Son, Inc., New York, New York 1997.

Hendricks, Dr. William with Barlett, Sam; Gilliam, Joe; Grant, Kit; Mackey, Jack; Norton, Bob, Siress, Jim; Stanley, Jim; and Wright, Randall, *Coaching, Mentoring, and Managing*, Career Press, Franklin Lakes, New Jersey, 1996.

Jacoba, Ronald L and Jones, Michael J., *Structured-On-The-Job Training*, Berrett-Koehler Publishers, San Francisco, California, 1995.

Larkin, TJ and Larkin, Sandar, *Communicating Change*, McGraw-Hill, New York, New York, 1994.

Peters, Tom, *Thriving on Chaos*, Alfred A. Knopf, New York, New York, 1988.

Piskurich, George M., *The ASTD Handbook of Instructional Technology*, McGraw-Hill, Inc., New York, New York, 1993.

Schank, Roger, *Virtual Learning*, McGraw-Hill, Inc., New York, New York, 1997.

Scherkenbach, William W., *The Deming Route to Quality and Productivity*, Mercury Press, Rockville, Maryland. 1991.

Senge, Peter; Kleiner, Art; Roberts, Charlotte; Ross, Richard; Roth, George; Smith, Bryan, *The Dance of Change*, Currency Doubleday, New York, New York, 1999.

Senge, Peter, *The Fifth Discipline*, Currency Doubleday, New York, New York, 1990.

Tobin, Daniel R., *The Knowledge Enabled Organization*, Amacom, New York, New York, 1998.

Zweiback, Meg, *Keys to Toilet Training*, Barron's Educational Services, Hauppauge, New York, 1998.

Chapter Six

Creating a Review and Communication Control Plan

A review and communication control plan (shortened to "the review plan") may seem new to many readers, though this type of plan is probably something that we have thought about at some time in our career. A review plan is a summary of reminders so the procedures analyst can stay current with potential changes to policies and procedures. Once policies and procedures are published, trained, and communicated, some kind of review plan should be created to ensure that the policies and procedures become and remain an integral part of the daily work-lives of the target audiences.

Unfortunately, some procedures analysts believe that their jobs are done once they publish new or revised policies and procedures. I have been trying to change this attitude throughout this book and I will continue to give the procedures analyst reasons he should become involved and be accountable for policies and procedures over their life cycle. The procedures analyst should want to be in control of his policies and procedures throughout their life, after all, he is accountable for them! When policies and procedures have been published, your job has just begun. Now it is time to measure the policies and procedures to confirm that data is not just an opinion and to ensure that the policies and procedures are being followed or complied with. The procedures analyst should want advance notice/warning of possible issues, changes, or problems. The review plan will also be used to give the procedures analyst information about ongoing communication and training strategies.

This review plan should be used by procedures analysts for two reasons:

1. The value of the procedures analyst is typically measured by his ability to be *proactive* and anticipate changes to policies and procedures to ensure that management has the latest information to make timely decisions. In reality, the procedures analyst often hears about internal and external events that could change policies and procedures months later, through the grapevine, a chance meeting, or some other source.

Receiving information after the fact is very frustrating and the review plan is one way the procedures analyst may be able to become "proactive" rather than "reactive."

2. With the addition of the communication and training information to the review plan, the plan can be used to continuously promote business processes, policies, and procedures to improve the compliance of published policies and procedures.

REVIEW AND COMMUNICATION CONTROL PLAN EXPLAINED

A review plan is a listing, database, or a spreadsheet used for scheduling and monitoring changes in taxes, laws, organizations, communications, and training activities. The plan is a summary of reminders for the procedures analyst. Maintaining control of hundreds, if not thousands, of policies and procedures is difficult. With this review plan, it is possible to monitor any number of events or dates. When you start creating a review plan, you might want to start with business processes and policies. Later, as you see the potential of the review plan, you can add procedures and forms. The size of the review plan is dependent on:

1. Number of employees in an organization and their physical locations throughout the world

2. Number of company manual holders for new or revised policies and procedures;

3. Number of persons responsible for policies and procedures in the company

4. Job duties and range of authority for the procedures analyst

5. Management's commitment to the policies and procedures infrastructure

6. Cooperation of legal and tax functions responsible for providing information to the procedures analyst for potential changes

7. Existence of training, communications, quality, or audit departments that are separate from the policies and procedures function

8. Budget and resources committed to policies and procedures, communications, and training

REVIEW AND COMMUNICATION CONTROL PLAN CATEGORIES

There are three main categories in the review plan: *General reviews, ongoing communications, and a training campaign.* Categories can be added, changed, or deleted as needed. Within each category are subcategories or sections that will vary depending on the decisions made by the procedures analyst and management as to the variables that are tracked using this review plan.

When I first developed a review plan, "general review" was the only category. During the past several years, I added communications and training as two more categories because I found it was easier to track dates and time lines of all reminders in a single spreadsheet. Managing three separate spreadsheets for hundreds of business processes, policies, and procedures can become unwieldy. The procedures analyst should find this review plan useful; he may also use it for other tracking purposes such as for keeping track of policy, procedure, or form baselines and revisions.

A sample review plan has been included in Table 6-1 following this section. The three categories of this sample review plan are:

1. General Review. In this category, the procedures analyst can keep track of external and internal events that may cause changes to business processes, policies, and procedures. There are three subcategories in the "General Review" category. These three categories are the minimum sections you should include within a general review category.

   a. Tax Changes. This section is dependent on when your government releases new tax laws in your country. For instance, in the United States, the month when new laws are announced is usually in January. This month, January, would be inserted in this column for the appropriate business processes, policies, and procedures. When this date is reached, the procedures analyst should confer with his contact in the Tax or Finance Departments and determine if there have been any new or revised tax changes that may affect the content of current or potential business processes, policies, and procedures.

b.   New Laws. This section is dependent on when your government announces new laws in your country. If the month is March, you would insert March in the appropriate column. When this month is reached, the procedures analyst should confer with his contact in the Legal or Administration Departments and determine if there have been any new or revised laws that may affect the content of business processes, policies, and procedures.

c.   Event Driven Changes. This section is dependent on events that occur in a company that could cause changes to titles of employees, department names or functions, forms, or records. These events could include an organization change, an internal audit report, change in vision or mission, merger, acquisition of another company, change in forms, or change in another business process, policy, or procedure.

Additional subcategories could include external events that may cause changes to business processes, policies, or procedures like ISO Quality Standards, Capability Maturity Model (CMM), or external audits. The procedures analyst and management can add as many categories and subcategories as they think necessary to capture information for the review plan. Both the procedures analyst and management will find more ways to use this kind of spreadsheet for monitoring and promoting business processes, policies, and procedures.

2.   Ongoing Communications. This category reflects the communication strategy you developed in Chapter 4. These are communication methods that should be continuously applied after the initial communication strategy has been executed. If you wrote a newsletter article on the initiation of a specific policy, you might want to consider writing newsletter articles every four months to remind employees to use the policy. Other communication methods might be added for long-term promotions.

Your choice of communication methods for this section will be dependent on the communication strategy developed and on other variables like budget, number of people available to coordinate the added communications, and management's commitment to this activity.

The communication methods illustrated in the sample review plan in Table 6-1 are typical methods for an ongoing communication strategy.

3. <u>Training Campaign</u>. This subcategory reflects the training strategy you developed in Chapter 5. The training methods included in the review plan in Table 6-1 are those methods that are typically used for ongoing training plans. Like the ongoing communication category above, this category is dependent on variables like budget, numbers of people available to train, and management's commitment to this activity.

PUTTING A REVIEW PLAN INTO PRACTICE

While I know that the use of the review plan may seem overwhelming, it is really very easy to prepare and monitor if you give it a chance. Can you honestly think that your business processes, policies, and procedures operate on their own without extra involvement on the part of the procedures analyst? We would like to think that the policies and procedures can run without our assistance, but they will run more efficiently if we review them on a regular basis and ensure users stay focused on those business processes, policies, and procedures that impact their work environment. We are accountable for business processes, policies, and procedures over their life cycle and we must continue to communicate, mentor, train, measure, and improve them. When policies and procedures are published, the procedures analyst becomes the focal point for questions and interpretations of the published documents. The users are his customers and the Policies and Procedures Department becomes customer service to them.

A review plan is a great tool for a procedures analyst because it gives him a method for anticipating changes to published policies and procedures and a method for laying out ongoing communication and training plans for policies and procedures. The execution of ongoing communication and training strategies will move the organization closer to 100% compliance of policies and procedures or to business processes that are stable or in control.

The review plan is not only reinforcing the efforts you have taken to communicate and train users but it also provides you with reminders about tax changes, new laws, or events that might affect the content of your business processes, policies, and procedures. The effective use of this review plan ensures that your policies and procedures stay current so that your management can make better decisions.

TABLE 6-1: *Review and Communication Control Plan*

Training Campaign

Method	Description
CDROM	The CDROM should be changed as often as the policy or procedure changes
CBT/WBT	CBTs or WBTs should be changed as often as the policy or procedure changes, time permitting
Dept Meeting	Department meetings should be held weekly to discuss department matters and to discuss policies and procedures
Work Shops	Workshops should be held at least every month to discuss new, or revised, policies and procedures
Lecture	Lectures can be repeated as often as you like, with the minimum being once per year

Ongoing Communications and **General Review**

	Newsletter	Paycheck Insert	Posters	Bulletin Boards	Company Meeting	Email Broadcast	FAX Broadcast	Event Driven	New Laws	Tax Laws
Processes										
Customer Service	1/YR	NA	1/YR	NA	AR	NA	2/YR		NA	NA
Benefits	6/YR	4/YR	4/YR	AR	2/YR	4/YR	4/YR		AR	2/YR
Accounting	2/YR	NA	AR	AR	AR	NA	1/YR		AR	2/YR
Policies										
Hiring Practices	4/YR	NA	2/YR	AR	AR	NA	1/YR		AR	NA
Travel Guidelines	4/YR	6/YR	1/YR	4/YR	2/YR	2/YR	4/YR	Refer to text on events that affect content	AR	2/YR
Engineering Change Control	1/YR	1/YR	AR	AR	AR	AR	NA		AR	NA
Procedures										
Purchasing System	4/YR	4/YR	2/YR	2/YR	3/YR	2/YR	4/YR		AR	2/YR
Quality Reviews	1/YR	NA	AR	NA	AR	NA	NA		AR	NA
Job Transfer Request	1/YR	2/YR	2/YR	AR	NA	NA	NA		AR	NA

110

CHECKLIST FOR CHANGE:

✓   Create a review plan for monitoring tax changes, new laws, or events affecting the organization.

✓   Establish an ongoing communication campaign and training strategy as a part of the review plan.

✓   Develop categories for your review plan that match your organization's culture and management style.

✓   Fill in the dates of the review plan for general reviews. Identify the policies and procedures that will be initially transferred onto the review plan. Fill in the frequency by which the ongoing communications and training activities will be executed.

APPLYING WHAT YOU HAVE LEARNED:

Discuss the idea of using a review plan with your management. Decide if you want to make changes to the categories and sections presented in this chapter. Determine if the review plan will be based on high level business processes, policies, or procedures in your organization or if it will be based on all of the published documents within your policies and procedures infrastructure. Prepare a "Review and Communication Control Plan" and put it into practice. Make adjustments to the categories as you gain experience with the categories selected. Measure the effectiveness of the review plan and report the results to management.

ACHIEVE 100% COMPLIANCE:

With the creation of a review plan, and the reinforcement of business processes, policies, and procedures through a review process, ongoing communication and training strategies, you will build a stronger foundation for the deployment of a compliance plan that should take you closer to 100% compliance.

REFERENCES:

Alessandra, Tony, Ph.D. and Hunsaker, Phil, Ph.D., *Communicating at Work*, Fireside Book, Prentice-Hall, Inc., Englewood Cliffs, New Jersey, 1993.

Hultman, Ken, *Making Change Irresistible*, Davies-Black Publishing, Palo Alto, California,. 1998.

Larkin, TJ and Larkin, Sandar, *Communicating Change*, McGraw-Hill, New York, New York, 1994.

Page, Stephen B., *Establishing a System of Policies and Procedures*, BookMasters, Inc., Mansfield, Ohio, 1998.

Scherkenbach, William W., *The Deming Route to Quality and Productivity*, Mercury Press, Rockville, Maryland. 1991.

Part Two

DESIGNING AND CARRYING
OUT A COMPLIANCE PLAN

Part Two shows how to design a compliance plan and use it through self-assessment checklists, continuous improvement tools, and audits. Each of the compliance methods will aid in the discovery of non-compliant tasks and activities. These results will lead to improvements in business processes, policies, and procedures.

Chapter 7

Establishing a
Compliance Plan

After policies and procedures are published, communicated, and trained, procedures analysts naturally assume that the policies and procedures will be followed and applied in the user's work environment. Procedures analysts often take for granted that users will follow these policies and procedures because they believe they have done everything necessary to write, publish, and train effective policies and procedures, including but not limited, to:

1.　The policies and procedures have been researched and well-coordinated by the procedures analyst and the cross-functional team with users, process owners, and customers.

2.　The policies and procedures represent the best solution from the analysis of flow charts, existing business processes, and other sources.

3.　The policies and procedures have been reviewed and approved by senior management.

4.　The users were provided communication about the new or revised policies and procedures and they have received relevant training.

Unfortunately, procedures analysts really do not know if their policies and procedures are being accepted, understood, and applied unless an effort is put forth to meet with the users (after the publication of policies and procedures) and verify that the policies and procedures are being used and to what extent. From Chapter 4, *Establishing a Communication Strategy,*" we saw the importance of communicating first to the frontline supervisors and then to the employees. Still, the procedures analyst has no way of knowing how the published policies and procedures are being received and applied without performing some kind of survey, questionnaire, or measurement of the user's reactions and feedback to the published documents. The procedures analyst must use a verification process to determine the extent of compliance and to show management and the users that the published policies and procedures are effective and represent "fact" and not just the opinions of those researching and writing the policies and procedures.

VERIFICATION PROCESS FOR POLICIES AND PROCEDURES

"*Data without being measured is just an opinion*" is a commonly used phrase about data and opinions. This phrase implies that just because someone makes a statement (or writes policies and procedures), it does not mean that the information is valid without any doubts: *It is just the opinion of that person or group of people.* An opinion only becomes fact when measured, and then applied. The phrase should be reworded as "*data is only an opinion until measured and applied.*" Measurements are still worthless unless they reported and acted upon.

You may be wondering — what does this discussion have to do with policies and procedures? Policies and procedures cannot just be published, communicated, and trained; the phrase means that procedures analysts must measure (verify) their policies and procedures using quality tools to ensure they are being properly used as intended. The results must be published and displayed throughout the company as proof, or evidence, that the published policies and procedures work, are stable, and are in compliance, or at least, acceptance is increasing with each incremental improvement.

> Too often procedures analysts think their job is done after policies and procedures are published, communicated, and trained. Measuring and auditing policies and procedures to ensure that policies and procedures are understood and being applied is an important role for the procedures analyst.

Next time you hear someone say, "*Our procedures are very effective,*" ask him how he knows they are effective. If he says, "*I just know, I have watched my people and they are doing it right.*" Tell him that "*Without facts, you cannot be sure of anything.*" If he says he measured the process, ask him by what method and how he gathered the data and measured it. While it is possible that he used the correct quality tool to measure the processes in his department, it is unlikely. Learning to do process measurements often requires formal training and/or considerable experience or practice with theoretical and real data.

116

Many of my peers have been writing policies and procedures for most of their career and yet few have tried to determine if their published policies and procedures really work. A plan of action called a "compliance plan" will be introduced in this chapter for measuring policies and procedures for the purpose of showing that the policies and procedures are properly communicated, trained, and are being used and applied by the majority of users within the target audiences. The compliance plan will also help the procedures analyst determine strengths and weaknesses of the policies and procedures infrastructure; and help to point out areas that need greater assistance. The results of the compliance plan are discussed in Chapter 11, "*Conducting Profitable Continuous Improvement Activities.*"

The term *compliance* means to conform or to apply to a rule. The rule in this case is a standard or baseline of a business process, policy, or procedure. Using this logic, a *compliance plan* can be defined as conforming to a standard or baseline. The compliance plan will provide the procedures analyst with empirical methods to determine if his published policies and procedures are really effective and are in compliance! As shown above, you cannot just say your policies and procedures are effective — you have to prove it! The application of compliance methods to measure business processes, policies, and procedures should provide this proof.

MEASUREMENTS ARE KEY TO IMPROVEMENT

Measurements stand as one of the great inventions of all time. Every day we make hundreds of decisions — what to wear in the morning, what to eat, which way to go to work, when to go to a meeting, or what to say in a letter. Many of our everyday decisions contain the questions "How much?" or "How many?" The answers to these and other questions involve measurements and numbers. We use measurements every day and probably never know it. For instance, in our daily lives, we may use a ruler or a measuring cup or a watch or clock. Each of these instruments relies on internationally regulated standards (Harrington, 1991).

Measurements track process performance over time. They enable you to tell if something is wrong or if your efforts have improved the process. Measurements provide a clear idea of how well a process is working. Performance measures need to begin once the business process, policy, or procedure has been published and implemented. Numbers are powerful tools for making better decisions, but numbers alone cannot make decisions. People must make decisions. Numbers help to answer three basic questions about every decision (Harrington, 1991):

1. Am I getting the results I want?

2. Is there too much variation in the results I get?

3. Are the results I get stable over time?

Once business processes, policies, and procedures become stable and are considered in control, they need to be maintained so they do not get out of control. Procedures analysts cannot become lax when they know their policies and procedures are stable: they must continue to take measurements so the policies and procedures remain in control. Procedures analysts must continually strive to make improvements to policies and procedures so that his organization stays ahead of its competition. The procedures analyst can use both the compliance plan and the improvement plan that will be introduced in Chapter 11, *"Conducting Profitable Continuous Improvement Activities,"* to ensure the strategic goals of the organization are met.

A well-executed compliance plan helps an organization stay ahead of the competition.

MEASURES, MEASUREMENTS, & METRICS

Measures, measurements, and metrics can be nebulous terms but their definitions are important in understanding how policies and procedures can be measured and applied to ensure continuous improvement activities are profitable and can lead to 100% compliance of policies and procedures. Definitions for *measures* and *measurements* can be confusing because both words can be a noun or a verb. A *measure* provides a quantitative indication of the extent, amount, dimensions, capacity, or size of some attribute of a product or process. A *measurement* is the act of determining a measure. A *metric* is a quantitative measure of the degree to which a system, component, or process possesses a given attribute. While these definitions may seem confusing, they are straight from a dictionary; the application of these terms may become clear in the next few paragraphs.

When a single data point has been collected, e.g., the number of errors uncovered in the review of something, a *measure* has been established. *Measurement* occurs as a result of the collection of one or more data points. A *metric* relates the individual measures in some way, like the average number of errors found per review or the average number of errors found in memoranda over a period of thirty days. In summary, a metric uses measurements to display a result and measurements are made up of measures. For instance, if you see a graphic (i.e., metric) that shows the average number of purchase requisitions rejected by Purchasing each week, you know that measures and measurements were involved. Sample metrics are discussed in Chapter 9, "*Using Continuous Improvement Tools to Measure Compliance.*"

Since the only rational way to improve any process is to measure specific attributes of the process, a set of meaningful metrics must be developed that will lead to a strategy for improvement. Process metrics enable an organization to take a strategic view by providing insight into the effectiveness of a process. There are some important points to remember when doing measurements of specific attributes in an organization. These include:

1. Using common sense and organizational sensitivity when interpreting metrics data

2. Providing regular feedback to the individuals and teams who have worked to collect measures and metrics

3. Never using metrics to appraise or threaten individuals or teams

4. Working with individuals and teams to set clear goals and metrics that will be used to achieve them

5. Not considering problem areas as "negative." These data are merely an indicator for process improvement

6. Not focusing obsessively on one metric

COMPLIANCE PLAN DEFINED

A compliance plan consists of guidelines to help the procedures analyst distinguish fact from opinion. Published policies and procedures are statements of opinions until measured using standard compliance methods. The goals of a compliance plan are:

1. Distinguishing fact from opinion for business processes, policies and procedures

2. Achieving 100% compliance (i.e., total acceptance of a business process, policy, or procedure by each individual within the target audiences) of business processes, policies, or procedures, establishing a business process, policy, or procedure that is in statistical control, or establishing a "comfort level" acceptable by the management of an organization.

3. Showing how results of this compliance plan can be used to support streamlining efforts and improvement strategies for business processes, policies, and procedures.

4. Repeating the steps in the "Policies and Procedures Improvement Cycle" (PPIC) to ensure continual changes and improvements occur during any effort to develop new or revised policies and procedures. The compliance plan is one component of the third phase (i.e., Check & Audit) of the PPIC.

The compliance methods used in this book include the self-assessment checklist, scatter diagram, run chart, control chart, histogram, Pareto chart, and the systems audit. All of these methods are metrics except for the checklist and the audit. The results of the execution of the compliance methods will provide the following:

1. For the self-assessment checklist and the systems audit, questions that have a "Yes" or "No" answer are typically used. The number of "Yes" answers represents your compliance number. By dividing the total number of "Yes" answers by the total number of users responding to the checklist or audit questions, the resulting percentage will show how close you are to achieving 100% compliance of policies and procedures. The number of "No" answers becomes your variation. If you can change all of the "No" answers to "Yes" answers, you will have 100% compliance.

2. For the scatter diagram, run chart, control chart, histogram, and Pareto chart, the stability of the business process, policy, or procedure can be derived from an analysis of these graphs. These compliance methods will show the source of the problems that could be causing business processes, policies, and procedures to show wide variation and to be out of control.

120

COMPLIANCE PLAN LAYOUT

A compliance plan consists of tools or methods used to measure business processes, policies, or procedures to distinguish fact from opinion. The compliance plan referenced in the next three chapters is described in Table 7-1 below. The selection of the appropriate compliance methods is the key to the compliance plan.

The compliance methods presented in the table below are the most commonly used by procedures analysts for measuring compliance of business processes, policies, or procedures. The procedures analyst should experiment with all available continuous improvement tools to determine which methods are best for his organization. Some of these methods may be difficult to use and even to understand. The procedures analyst should use tools that make sense to him. Fifteen possible continuous improvement tools will be presented in Chapter 9, "*Using Continuous Improvement Tools to Measure Compliance.*"

TABLE 7-1: *Commonly Used Compliance Methods for Policies and Procedures*

NO	METHOD	DESCRIPTION
1	Self-Assessment Checklist	A checklist is a data gathering tool for soliciting responses to questions. The checklist is completed by the target audiences and submitted to the procedures analyst. The procedures analyst uses another quality tool, a *check sheet*, to summarize results from the self-assessment checklist. Refer to Appendix "A" for a completed check sheet based on a example illustrated in Chapter 8.
2	Scatter Diagram	A scatter diagram is a data interpretation tool used to look at how strong the relationship is between two variables.
3	Run Chart	A run chart is a line graph used to create a picture of what is happening in a situation you are analyzing; it will help you find patterns that will yield valuable insights into problems and solutions.
4	Control Chart	A control chart is a line graph depicting acceptable and unacceptable variations within a process. The control chart is the most effective and most widely used quality tool for measuring business processes, policies, and procedures.

5	Histogram	A histogram is a process variation and decision-making bar chart tool that focuses on business process improvement efforts.
6	Pareto Chart	A Pareto chart is a bar graph for determining the relative frequency or importance of different problems or causes. It will help you focus on vital issues by ranking them by significance.
7	Systems Audit	An audit is a formal, methodical examination or review of business processes, policies, or procedures. A questionnaire with "Yes" and "No" answers is presented in Chapter 10, *"Conducting Systems Audits."*

USING THE COMPLIANCE PLAN

The procedures analyst should design a flow chart similar to the one in Figure 7-1 below as a visual representation of the compliance methods selected. The methods you use to execute the selected compliance methods are your choice, though I would recommend seeking assistance from individuals from the Quality Department which might have experience with using continuous improvement tools like the control chart, run chart, histogram, scatter diagram, or Pareto chart. These compliance methods that are discussed in the next three chapters are summarized below:

1. Chapter 8, *"Developing Self-Assessment Checklists,"* explains how a checklist is used by members of the target audiences to verify they are correctly applying a business process, policy, or procedure as it was originally intended. The users perform a self-inspection of the business process, policy, or procedure they are using.

2. Chapter 9, *"Using Continuous Improvement Tools to Measure Compliance,"* explains the use of five quality tools (metrics) and their applications when determining the compliance and stability of business processes, policies, or procedures.

3. Chapter 10, *"Conducting Systems Audits,"* explains the use of systems audits as they relate to business processes, policies, and procedures. Systems audits help to identify system failures and operating deficiencies. Audits will result in value being added to the organization.

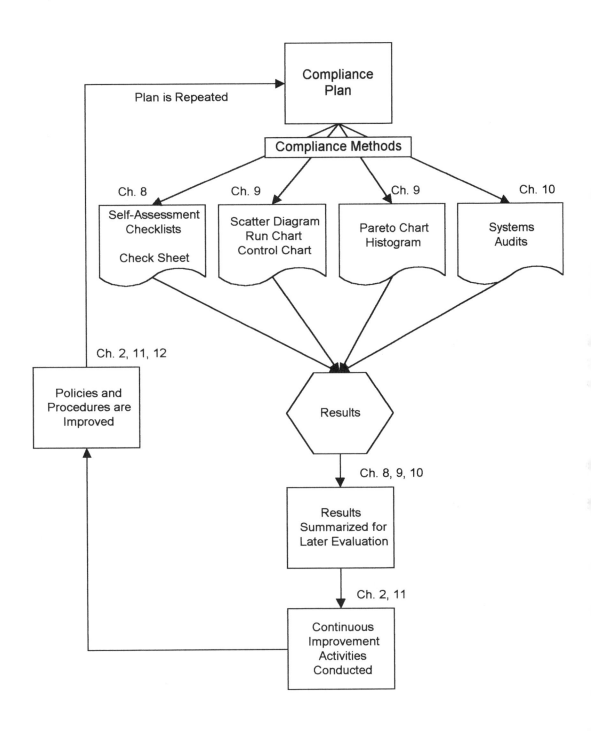

FIGURE 7-1: *Compliance Plan — A Visual Reference*

Keep a copy of this flow chart where you can view it daily.

When the compliance methods are executed, the results should be summarized within 48 hours. Depending on the number of individuals doing policies and procedures in an organization, there may or may not be enough time to properly analyze these results. If the results are put aside until another time, then a summary should be written about the information along with notes on the actions that need to be taken.

If the results of the execution of specific metrics indicate that improvements are urgently needed, then the procedures analyst should establish a cross-functional team to review the results and find a solution to the problems. Additional interviews could be conducted with present users and new users to validate the data. Once the information has been reviewed, calculated, and summarized, the cross-functional team can make a recommendation to management. Upon approval, the procedures analyst should make the necessary corrections to the policies and procedures, do the necessary coordination between the users and management, obtain approvals, publish, communicate, and train the policies and procedures. The process continues through the "Policies and Procedures Improvement Cycle" (PPIC).

If you feel overwhelmed with these compliance methods, you may consider asking for help from departments who specialize in these areas. For instance, the Finance Department often conducts internal audits, you could ask for their guidance or they may be able to do the audits for you. There may also be local associations where you can seek help and attend their meetings.

The Quality Assurance Department is usually responsible for collecting information for continuous improvement tools like the run chart, control chart, Pareto chart, scatter diagram, or histogram. You can also visit "Quality" web sites like the American Society for Quality (ASQ) at http://www.asq.org or self-help sites like http://www.quality.org maintained by quality professionals.

CHECKLIST FOR CHANGE:

✓   Discover the definitions, benefits, and usefulness of measures, measurements, and metrics to business processes, policies, and procedures.

✓   Understand the goals and objectives of a compliance plan.

✓   Establish a compliance plan and compliance methods that can yield realistic results for the improvement of business processes, policies, and procedures

✓ Learn how to apply the results of the execution of compliance methods.

✓ Understand that continuous quality improvement is a cyclical process for achieving improvement.

APPLYING WHAT YOU HAVE LEARNED:

Develop a high-level compliance plan and obtain approval from your management. Determine if there are other groups that could help you with your compliance activities. Use some of the books referenced in this book as training aids for using these quality tools. Visit the American Society of Quality (ASQ) web site and follow some of the links they provide to other Quality-related web sites. Begin with those compliance methods in this chapter and add or subtract ones with which you are comfortable. Work with the results and make improvements as appropriate. As your learning curve increases, work with the compliance methods that need a knowledge of statistics and mathematics because they will yield more meaningful results, e.g., a control chart or histogram. Experiment with different continuous improvement tools to identify the tools that work best for you and your organization.

ACHIEVE 100% COMPLIANCE:

With the establishment of this compliance plan, you should get a clearer picture of how you are going to achieve 100% compliance of published policies and procedures. The compliance plan will direct you in the right direction for doing the necessary activities for achieving compliance of your business processes, policies, and procedures. The preparation of the "visual" flow chart for the compliance plan will provide a daily visual reference to compliance methods that you need to constantly keep in mind.

REFERENCES:

Bhote, Keki R., *World Class Quality*, AMACOM, New York, New York, 1991.
Catapult, *Step by Step Microsoft Project 98*, Microsoft Press, Seattle, Washington, 1997.
Chang, Richard Y. and Niedzwiecki, Matthew E., *Continuous Improvement Tools, Volumes 1 and 2*, Richard Chang Associates, Inc, Publishing Division, Irvine, California, 1993.
Dobyns, Lloyd and Crawford-Mason, Claire, *Thinking about Quality*, Times Books, New York, New York, 1994.
Fink, Arlene and Kosecoff, Jacqueline, *How To Conduct Surveys*, Sage Publications, Thousand Oaks, California, 1998.

Harrington, H. James; Hoffherr, Glen D; and Reid, Robert P., *Statistical Analysis Simplified*, McGraw-Hill, Inc., New York, New York, 1998.

Lindberg, Roy A. and Cohn, Theodore, *Operations Auditing*, AMACOM, New York, New York, 1972.

Peters, Tom, *The Circle of Innovation*, Alfred A. Knopf, New York, New York, 1997.

Poirier, Charles, C. and Houser, William, F., *Business Partnering for Continuous Improvement*, Berrett-Koehler Publications, San Francisco, California, 1993.

Scherkenbach, William W., *The Deming Route to Quality and Productivity*, Mercury Press, Rockville, Maryland. 1991.

Shewhart, Walter A., *Statistical Method from the Viewpoint of Quality Control*, Dover Publications, Inc., New York, New York, 1986.

126

Chapter 8

Developing Self-Assessment Checklists

The "Self-Assessment Checklist" is the first compliance method outlined in the compliance plan in the previous chapter. The checklist provides a form of feedback about a business process, policy, or procedure. According to quality definitions, the word *checklist* means a data gathering tool. As the name implies, it provides a list to be checked. For our purposes, the checklist will be used to check "Yes" or "No" answers to a list of questions about a business process, policy, or procedure. The word *assessment* means to determine the importance or value of, to analyze, or to identify. The word *self* means one self. Putting these words together, the phrase *self-assessment checklist* means a data gathering tool for analyzing a situation, filled out by oneself. The user will complete a checklist by answering questions about a business process, policy, or procedure. The benefits of using a checklist include:

1. Providing a self-help tool to the user when applying the guidelines of a policy or procedure

2. Assisting the user's management in determining if their subordinates are using the published policies and procedures

3. Providing feedback and data for the procedures analyst to use in determining the compliance level of policies and procedures

4. Providing the procedures analyst with insight for making improvements to the policies and procedures as well as for improving the communication and training strategies for the policies and procedures

The self-assessment checklist is the easiest compliance method to prepare and use because it is the user who completes the checklist, not the procedures analyst. The procedures analyst only develops the checklist for the user. This checklist is used to answer questions about a business process, policy, or procedure, or any combination of business processes, policies, procedures, or other documents like forms and reports. The checklist helps the user decide if he using the policy or procedure as intended. These checklists can be beneficial to both the users and their management in determining if a business process, policy, or procedure is being followed. The users' management can use these checklists to ensure their subordinates are following company standards. If these checklists are being properly communicated through the frontline supervisors and through various company media, then it is a high probability that most users within the target audiences will use the checklists and return their results to the procedures analyst for analysis and feedback.

The procedures analyst will distribute self-assessment checklists periodically to determine procedural compliance. While there could be checklists for all business processes, policies, and procedures, the procedures analyst should primarily prepare checklists for major business processes, policies, procedures, and forms. If checklists are prepared for all of the policies and procedures within the policies and procedures infrastructure, the preparation, distribution, collection, calculation, and processing of tasks could become a major effort for both the users and the procedures analyst. The likelihood of users completing a checklist for each process, policy, procedure, or form used is low. The procedures analyst should concentrate on major business processes, policies, and procedures and not flood the users with too many checklists.

DESIGNING A SELF-ASSESSMENT CHECKLIST

A step-by-step process for designing a self-assessment checklist is defined below. In the next section, I will use the *Purchasing System* case study from Chapter 3 to show how to create a checklist. The goal is to create a listing of questions with a "Yes" or "No" response for data collection purposes. The questions must be phrased so that all the "Yes" answers are the correct way to do a task within a procedure. The "No" answers should be an incorrect way to do a task. When the data is tabulated and calculated, the total number of "Yes" answers will be compared to the total number of questions.

There should be about 5 to 15 short questions for each role (e.g., an employee, supervisor, and manager represent three distinct roles) identified in a specific policy or procedure. While more questions could be created, statistics have shown that employees are more likely to complete a checklist when the list is short and the questions are easy to understand. If the content is long, you could exceed 15 questions once in awhile but it should not become practice.

128

STEPS FOR DESIGNING AND PROCESSING A CHECKLIST

1. Select a Document(s) to be Reviewed. One or several documents could be reviewed including business processes, policies, procedures, forms, figures, tables, flow charts, reports, and any section of a business process, policy, or procedure. Questions can be formulated from each document and for each role within a document.

2. Create an "Assessment Preparation Table" to Record the Statements from the Selected Documents (Refer to Table 8-1). Using the selected document(s), pick relevant statements and record them and the corresponding policy and procedure section numbers in this table. Write questions based on these statements in such a way that the correct way of doing a task is always "Yes." While writing questions in one specific way is not easy, the resulting answers may yield inaccurate results if the answers are mixed. If you have difficulties writing "Yes" questions that always reflect the correct way to do a task, review the sample questions in Table 8-2 to give you some ideas for phrasing questions.

3. Design a "Self-Assessment Checklist" (Refer to Table 8-2). Using the "Assessment Preparation Table," transfer the questions to this checklist. Preferably, they are transferred one for one, however, the questions can be altered to fit the language expected by the target audiences as long as the intent is the same. Instructions for returning the checklist should be indicated at the top of the form when the checklists are distributed to supervisors and/or employees.

4. Determine the Individuals to Whom the Checklist will be Distributed. Review the original business process, policy, procedure or flow chart and determine the roles of all users within the target audiences. Work with management or Human Resources to obtain the users' names.

5. Communicate and Distribute the Checklist. As a part of the communication strategy developed in Chapter 4, communicate to the frontline supervisors that a "Self-Assessment Checklist" has been developed for a major business process, policy, or procedure and that it is important for their subordinates to use the checklist and return it either to them or to the procedures analyst by a specified due date.

6.   <u>Collect the Checklists and Summarize the Data</u>. Analyze the returned checklists and perform the necessary calculations. Summarize the data using a "Summary Report Check Sheet." Refer to Appendix "A" for a completed check sheet based on the example in Table 8-2.

AN EXERCISE - CREATING A SELF-ASSESSMENT CHECKLIST

This section has been included to show you how a "Self-Assessment Checklist" is created using a written procedure as the primary source document. Three forms will be completed: *"Assessment Preparation Table," "Self-Assessment Checklist,"* and a *"Summary Report Check Sheet."* The first two forms will be explained and illustrated in this chapter; the third form is illustrated in Appendix A but explained in this chapter. The *Purchasing System* procedure written as a part of the case study in Chapter 3, will be the source document for the checklist.

STEPS FOR CREATING A "SELF-ASSESSMENT CHECKLIST" FOR THE PURCHASING SYSTEM

1.   <u>Select a Document(s) to be Reviewed</u>.

    The document selected is the *Purchasing System* procedure as described in Chapter 3. The flow chart created for the *Purchasing System* will be also referenced.

2.   <u>Create an "Assessment Preparation Table" to Record the Statements from the Selected Documents</u>.

    A sample "Assessment Preparation Table" for the *Purchasing System* case study has been created in Table 8-1 to record the statements for the checklist. In this sample, I have referenced the procedural steps in the first column; I have copied, or paraphrased, the statements from the procedural step in the second column; in the third column, I have created questions based on the statements in the second column. I used a "NA" or "Not Applicable" notation in the first column when the reference is general and is not directly tied to a statement that can be referenced. If the audience is small and the "Assessment Preparation Table" is short, it is possible to bypass this table and write statements directly on the checklist.

3.   Design a "Self-Assessment Checklist."

A checklist is designed that will include questions prepared from the "Assessment Preparation Table" in Table 8-1. The questions formulated in the "Questions to Ask" column will be used to create a checklist. Refer to Table 8-2 for the checklist.

4.   Determine the Individuals to Whom the Checklist will be Distributed.

The key roles in the *Purchasing System* procedure are requesters, purchasing assistants, purchasing managers, buyers, receiving personnel, and accounting personnel. For this checklist, we will focus on the requesters, purchasing assistants, buyers, and receiving personnel. Checklists will be distributed to each role category and a deadline will be set for the return of the completed checklists. As there are a small number of users within each category, each individual within the target audience is expected to return "filled in" checklists. For larger groups of users, sampling techniques could be used. References for "sample" techniques can be obtained from libraries or from online bookstores like Amazon.com or Barnes & Noble.

5.   Communicate and Distribute the Checklist.

When the checklist has been completed, use voice mail, email, and/or FAX messages to broadcast to all supervisors and managers of the selected roles identified above, that a "Self-Assessment Checklist" for the *Purchasing System* is going to be distributed. Through discussions with the supervisors, the checklists could be delivered to the supervisors for distribution to their employees or the checklists could be delivered directly to the employees. This decision should be made by the supervisor, not the procedures analyst.

The supervisor will receive a better response if he is aware of the checklist, its benefit, and its purpose before the checklist is distributed to all target audiences. The supervisors should be provided with the return date regardless of which method of delivery is selected, thus they can monitor their employees to ensure that they understand, complete, and return the checklist by the due date on the checklist. The supervisor should announce to his subordinates that he is available for questions about the use, purpose, and benefits of the checklist.

6. Collect the Checklists and Summarize the Data.

Pick a date when checklists can no longer be accepted. This should be three or four working days after the return deadline date. The checklists can be sorted by function; the question numbers and responses could be entered in a check sheet to tabulate the total number of "Yes" answers and the total number of checklists sent out and returned. Refer to the *"Purchasing System* Summary Report Check Sheet" in Appendix "A" for an analysis of the results from the answers to the checklist questions.

TABLE 8-1: *Assessment Preparation Table*

PURCHASING SYSTEM ASSESSMENT PREPARATION TABLE Dated: (Preparation Date)		
NO.	**STATEMENTS**	**QUESTIONS TO ASK** (Transfer to Checklist)
Requester or Originator of Purchase Requisition		
4.a.	All expenditures of company funds for goods and services are properly reviewed and approved prior to commitment.	Was your requisition properly reviewed and approved in accordance with this procedure? Was the value of the requested items within your department's budget? Were any requisitions rejected as a result of a disapproved request from your management? Were all requisitions accepted by the user's management?
4.d.	The Purchasing Department is the only department authorized to obligate suppliers for orders or enter in contracts.	Did you call suppliers for prices, check published sources, or review department history records before writing down your specific items on the requisition?

5.b.	MRO items are used by employees to help them perform their jobs. These include, but are not limited to small tools, cleaning supplies, office supplies, and a wide variety of other consumable items that are not-for-resale.	Is this requisition for MRO items only?
6.b.	Employees are expected to select the most current requisition form and adhere to the guidelines of this procedure when describing a request for MRO items.	Did you obtain this purchase requisition from the designated company forms stockroom?
7.a.2)	The employee will complete the purchase requisition and obtain signatures for the estimated value of the order.	Did you obtain one approval signature for requisition values under $250.00? Did you obtain two approval signatures for values from $251.00 to $500.00?
7.a.4)	Once approved, the employee will remove the last copy of the purchase requisition for his records.	Did you remove the last copy of the requisition for your records?
NA	After the Receiving Department receives your order from the supplier, they will deliver the items to you or ask that you pick them up.	Did the items you received match what you requested? Were the items delivered to you in a timely manner? Were the items received undamaged?

NA	Procedure in general	Are you satisfied with this procedure? Were the guidelines easy to use and not cumbersome? Was the approval process clear and easy to use? Are you satisfied that Purchasing can make a better supplier selection than you?
Purchasing Assistant		
6.c.	The Purchasing Assistant shall review all Purchase Requisitions to ensure they are completed in accordance with this procedure.	Did you review all incoming purchase requisitions? Did you review the requisitions in accordance with the guidelines in this procedure? Did you initial the requisition indicating that you have reviewed it? Did you accept all requisitions? Did the requisitions have the correct signatures for the estimated value? Were the signatures on the requisition the correct signatures? Did the requester remove the last copy of the requisition before delivering or mailing the original and one copy to you?
NA	The requester shall use the most current purchase requisition form.	Did the requester use the most current requisition form? Did you reject the requisition if the wrong form was used?
NA	Procedure in general	Are you satisfied with this procedure? Were the procedural statements easy to use? Were you able to find answers to questions quickly? Did your job functions match the duties described in the *Purchasing System* procedure?
Buyer		
NA	The Purchasing Manager selects an MRO Buyer.	Were all requisitions for MRO items? Did the Purchasing Assistant and Purchasing Manager initial the requisition before it came to you?

7.b.3) a)	The Buyer will contact at least three suppliers.	Did you call at least three suppliers?
7.b.3) c)	A Purchase Order is awarded to the selected supplier. A Purchase Order form is generated and copies are distributed to the supplier, Accounting, Receiving, and the Buyer's open-order follow-up file.	Did you select one supplier to fill the order? Did you (or a purchasing clerk) file a copy of the Purchase Order in your open-order follow-up file?
NA	Procedure in general	Were you satisfied with this procedure? Were the users of the procedure satisfied with the way the Purchasing Department handled the order? Were the instructions clear and relevant to your job functions?
Receiving Department		
7.c.1)	Upon receipt of the purchase order, the Receiving Department will create a four-part Receiver set. The Purchase Order will be copied onto a four-part, pre-collated, colored paper.	Did you create a Receiver set from the Purchase Order?
7.c.2)	Upon receipt of the material, the inspection department matches the items received with the purchase order copy. If the documents do not match, then the Buyer is contacted.	Did the supplier's packing sheet match the material sent? Did the material received match the description on the purchase order?

NA	The material packaged by the supplier is expected to arrive in a standard shipping container.	Was a standard shipping container used? Was the shipping container inspected for damage? Were the contents of the shipment inspected for damage?
NA	The Receiving Department will deliver or mail the items to the requester.	Did the requester receive the shipment within 1-2 days after it passed inspection?
NA	Procedure in general	Were you satisfied with this procedure? Were the instructions clear? Were answers to questions easy to find?

After the "Assessment Preparation Table" is completed, the questions should be reviewed with several individuals from the Purchasing Department (e.g., Purchasing Manager, Purchasing Assistant, and Buyer). The questions should also be reviewed by other procedures analysts or department managers. In the case of a major business process, policy, or procedure, the procedures analyst should take extra care to ensure that the information is correct. The "Self-Assessment Checklist" will now be prepared based on the statements gathered using the "Assessment Preparation Table." If extra questions are generated while doing the checklist, the *Purchasing System* procedure should be examined to determine if additional procedural statements are needed.

TABLE 8-2: *Self-Assessment Checklist*

SELF-ASSESSMENT CHECKLIST Return Date: (Specify Date)		
Doc. Name: Purchasing System	**Doc. No:** 1001	**Date:** (Specify)
NO	**QUESTIONS**	**RESPONSES**
►Requester of Purchase Requisition		
1	Was your requisition properly reviewed and approved in accordance with this procedure?	□ Yes □ No

2	Was the value of the requested items within your department's budget?	☐ Yes ☐ No
3	Were requisitions rejected as a result of a disapproved request from your management?	☐ Yes ☐ No
4	Were all requisitions accepted by the user's management?	☐ Yes ☐ No
5	Is this requisition for MRO items only?	☐ Yes ☐ No
6	Did you call suppliers for prices, check published sources, and review department history records before completing the description of the order?	☐ Yes ☐ No
7	Did you obtain this purchase requisition from the designated company forms stockroom?	☐ Yes ☐ No
8	Did you obtain one approval signature for requisition values under $250.00?	☐ Yes ☐ No
9	Did you obtain two approval signatures for requisition values from $251.00 to $500.00?	☐ Yes ☐ No
10	Did you remove the last copy of the requisition for your records?	☐ Yes ☐ No
11	Did the items you received match what you requested?	☐ Yes ☐ No
12	Were the items delivered to you in the time period that you expected?	☐ Yes ☐ No
13	After receiving the order from the receiving department, were the items undamaged?	☐ Yes ☐ No
14	Are you satisfied with this procedure?	☐ Yes ☐ No
15	Were the guidelines easy to use and not cumbersome?	☐ Yes ☐ No
16	Was the approval process clear and easy to use?	☐ Yes ☐ No
17	Are you satisfied that Purchasing can make a better supplier selection than you?	☐ Yes ☐ No

	Purchasing Assistant	
18	Did you review all incoming purchase requisitions?	□ Yes □ No
19	Did you review the requisitions in accordance with the guidelines in this procedure?	□ Yes □ No
20	Did you initial the requisition indicating that you reviewed it?	□ Yes □ No
21	Did you accept all requisitions?	□ Yes □ No
22	Did the charge number (account number) format match the format designated as MRO items?	□ Yes □ No
23	Did the requisitions have the correct signatures for the estimated value?	□ Yes □ No
24	Were the signatures on the requisition the correct signatures?	□ Yes □ No
25	Did the requester remove the last copy of the requisition before delivering or mailing the original and one copy to you?	□ Yes □ No
26	Did the requester use the most current requisition form?	□ Yes □ No
27	Did you reject the requisition because the wrong form was used?	□ Yes □ No
28	Are you satisfied with this procedure?	□ Yes □ No
29	Were the guidelines easy to use and not cumbersome?	□ Yes □ No
30	Were your job functions clearly stated?	□ Yes □ No
	Buyer	
31	Were all requisitions for MRO items?	□ Yes □ No
32	Did the Purchasing Assistant initial the requisition?	□ Yes □ No
33	Did the Purchasing Manager initial the requisition?	□ Yes □ No
34	Did you call at least three suppliers?	□ Yes □ No

138

35	Did you (or a Purchasing Clerk) file a copy of the Purchase Order in your open-order follow-up file?	☐ Yes ☐ No
36	Were you satisfied with this procedure?	☐ Yes ☐ No
37	Were the users of the procedure satisfied with the way the Purchasing Department handled the order?	☐ Yes ☐ No
38	Were the instructions clear and relevant to your job functions?	☐ Yes ☐ No
►Receiving Department		
39	Did you create a Receiver set from the Purchase Order?	☐ Yes ☐ No
40	Did the supplier's packing sheet match the material sent?	☐ Yes ☐ No
41	Did the material received match the description on the Purchase Order?	☐ Yes ☐ No
42	Was the shipping container inspected for damage?	☐ Yes ☐ No
43	Were the contents of the shipment inspected for damage?	☐ Yes ☐ No
44	Did the requester receive his shipment within 1-2 days after it passed inspected?	☐ Yes ☐ No
45	Were you satisfied with this procedure?	☐ Yes ☐ No
46	Were the instructions clear?	☐ Yes ☐ No
Ref. No.	Comments (insert relevant number) Write on the back if you have more comments.	

EVALUATING THE RESULTS

The results are compiled in a summary report in Appendix A. Possible improvements, based on these results, are discussed in Chapter 11, "*Conducting Profitable Continuous Improvement Activities.*" The results should be summarized so relevant information is not forgotten when the information is reviewed at a later date. If you have instituted an improvement plan, these results could be assigned to other procedures analysts for investigation purposes if your department is large enough to warrant extra people.

SUMMARY OF RESULTS — APPENDIX "A"

The highest compliance percentage was 73%. This percentage figure suggests that the requesters thought that they were completing the requisitions properly. The lowest compliance was 61%. This percentage figure suggests that the Purchasing Assistants were having difficulties following the *Purchasing System* procedure. A proper analysis of these, and other numbers, could yield some interesting results. These percentages may be satisfactory or unsatisfactory depending on the strategic goals of the organization. If the goal is 99.99966%, or Six Sigma, then 67% is poor. If management is comfortable with 80%, then an average compliance level of 67% is a good result for the first measurement. With the completion of one or two cycles of the "Policies and Procedures Improvement Cycle" (PPIC) as introduced in Chapter 1, "*Introducing the Policies and Procedures Improvement Cycle,*" and two iterations of improvements, a compliance figure of 80% or higher might be reached. This conclusion is based on the assumption that improvements will lead to better policies and procedures, however, it may be that an improvement made the process harder to understand and apply and so the compliance level could decrease. Improvements do not always lead to high compliance levels. For the purposes of examples in this book, the assumption is being made that all improvements will produce high compliance levels.

CHECKLIST FOR CHANGE:

✓   Identify the benefits of users completing a "Self-Assessment Checklist" to "self-evaluate" their application of specific policies and procedures.

✓   Analyze policies and procedures to identify which statements can be translated into questions for use in checklists.

140

✓ Design an "Assessment Preparation Table" for extracting questions from a policy or a procedure that will then be used to create a "Self-Assessment Checklist."

✓ Develop a "Self-Assessment Checklist" that reflects the questions developed from the "Assessment Preparation Table."

✓ Create a "Summary Report Check Sheet" for analyzing the results of the completed checklists.

✓ Evaluate and investigate the results of completed checklists.

APPLYING WHAT YOU HAVE LEARNED:

Select the business process, policy, or procedure you wish to review for compliance. Design an "Assessment Preparation Table" using a word processing program to use as a collector of information. Develop questions based on the procedural statements in your selected documents. Develop a "Self-Assessment Checklist" to develop a checklist for distribution to the target audiences for eliciting answers to questions about the use of business processes, policies, procedures, tasks, or activities. Create a "Summary Report Check Sheet" to summarize results from completed checklists and to calculate compliance levels for each question, each role, the total audience, and the mathematical average of the business process, policy, or procedure being applied.

ACHIEVE 100% COMPLIANCE:

This chapter has been the first important step toward determining the effectiveness of published policies and procedures. With the results from the "Self-Assessment Checklist" you have identified areas for possible improvement. You have also determined that the *Purchasing System* procedure is not being applied as intended. Through the use of improvement methods (Chapter 11), you should be able to make progress toward raising the level of compliance for business processes, policies, and procedures, and even achieving 100% compliance!

REFERENCES:

Chang, Richard Y and Niedzwiecki, Matthew E, *Continuous Improvement Tools, Volumes 1 and 2,* Richard Chang Associates, Inc, Publishing Division, Irvine, California, 1993.

Harrington, H. James; Hoffherr, Glen D; and Reid, Robert P, *Statistical Analysis Simplified*, McGraw-Hill, Inc., New York, New York, 1998.

Larkin, TJ and Larkin, Sandar, *Communicating Change*, McGraw-Hill, New York, New York, 1994.

Lockamy, Archie, III and Cox, James F., *Re-engineering Performance Measurement*, Irwin Professional Publishing, New York, New York, 1994.

Owen, D. B., *Beating Your Competition Thru Quality*, Marcel Dekker, Inc., New York, New York, 1989.

Swindle, Robert E. and Swindle, Elizabeth M., *The Business Communicator*, Prentice-Hall, Inc., Englewood Cliffs, New Jersey, 1989.

Vicker, Lauren and Hein, Ron, *The Fast Forward MBA in Business Communication*, John Wiley & Sons, Inc., New York, New York, 1999.

Chapter 9

Using Continuous Improvement Tools to Measure Compliance

The tools used to measure the compliance level of business processes, policies, and procedures include diagrams, charts, forms, and metrics. The literature defines these tools as continuous improvement tools, statistical process control (SPC) methods, and quality control tools. SPC helps improve processes by summarizing data, providing insight into variability, and clarifying decisions and understanding risks. Both phrases, *continuous improvement tools* and *quality tools* will be used interchangeably in this book. Fifteen continuous improvement tools will be presented in this chapter. Five of these tools will be selected to illustrate examples of how they can be used when applied to the *Purchasing System* flow chart and procedure as presented in Chapter 3, "*Focusing on a Case Study to Apply the Principles of this Book.*" We have already discussed a few of these tools including brainstorming, flow charts, check sheets, and checklists.

Measuring the compliance of business processes, policies, and procedures is best achieved with those continuous improvement tools that use numbers and statistics. Statistics help improve processes by summarizing data, providing insight into variability, clarifying decisions, and understanding risks. The computer has virtually eliminated the pencil, paper, or calculator for making the complex calculations for deriving the statistics required to measure a business process. There is so much to be gained from the measurement of business processes, policies, and procedures. Through measurements we can gain increased knowledge. Often, we hear that companies cannot afford the time and resources to measure their business processes. In reality, this belief is furthest from the truth.

METRICS AND MEASUREMENTS

Metrics create a common language for communication and allow process measurements to be communicated openly and candidly. We need metrics to (Harry, 2000):

1. Establish the difference between perception, intuition, and reality.

2. Gather the facts for good decision making and provide the basis for sound implementation of those decisions.

3. Identify and verify areas of problems, issues, and concerns that have remained undetected.

4. Better understand our business processes and determine which factors are important and which are not.

5. Validate our processes and determine whether they are performing within the required specifications.

6. Document our business processes and then communicate them to others.

7. Provide a baseline for process performance and cost correlation.

8. See if our processes are improving and retain the gains for those processes that are improving.

9. Decide if a process is stable or predictable, and determine how much variation is inherent in the process.

A set of metrics must be developed as a strategy for improvement. Process metrics enable an organization to take a strategic view by providing insight into the effectiveness of a process. There are some guidelines for performing measurements of specific attributes in an organization. These include:

1. Using common sense and organizational sensitivity when interpreting metrics data

2. Providing regular feedback to the individuals and teams who have worked to collect measures and metrics

3. Working with individuals and teams to set clear goals and metrics that will be used to achieve them

4. Not using metrics to appraise or threaten individuals

5. Recognizing metrics as indicators of an opportunity for improvement, not as problem areas

6. Experimenting with a variety of metrics, not just one or two that are easy to measure and calculate

STATISTICS ARE NOT BORING!

Understandably, most people believe that statistics are boring and complicated. But some of the most interesting phenomena that occur within organizations can be best captured and explained with the simplicity and beauty of statistics. Once people get beyond the symbols, formulas, and charts, they usually find that statistics make problems (and the solutions) much clearer and simpler. Statistics can be creative, simple, important, and relevant, yet many people think statistics only muddy the waters. The simplicity of statistics allows us to measure, improve, and monitor business processes, policies, procedures, forms, and other information within organizations. Statistics can be fun. Refer to H. James Harrington's 1998 book on "Statistical Analysis Simplified." He provides "fun" exercises in each chapter.

The goal of statistics is to get where you want to go by reducing variation and driving processes to meet their targets. Statistics allow companies to solve problems and form the framework for how they educate their employees. They allow companies to collect data, translate that data into information, and then interpret the information so that decisions can be made based on fact, rather than intuition, or past experience. Statistics create the foundation for quality, which translates to profitability and market share. They help summarize data, provide insight into variability, clarify decisions, and help understand risks. Statistics are needed to make the calculations for metrics like averages or standard deviations.

Managers need to become more literate in statistics, but it must also be realized that statistical knowledge needs to be communicated in a format that makes it usable, so that managers can extrapolate key data and apply it to their day-to-day work. The full benefit of statistics can be achieved in a culture that has people with the right skills reviewing and analyzing data. The more knowledgeable the organization becomes, and the more it allows its employees to use that knowledge, the more profitable it will become. Knowledge put to use creates wisdom. With wisdom come better decisions.

IMPORTANCE OF VARIATION

Variation is a part of everyday life, including the workplace. Variation is simply the difference between numbers. One goal in using numbers for making decisions is to hold the variation in your business process to a minimum. If variation becomes equal to your target, you will have achieved 100% compliance. Variation in your product's quality often results in waste, which in turn, results in your overall organization becoming less efficient. You are less efficient because of lost time and material. For instance, there is variation in the length of time it takes to complete a form, variation in the weight and volume of tangible products, and so on. Boundaries or variation limits must be set for all business processes, policies, and procedures. The amount of acceptable variation is the key to achieving 100% compliance. The more variation permitted, the further away you will be from achieving 100% compliance. You can now appreciate how difficult it is to achieve Six Sigma, or 3 parts per 1 million: *This is clearly a very small number!* Six Sigma is equal to 99.99966% compliance.

VARIATION EXAMPLE

For instance, let us look at a process for completing a step within a procedure. Suppose we have determined that one task is to process a form and it has been calculated that it takes 60 minutes to process the form. When the procedure to complete the form is published, a baseline is taken of the procedure. The boundaries of the "form process" can be ± 10 minutes, or a range from 50 to 70 minutes. Anything outside of this range would be unacceptable. If we complete the form within this 20-minute spread, then it is considered to be statistically stable. If one or more users process their forms in 71 minutes or more, it would mean that the process is out of control. When investigated, it may show that the form is too complex or takes too long to complete.

If the form, on the other hand, only took 40 minutes to process, the process would also be considered out of control. You may be wondering, *"What is wrong with processing a form too quickly?"* If a form has been carefully calculated to take an average of 60 minutes to process and it takes only 40 minutes, then the user is probably not spending enough time on completing the form and may be rushing or skipping form fields. In this case, the results of the form would also be invalid. Whether the form takes 40 or 71 minutes to process, the event would trigger a cause for investigation. By improving the way the form is processed, we could tighten the variation limits to 55-65 to bring us closer to 100% compliance. With Six Sigma, the variation is 59.97 to 60.02 minutes. You can now see how hard Six Sigma is to achieve! Six Sigma is an admirable goal but it is very difficult, if not impossible, for some companies to achieve.

IMPORTANCE OF NUMBERS

Organizations that cannot describe their business processes in the form of numbers cannot understand their processes. If they do not understand their processes, they cannot control them. When you can measure what you are speaking about, and express it in numbers, you know something about it, when you cannot express it in numbers, your knowledge is unsatisfactory. Numbers are powerful tools for making better decisions, but numbers alone cannot make decisions. People make decisions. People run business processes. People manage organizations. By looking at numbers, you will know whether your operation is running smoothly or whether it needs to be adjusted. More importantly, you will learn to predict how the operation will run in the future (Harrington, 1998).

> Numbers are powerful tools for making better decisions, but numbers alone cannot make decisions. People make decisions.

Using numbers to help you make better decisions involves a lot more than the arithmetic and calculations needed to manipulate them. Numbers occur in different contexts and mean different things to different people. Using numbers to help make decisions is important for many reasons including, but not limited to:

1. Numbers can focus your attention on whether you are attaining your goal

2. Numbers provide input and insights that help you analyze and understand why things appear as they do

3. Numbers help find and correct problems with your business processes, policies, and procedures

4. Numbers can connect people, business processes, and ideas and give everyone a sense of accomplishment

To learn from numbers, you must look for and recognize patterns. Understanding the underlying cause of patterns helps to make more informed decisions. For instance, we may find an interesting pattern when we measure the "training time spent on learning how to complete a purchase requisition form" versus "mistakes made when using the purchase requisition form." If we measured the time spent on completing hundreds of requisitions, and the time spent by employees for learning how to use a purchase requisition, we should see some interesting patterns. Examples of these patterns will be addressed later in this chapter when we discuss histograms. Understanding patterns is a key to interpreting metrics (Harrington, 1998).

FIFTEEN (15) CONTINUOUS IMPROVEMENT TOOLS (also, called "Quality Tools")

There are fifteen quality tools (refer to Table 9-1) that could be used to assist with the processing and improvement of business processes, policies, and procedures. These fifteen continuous improvement tools represent the total number of tools that could be selected for your compliance plan (established in Chapter 7, *Establishing a Compliance Plan*"). Five of these tools have been selected to show you how to improve the compliance level of your business processes, policies, and procedures and to move closer to 100% compliance. The quality tool and the descriptions for this table came from Richard Chang's two volumes on Quality and from H. James Harrington's book on "Statistics."

TABLE 9-1: *Continuous Improvement Tools*

QUALITY TOOL	DESCRIPTION
Brainstorming	Brainstorming is a communication method for a team to generate a high volume of ideas on a topic by creating a process creatively and efficiently that is free of criticism and judgment.
Affinity Diagram	An affinity diagram allows a team to generate many ideas and issues creatively and to organize them in natural groupings to understand the essence of a problem and breakthrough solutions. Brainstorming sessions typically precede affinity diagram discussions. This exercise is generally lead by the team leader.

Matrix Diagram	A matrix diagram permits a team to systematically identify, analyze, and rate the presence and strength of relationships.
Force Field Diagram	A force field diagram is used to identify the forces and factors in place that support, or work against the solution of an issue or problem, so that the positives can be reinforced and/or the negatives eliminated or reduced.
Cause and Effect Diagram (also called the "Fishbone" Diagram)	A cause and effect diagram permits a team to identify, explore, and graphically display, in increasing detail, the possible causes related to a problem or condition to discover its root cause(s). The diagram focuses on causes, not symptoms.
Check Sheet	The check sheet is a tally or record of observations. The check sheet allows a team to record systematically and compile data from historical sources, or observations as they happen, so that patterns and trends can be detected and shown. The check sheet is a good starting point to solve most problems.
Checklist	The checklist is a data gathering tool; it provides feedback about business processes, policies, and procedures. The check sheet is often used to tabulate results for the checklist. (Note: While the checklist is normally not considered a quality tool, I believe that it should be added to the list because it is often used in conjunction with the check sheet.)
Tree Diagram	The tree diagram is used to break down broad goals, graphically, into increasing levels of detailed actions that must or could be done to achieve the stated goals.
Pareto Chart	Pareto charts are used to analyze data from a new perspective, to focus attention on problems in priority order, and to compare data changes during different times. The Pareto Principle states that 20% of the sources account for 80% of the causes.
Sequence Flow Chart	The sequence flow chart is a planning and analysis tool used to analyze the flow of work in your business processes and produce a visual picture of a business process. The sequence flow chart is another version of a flow chart to display steps sequentially.

Flow Chart	A flow chart is a planning and analysis tool used to define and analyze manufacturing, assembly, or service processes, build a step-by-step picture of a process for analysis, discussion, or communication purposes, and define, standardize, or find areas for improvement in a process.
Scatter Diagram	A scatter diagram is a data interpretation tool used to look at how strong the relationship is between two variables (*e.g., the relationship between advertising costs and sales, years of experience and employee performance, etc.*), to confirm hunches about a cause-and-effect relationship between types of variables, and to determine the kind of relationship (*positive, negative, etc.*).
Run Chart	A run chart is a type of line graph used as an analysis tool to collect and interpret data over time; to create a picture of what is happening in the situation you are analyzing; to find patterns yielding valuable insights; and to compare one period of data with another, checking for changes.
Control Chart	A control chart is a special type of line graph you can use to interpret data about a process by creating a picture of the boundaries of acceptable variation and objectively determine if a process is in control or out of control. Control charts help you get the feel of your process. These charts tell you when to change things and when to leave things alone.
Histogram	A histogram is a special type of bar chart you can use to communicate information about variation in a process and make decisions on the focus of improvement efforts. The histogram can be used to summarize data from a process that has been collected over a period of time.

FIVE (5) CONTINUOUS IMPROVEMENT TOOLS

The five tools that are most frequently used for measuring the compliance of business processes, policies, and procedures are: *The Scatter diagram, run chart, control chart, histogram, and Pareto chart.* The *Purchasing System* procedure from the case study presented in Chapter 3, *"Focusing on a Case Study to Apply the Principles of this Book,"* will be used as the basis for the examples of each tool. The results of each tool will be addressed in Chapter 11, *"Conducting Profitable Continuous*

Improvement Activities," and evaluated when the cross-functional team seeks alternate solutions to the paperwork, labor intensive, *Purchasing System* case study. In each of the five examples of quality tools, we will identify:

1.   The purpose for using the tool

2.   The basic steps for creating a metric using the tool

3.   A description of the metric including a scenario, hypothesis, and variables

4.   A diagram or chart based on the hypothesis

5.   An interpretation of the completed metric

➤The mathematics used to calculate the charts will not be presented. Entire books have been written on the complex calculations of these five tools. The mathematics is nothing to fear because there are many software programs that can do calculations for you.

The five continuous improvement tools are included below:

1.   SCATTER DIAGRAM

The scatter diagram is a data interpretation tool used to show strong relationships between variables. The scatter diagram provides both a visual and statistical means to test the strength of a possible relationship. These relationships supply the data to confirm a hypothesis that two variables are related.

Basic Steps

1.   Determine a hypothesis for the correlation.

2.   Collect 50-100 paired samples of data that you think may be related.

3.   Determine the variables to use.

4.   Draw the horizontal and vertical axes of the diagram.

5.   Plot the data on the diagram and use a circle for overlapping data.

6.   Interpret the data.

Refer to Figure 9-1 on the next page for a sample scatter diagram.

Example

Our hypothesis is that there is a strong relationship between the training time an employee receives for a purchase requisition with the time it takes this same employee to complete the requisition in accordance with the *Purchasing System* procedure. The variables for this correlation are as follows:

1.   X-Axis. Number of hours of training on the purchase requisition.

2.   Y-Axis. Number of minutes to complete the purchase requisition.

Our focus is on the relationship of hours an employee spends on training with the number of minutes the same employee spends completing a purchase requisition. A decrease in the time spent completing a purchase requisition is expected as training hours increase. The key to remember is that the scatter diagram does not predict cause and effect relationships.

The scatter diagram shows only the strength of the relationship between two variables. The stronger the relationship, the greater the likelihood that change in one variable will affect change in another variable. The scatter diagram is a good tool to use for a variety of comparisons, for example, you could compare the quantity of purchase requisitions that are rejected by the Purchasing Department for not following the current procedure over a specific period.

Interpretation of Data

When a scatter diagram is interpreted, possible causal relationships are shown, not actual causal relationships. More advanced statistical tests are needed if you want to determine the exact degree of the relationship. In Figure 9-1 above, the metric shows a strong correlation is exhibited: *As training hours increase, the minutes to complete the requisition decrease.* There are several conclusions about this relationship. First, if we can find a way to improve the requisition process or form, we may be able to reduce the number of training hours needed, and consequently, training hours. The reduction of training hours would also reduce training costs. Second, we could also work on streamlining the training process to reduce training hours and the number of minutes it takes to complete a requisition. Changing the training method may also have an effect on the process. Any savings on either variable would be worthwhile.

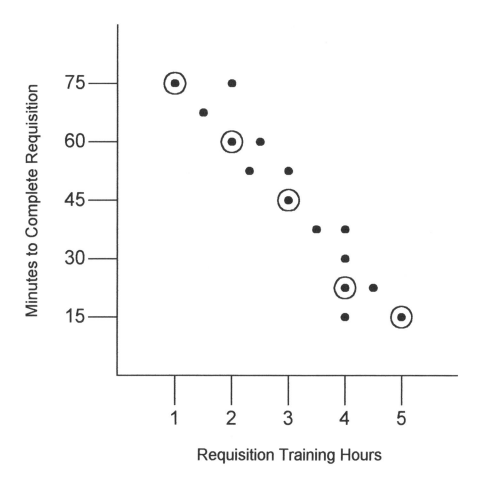

Figure 9-1: *Scatter Diagram*

2.   RUN CHART

The run chart is a type of line graph used as an analysis tool to identify trends or shifts in the output of a process over a period of time. Run charts are the simplest of the numerical problem-solving tools to use and master. You can plot run charts in seconds, minutes, hours, days, or some longer or shorter increments. The time increment must be relevant to the process.

Waste, errors, or inefficiencies are common results from a business process as it varies over time. Run charts show patterns, positive or negative, and like the scatter diagram, can be very useful in finding out possible problems and solutions. Possible measures for run charts include:

1. Volume (*i.e., how much over a specified period of time*)

2. Cycle Time (*i.e., how long something takes*)

3. Errors (*i.e., how many are incorrect over a period of time*)

4. Waste (*i.e., how much is reworked or rejected*)

Basic Steps

1. Gather data and determine the variables to be defined.

2. Create a graph with the "x" and "y" axes.

3. Plot the data.

4. Calculate the average line.

5. Interpret the chart.

Example

In this example, we want to find out the quantity of requisitions rejected during the first two weeks the *Purchasing System* becomes effective. The variable, "rejected purchase requisition," will be measured over ten working days. This will help us determine two things: *(1)* How well the users were trained and (2) How well the Purchasing Assistant applied the new Purchasing System procedure to incoming purchase requisitions. Refer to Figure 9-2 for a sample chart. The variables are:

1. <u>X-Axis</u>: Number of business days in 2 weeks (10 working days)

2. <u>Y-Axis</u>: Number of requisitions rejected

154

The Purchasing Assistant will abide by the rules of the *Purchasing System* procedure and will reject requisitions for the following reasons:

1   Old purchase requisition form (wrong form being used)

2   Incomplete description of purchase request

3.   Preselected supplier

4.   Preliminary discussions with suppliers

5.   Mandatory fields not being completed (e.g., telephone number and extension, estimated price of items being ordered, etc.)

6.   Incorrect charge number

7.   Wrong signatures

8.   Incorrect signatures

9.   Sloppy or illegible writing or typing

10.   Incomplete information of any kind

For simplicity, the results will be plotted for ten working days. After the data is plotted, lines can be connected for easier interpretation. You can:

1.   Search for patterns in the data (*e.g., errors are higher on Tuesday during the second shift*)

2.   Discover the root cause of the error (*e.g., a new employee is working Tuesday's second shift and has yet to be trained*)

3.   Investigate highs or lows in data points (*e.g., extreme variation around the average line indicates opportunity for improvement*)

4.   Continue measuring to track the effect of changes (*e.g., you can prove that the changes are working by tracking the data*)

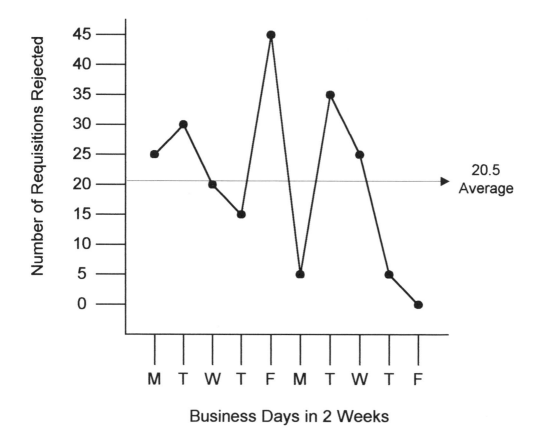

FIGURE 9-2: *Run Chart*

Interpretations

In this example, there are several interpretations that can be made. Each of these interpretations would normally be thoroughly investigated to determine their validity but because these are exercises for this book, the few interpretations presented are not analyzed in any detail. You can look at the chart and make your own interpretations for better understanding.

1.   There is a high rejection rate on Friday of the first week. Further investigation may show that the normal Purchasing Assistant was sick, on vacation, or perhaps an untrained employee filled in for the day.

2.   The number of requisitions on Monday of the second week is low. Further investigation may show that few requisitions came in the department or that most of these requisitions were returned requisitions, from requesters that corrected "rejected" requisitions.

3.   The number of requisitions on Tuesday of the second week jumped up considerably. Further investigation may show that there were a number of new requisitions that had been waiting to be reviewed.

4.   On Friday of the second week, the number of requisitions rejected is zero. Further investigations could reveal that the Purchasing Manager provided on-the-job training and found that the Purchasing Assistant had been rejecting too many requisitions for the wrong reasons. Another interpretation could be that the entire Purchasing Department went to an all day meeting or to an off-site seminar, and requisitions were not checked for that day. A preferred interpretation is that all the requisitions submitted on that Friday had no errors which could lead to a conclusion that the users were becoming more proficient at completing purchase requisitions. (Normally, it would take a longer period of time to come to this kind of conclusion.)

3.   <u>CONTROL CHART</u>

This is the most powerful method for determining compliance of business processes, policies, and procedures. The chart can tell you when to change things and when to leave them alone. A control chart provides a picture of the way your business process is performing. This special type of line graph can be used to interpret data about a business process by creating a picture of the boundaries of acceptable variation. The chart tells if the process is in control, you cannot tell if a chart is in control just by looking at the numbers. A control chart has control limits and plotted values that are a statistical measure of the output of your business process. For the math behind this chart, refer to H. James Harrington's or Richard Chang's books in the "References" section at the end of this chapter.

> You cannot tell if a chart is in control just by looking at the numbers. Statistics and mathematics must be applied to determine the amount of variation in any process, policy, or procedure.

The following terms are some basic definitions that will help you understand what control charts are trying to tell you:

1. Variable data is a measurement that can take on a continuous set of values (e.g., the temperature in your living room or the miles per gallon of your car).

2. An in control process is when data points fall within the upper and lower boundaries of the control chart, or control limits. Common causes are present.

3. An out of control process is when data points fall beyond the upper or lower control limits. Common and assignable causes are present.

4. An assignable cause is something that contributes to the variations in your process that can be identified and tracked. Assignable causes are found in out of control processes.

5. A common cause is part of the random variation that is present within every process or system. Variation (i.e., common cause data points) within the control limits is expected and there is no cause for alarm or investigation.

6. Control limits provide criteria for action based on judging the significance of variations from sample to sample. These limits are used as criteria for signaling the need for action and for identifying if a set of data represents a "state of statistical control," (i.e., being in control). The control limits set the upper and lower boundaries of acceptable variation of a process. The upper and lower limits are generated statistically and show how your process is working. Abbreviations for these are: UCL = Upper Control Limit and LCL = Lower Control Limit.

   Control limits will tell you if your business process is in statistical control (i.e., the business process is exhibiting only the usual day-to-day variation you expect from common causes). As long as the data points are within the control limits, the business process is stable. If the data points fall outside of the limits, there should be a cause of alarm as the business process is not in compliance or is considered out of control.

There are many types of control charts but for the purposes of this example, I will present the "P-Chart" (i.e., percent defective) only. The *average percent defective* of an entire sample is calculated and the average line is drawn. After the data is plotted and the average line is calculated and drawn, the control limits can be calculated.

EXAMPLE OF "PERCENT DEFECTIVE" CALCULATION

> For instance, if 10 errors of any type are found in a single day and the sample is 50, then the percent defective for that day would be 20 percent (10 divided by 50 = 20%). The sample size should not vary day to day; 20 sets of samples should be taken at a minimum (in our example, 10 sets of samples were taken). The sample size for a standard P-Chart is 50 or less. These samples should be collected before the statistics and control limits are calculated.

Basic Steps

1. Determine the business process to be charted.

2. Identify the critical components of the process (those items that lead to the most defects). Quality expert, Juran says that just a few items account for 80% of the defects and many items account for 20% of the defects. The goal is to identify the critical few and concentrate on them. The cause-and-effect diagram can be useful in identifying these defects.

3. Identify measurements that may be taken to determine how the process is operating and apply one of the standard control charts to those measurements.

4. Determine sampling method and initiate data collection.

5. Calculate the appropriate statistics.

6. Calculate the control limits and average line.

7. Create a graph with the "x" and "y" axes.

8. Plot the data on the control chart.

Refer to Figure 9-3 for a sample control chart.

Example

In this example, the *Purchasing System* is assumed to have been in operation for one year and that an employee survey recently revealed that the *Purchasing System* was very important to the organization and that the process received the most complaints. Management wants the *Purchasing System* investigated to determine the validity of the survey before authorizing resources to investigate the complaints and make improvements. Data will be collected on the number and types of purchase requisition errors to determine if the *Purchasing System* is in control and to see where improvements could be made.

The kinds of errors to be observed are listed below:

1. An earlier version of a requisition is used

2. Incomplete item descriptions

3. No dollar estimates of order

4. Incorrect signatures or wrong signatures

5. No signatures

6. Incorrect charge number or account number

7. Dollar amount over the MRO limit of $500.00

8. Incomplete information

9. Preselected supplier

The variables for this chart are:

1. <u>X-Axis</u>. Date, or ten working days

2. <u>Y-Axis</u>. Percent defective (of purchase requisitions)

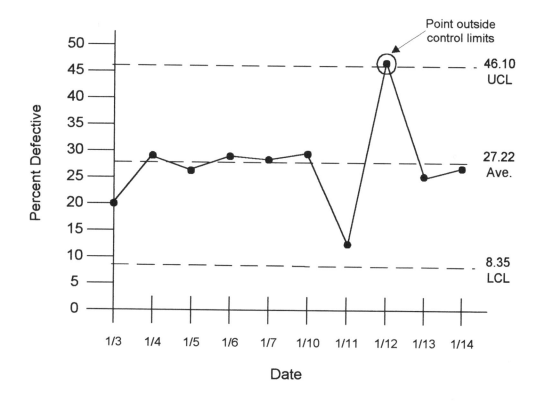

FIGURE 9-3: *Control Chart*

Interpretation of Data

Variation is the key to the interpretation of a control chart. Many processes may appear under control on the surface, but in reality they are out of control. Under these circumstances, management tends to blame the worker for the problems when, in fact, the worker has no control over the situation. In this control chart, one data point (assignable cause) fell outside of the control limits. This single data point (i.e., an assignable cause) on January 12 needs further investigation. These special causes need to be eliminated before the process can be considered in control. Management appears to have a valid concern about the business process being out of control. If the data points had been between the control limits, the chart would have been considered stable or in compliance and management would have reason to doubt the validity of the survey. There is a normal tendency for management to doubt a survey when it seems to yield negligence on their part; as mentioned earlier, complaints are good because they are opportunities for improvement. Refer back a few pages to the guidelines listed for doing data collection or taking measurements. The problem is the process, not the people.

> Process improvements cannot take place until all special causes, those that caused the ·data to be outside the control limits, have been identified and eliminated.

Finding Special Causes

When one or more points are outside the control limits, we must look carefully at the process to try to determine the causes. Sometimes, it is as simple as the manner in which data was collected. The usual rule is to call a process out of control if there are seven or more points in a row on one side of the center line or seven points in a row with each point larger (or smaller) than the preceding one (a trend is present). Points outside of the control limits come from a special cause (e.g., human errors, unplanned events, freak occurrences) that is not part of the way the business process normally operates.

In our example, we did not use enough data points to justify using this rule. To find assignable causes, we must gather evidence from whatever sources are available and make inferences much like a detective. Enlisting the aid of everyone who has information about the process can be helpful to an investigation. Sometimes a worker may know of some event that seemed unimportant at the time it occurred, and that event can be the key to the problem. When doing this investigation, the process is generally halted but there may be cause to continue the process even though it is out of control.

When a control chart has been initiated and all special causes have been removed, you can plot the new data on a new chart but you cannot recalculate your control limits. As long as the business process does not change, the limits should not be changed. Control limits should only be recalculated when a permanent, desired change has occurred in the business process, and only using data after the change occurred. Control charts are powerful tools for measuring the validity of business processes but care must also be taken to follow the rules about control charts. As the top and bottom boundaries of the control chart get closer together, the variation will decrease and this will result in a process with fewer common causes — and your compliance levels will increase.

Improving the Process

Even when a process is in control, the variation in the output may be more than management wants. Recalling the discussion of Six Sigma in the "Introduction" of this book, the control limits in a "Six Sigma Environment" would be ± 0.00017: *These are incredibly tight limits!* If your company is striving for Six Sigma, then major resources must be put forth to achieve these goals. Procedures analysts should always have the goal in mind to tighten up a process by searching for the causes of variation in the product. Everyone who has any involvement with a process should be consulted and asked, "What do you think might be the causes of variation of this process? In non-quality terms, this question could read, "What do you think might be the causes of the inconsistencies of this process?" Seeking sources of variation of a process in control is a management responsibility. The worker cannot change those things that are not under his control. Senior management must take the lead in quality matters and <u>must</u> not send out signals that a poor quality product is acceptable.

4.   <u>HISTOGRAM</u>

A histogram is a special type of bar chart that can be used to communicate information about variation (extent to which things differ, from one to the next) in a business process and make decisions that focus on improvement efforts. Histograms are used mainly to show patterns, that are the result of business processes, to help people make decisions about what is occurring in their business processes and to help them examine what to improve for greater efficiency. There are a number of histogram patterns and each has its own explanation. For instance, if the chart is skewed to the left or right, it has a different meaning than if the histogram is perfectly centered. In the ideal business process, variation is minimized and under control. This situation is reflected in a histogram showing a normal, symmetric distribution, or bell-shaped curve. Histograms are used to group measures like time, weight, or size, on the frequency of a specific occurrence in clusters (or intervals) around an average of observations. The more data used to calculate the average, the more accurate your histogram.

Basic Steps

1.   Gather and tabulate the data in a frequency table.

2.   Calculate the range and interval width.

3. Draw the horizontal and vertical axes.

4. Tabulate the data by intervals.

5. Plot the data.

6. Interpret the histogram.

Refer to Figure 9-4 on the next page for a sample histogram.

Example

In the example below, we will use the histogram to analyze variation for the time it took a Purchasing Department to review an incoming purchase requisition to the point when the Purchase Order is generated. The two variables include:

1. X-Axis. Number of days to process a requisition.

2. Y-Axis. Number of requisitions processed.

Interpretation of Data

There are three patterns to look for during analysis:

1. *Centering*. Where is the distribution centered? Is the process running too high? Too low?

2. *Variation*. What is the variation or spread of the data? Is there too much variation?

3. *Shape*. What is the shape? Is it bell-shaped distribution? Is it positively or negatively skewed, i.e., more data values to the left or to the right?

In our example, the histogram is not centered and suggests that the business process has too much variation. The shape is positively skewed. Had the histogram been concentrated in the middle, the variation would have been under control and manageable. A heavier distribution on the right side may be caused by a new employee taking a longer time to complete a task or from an employee having

164

difficulties understanding a procedure. When there is heavier distribution on the left side of the chart, it could mean that the process is being rushed. When you add the average line to the chart and investigate the distribution of the data, the results could be interpreted differently.

The average time to process a requisition is 4.5 days. The largest grouping is in the interval from 3.6 to 4.3 days, which was close to the average, and makes sense. The question arises about the quicker turnaround times and the slower turnaround times at the end of the chart. One possible answer is that "rush" requests from senior managers account for the requests being turned around in a day or two. This would explain the relatively high number of requests in the interval of 1.5 to 2.2 days. When the "rush" requisitions receive the highest priorities among the buyers, it means that another employee's requisition is being held unnecessarily and this would account for the longer times for some requisitions. The slower turnaround seems to be due to the special treatment that the Purchasing Department has been extending to senior managers for "rush" orders.

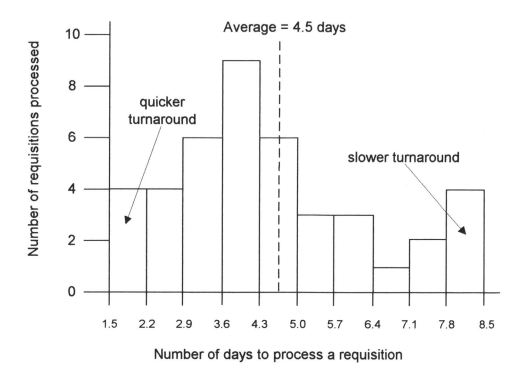

FIGURE 9-4: *Histogram*

5.   PARETO CHART

The Pareto chart is a special type of bar graph you can use as an interpretation tool to determine the relative frequency or importance of different problems or causes. This bar graph can help a team to examine those causes that will have the greatest impact if solved. The Pareto principle states that 20 percent of the sources cause 80 percent of any problem. A Pareto chart is often used when conducting continuous improvement activities because it is a way to measure the results of adjustments that are made to business processes, policies, and procedures. This chart displays the relative importance of problems in a simple, quickly interpreted, visual format. Progress is measured in a highly visible format that provides an incentive to push for more improvement.

The Pareto graph results enable you to concentrate on vital issues by ranking them according to significance. Pareto charts are used to analyze data from a new perspective, to focus attention on problems in a prioritized order, to compare data changes during different time periods, and to provide a basis for showing the cumulative effect of a problem. Pareto charts are an excellent method for determining the most significant areas or issues to work on when doing any kind of problem-solving exercise. Once you start using these charts for your everyday work, I believe that you will use them for most of your day-to-day problems.

A Pareto chart helps the user prioritize problems so that he can focus on the right problems and work on the right solutions. Doing a Pareto chart requires a discipline that forces users to qualify and quantify problems and their causes. This removes guessing and assumptions and introduces objectivity and analysis in the evaluation process. Removing subjectivity from the problem-solving process allows the user to focus on facts.

Basic Steps

1.   Identify the categories of problems or causes to be compared.

2.   Select a standard unit of measurement and the time period to be studied.

3.   Collect and summarize data.

4.   Draw the horizontal and vertical axes.

166

5.   Plot bars on the Pareto Chart.

6.   Calculate the percentages and label the bars and the cumulative percentage line.

Refer to Figure 9-5 in the next few pages for a sample Pareto Chart.

Example

In this example, we will focus on a lesser known problem that occurs in some purchasing departments — analyzing frequent typos, misspelled words, and other errors on purchase orders that may give customers and suppliers a negative image of the organization. As information is either typed or keyed in a computer, spelling and grammatical errors can happen. We would hope that the company's policy would be to double-check any official document that will be viewed by a customer. Spelling and grammar mistakes can be very serious to some customers.

When customers or suppliers start noticing sloppy forms, sloppy typing, misspelled words, or other errors on an important contractual document, they begin to wonder about the integrity of the purchase order contract and of the organization. This may be enough for the customer and/or supplier to seek other business. I remember working in a consultant position for the largest film maker in the world who used a form that had been reproduced 20 times: *The form had wavy lines and portrayed a poor image to customers.* Also, I can remember at least five companies that used some kind of poorly designed visitor form — these sloppy forms project a poor image to the customer. If I were their customer, I would wonder about the quality of the products and services of the company. In our Pareto analysis, we will look at the following errors:

1.   Grammar.

2.   Spelling.

3.   Typos.

4.   Sloppiness.

5.   No signatures.

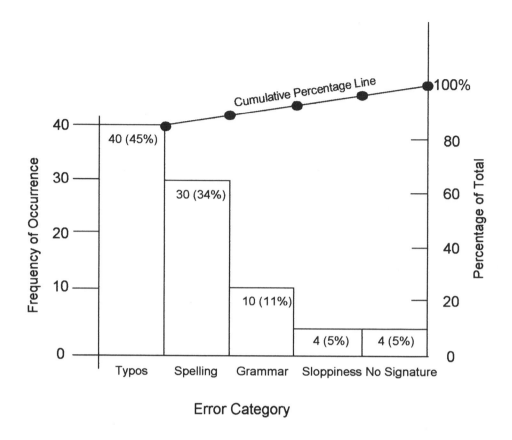

FIGURE 9-5: *Pareto Chart*

The variables in this example are:

1. <u>X-Axis</u>. Error category

2. <u>Y-Axis</u>. Frequency of occurrence

Interpretation of Data

With the chart plotted, the most significant issues are easy to spot. Two sources, typos and spelling, together accounted for 79% of the problems. (Notice that the figures do not always have to be exactly 80/20%, it is acceptable if the ratio is close.) The other three bars represent 21% of the errors. Typos and spelling errors should be the first problems investigated. The procedures analyst should spend some time on the other problems as well but the major emphasis should be on typos and spelling errors.

You can also discuss your findings with your largest customers and suppliers and solicit their opinions about improvements and solutions. Even though the Pareto chart indicated that typos and spelling errors were the biggest problem, if a major customer was disturbed with grammar errors (i.e., 11%), then the procedures analyst should add this concern to his list of problems to correct.

CHECKLIST FOR CHANGE:

✓ Learn how continuous improvement tools can be used in any phase of the life cycle of a business process, policy, or procedure.

✓ Find out how the Pareto chart, run chart, scatter diagram, control chart, and histogram are applied to the analysis of business processes, policies, and procedures. Follow the steps of using quality tools for measuring the *Purchasing System* procedure from the case study introduced in Chapter 3.

✓ Interpret quality tools as they relate to a specific business process, policy, procedure.

✓ Learn more about measurements and why they are key to measuring, controlling, and managing metrics. Discover why measurements are worthless unless an effective feedback system exists. Recall the phrase, "If you cannot measure it, you cannot control it. If you cannot control it, you cannot manage it. If you cannot manage it, you cannot improve it. It is as simple as that," (Harrington, 1991).

✓ Discover excellent books on continuous improvement tools and statistical analyses to add to your reference library and use for developing and designing metrics and executing them.

APPLYING WHAT YOU HAVE LEARNED:

Decide if the continuous improvement tools presented in this chapter will become a part of your compliance plan. Buy and read the books specifically referenced in this chapter on using the continuous improvement tools and statistical analyses to measure your business processes, policies, and procedures. Continue to apply and reapply these tools to your business processes, policies, and procedures as data is collected, presented, and analyzed with the intention of making improvements.

ACHIEVE 100% COMPLIANCE:

The methods, tools, and plans presented in this book will help you analyze problems more efficiently and find solutions more quickly. The continuous improvement tools will provide insight into the stability of your business processes, policies, and procedures, and how well the different elements, tasks, or functions are operating within that business process. The results of the application of these continuous improvement tools will lead to adjustments of the published business processes, policies, and procedures to the extent that there will be limited variation within the business processes. This gradual reduction in the variation of a business process, policy, or procedure should result in higher compliance levels.

REFERENCES:

Amsden, Robert T; Butler, Howard, E.; Amsden, Davida M, *SPC Simplified, Practical Steps to Quality*, Quality Resources, New York, New York, 1998.

Bemowski, Karen and Stratton, Brad, *101 Good Ideas, How to Improve Just About Any Process*, ASQ Quality Press, Milwaukee, Wisconsin, 1998.

Bhote, Keki R., *World Class Quality*, AMACOM, New York New York, 1991.

Brassard, Michael and Ritter, Diane, *The Memory Jogger II, A Pocket Guide of Tools for Continuous Improvement & Effective Planning*, GOAL/QPC, Methuen, Massachusetts, 1994.

Chang, Richard Y and Niedzwiecki, Matthew E, *Continuous Improvement Tools, Volumes 1 and 2*, Richard Chang Associates, Inc., Irvine, California, 1993.

Gitlow, Howard S and Gitlow, Shelly J, *Total Quality Management in Action*, PTR Prentice-Hall, Englewood Cliffs, New Jersey, 1994.

Grieco, Peter L., Jr., *MRO Purchasing*, PT Publications, Inc., West Palm Beach, Florida, 1997.

Harding, Michael and Harding, Mary Lu, *Purchasing*, Barron's Business Library, Hauppauge, New York, 1991.

Harrington, H. James; Hoffherr, Glen D; and Reid, Robert P., Jr., *Statistical Analysis Simplified*, McGraw-Hill, New York, New York, 1998.

Larkin, TJ and Larkin, Sandar, *Communicating Change*, McGraw-Hill, New York, New York, 1994.

Lockamy, Archie, III and Cox, James F., *Re-engineering Performance Measurement*, Irwin Professional Publishing, New York, New York, 1994.

Owen, D. B., *Beating Your Competition Thru Quality*, Marcel Dekker, Inc., New York, New York, 1989.

Paulk, Mark C; Weber, Charles V; Curtis, Bill; and Chrissis, Mary Beth, *The Capability Maturity Model*, Addison-Wesley, Reading, Massachusetts, 1994.

170

Peach, Robert W. and Ritter, Diane S., *The Memory Jogger 9000, A Pocket Guide to Implementing the ISO 9000 Quality Systems Standard and QS-9000 Third Edition Requirements*, GOAL/QPC, Methuen, Massachusetts, 1996.

Pilachowski, Mel, *Purchasing Performance Measurements: A Roadmap to Excellence*, PT Publications, Inc., West Palm Beach, Florida, 1996.

Poirier, Charles, C. and Houser, William, F., *Business Partnering for Continuous Improvement*, Berrett-Koehler Publications, San Francisco, California, 1993.

Shewhart, Walter A, *Statistical Method from the Viewpoint of Quality Control*, Dover Publications, New York, New York, 1986.

Chapter 10

Conducting Systems Audits

The systems audit is the seventh compliance method from the sample compliance plan presented in Chapter 7, *"Establishing a Compliance Plan."* Systems auditing is used by procedures analysts to determine general compliance of published policies and procedures; systems auditing can also be used to verify the implementation of written policies and procedures. Systems auditing can also be used to support the results obtained from the other six compliance methods (i.e., a checklist, scatter diagram, run chart, control chart, histogram, and Pareto chart). The procedures analyst will use tools and techniques from traditional auditing methods like financial, internal, operational, process, compliance, functional, or quality auditing. Auditing is used to identify system failures and operating deficiencies so the auditee (i.e., person or group being audited) may initiate appropriate corrective or preventive actions.

The history of auditing is useful in understanding how the procedures analyst can provide value-added service by doing systems audits of major business processes, policies, and procedures. Auditing is almost as old as civilization. Audits were used in ancient Egypt, the Roman Empire, and the great mercantile establishments of the Middle Ages. The common areas of audit action throughout history have been examining, verifying, and reporting. Auditing has become a key factor in controlling virtually every kind of organization which has financial and economic aspects. Although auditing has traditionally focused on the correctness of accounting records and the property of activities reflected in those records, its subject matter has been changing in recent years. The objective has been to obtain more useful information about results than can be found in financial statements. Audits are changing their focus to achieving organizational effectiveness, conformance of business processes to policies and procedures, verification of the implementation of policies and procedures, economies and efficiencies of resource allocation, and quality systems.

The word *auditing* comes from the Latin *audire* which means the act of hearing: literally, an *auditor* is a person who hears or listens. When we say that a student audits a class, we still use the word in its oldest sense. The auditor merely listens to lectures without responsibility for the required class work.

SUCCESSFUL AUDITS

Audits provide management with accurate and valid information with which to make decisions. Successful audits require that the goals and objectives of an audit be clearly defined. There are four important components to successful audits:

1. <u>Knowledge of Auditee</u>. The auditee (i.e., the person or organization being audited) must be knowledgeable about processes, provide adequate resources for the audit program, and assure that the audits are planned to meet the expectations of the organization. The auditee should be a "subject matter expert" (SME) and/or an individual who is regarded as very knowledgeable about the functions, departments, activities, processes, policies, procedures, documents, forms, and reports being audited. There can be a team of auditees sponsored by the auditee management.

2. <u>Qualifications of Auditor.</u> The auditor must be qualified to do auditing. He must be independent of the processes, have knowledge of the company and processes, be trained in doing audits, and know about standards imposed on processes. The lead auditor organizes and directs the plan, coordinates preparation and issuance of audit reports, ensures his audit team is prepared, and reviews procedures and reports issued as a result of the audit scope. The lead auditor coordinates and prepares the audit plan, pre-audit interview, audit report, audit, post-audit interview, and follow up.

3. <u>Tools of Auditor</u>. Auditors must be equipped with the proper audit techniques, methods, and tools for assessing the quality of processes, policies, and procedures. The auditor must be trained in how to perform audits and possess various auditing skills like questioning techniques, selling the benefits of audits, handling difficult situations, patience, persistence, integrity, and other skills and abilities.

4. <u>Plan of Action</u>. The auditor's approach to audits can determine whether or not the audit will be a success. The auditor must view audits as an

174

opportunity to improve the system. With this point of view, the audit can be viewed as an independent assessment with positive potential for success and improvement. The audit must have the support of the auditee and his management. The auditee's management needs to work closely with auditors to ensure that their scope, goals, objectives, and expectations are clearly defined.

> The auditor must view audits as an opportunity to improve the system. The auditor should want to become a part of the solution, not the problem.

AUDITS ARE NOT ALWAYS SUCCESSFUL

Audits are effective methods for surfacing system and operating deficiencies. When audits are focused and judiciously used, they represent a valuable method for maintaining control and improve visibility. Unfortunately, audits are not always successful and supported by everyone. If the audit results are not properly conveyed, the auditor becomes a part of the organization's problem, not a part of the solution. Auditing is viewed differently by each organization involved. Senior management of some organizations views auditing as responding to mandatory licencing commitments or contractual requirements while others view it as a useful management tool. No matter which view is taken, the first reaction to any audit group or function is usually one of suspicion due to the tradition of audits uncovering fraud, deceit, or a gross lack of compliance.

Organizations being audited may also react negatively based on the connotation that an audit is directed solely toward uncovering deficiencies rather than showing the degree of compliance to published standards and practices. Auditees can sabotage audits from the start if auditees do not think the audits will be beneficial. Auditees do not have to be cooperative. They may have hidden agendas or they might not like feeling bombarded by a team of auditors as though all are against him. This experience can make some auditees nervous, especially if the auditee is not certain of the final outcome of the audit: *The auditee may feel like he is being interrogated!* The auditors can alleviate this problem by interviewing two auditees at the same time.

The fundamental problem with most audit programs is how audit results are used. Traditionally, auditors present their results to the auditee's organization and management uses the findings to support financial and economic conclusions about the company. While the audited organization is supposed to take corrective and preventive actions, the result is typically inaction. Several reasons for this attitude include (Russell, 1996):

1.   The "problem" was not thoroughly investigated by the auditors or the problem was not properly presented to the auditee.

2.   The results of the audit were not communicated effectively to the auditee and his management.

3.   The guidelines or processes for correcting a problem, or preventing its recurrence, have not been properly presented to the auditee and he may not understand his role after the audit results are completed.

4.   The auditee does not understand the auditor's role in this process. If this relationship is not clear, then friction and mistrust can result. Any audit activities in this situation are difficult for both the auditor and the auditee. Care must be taken to avoid these kinds of confrontations.

AUDITOR SELECTION

When we think of auditors, we generally think of an "external" auditor like an auditing firm, or an independent auditor, that has been hired to conduct an audit of a department, function, or organization for some specified purpose. A major advantage of using external auditors is that they do not know the employees and can be objective in their approach whereas this is not always possible for internal auditors.

"Internal" auditors are employees of a company. They generally work for an Accounting Department or an internal Auditing function. Internal auditors have the advantage of being employees and they may not be treated as strangers like external auditors. Also, the internal auditors might know the individuals within the department they are auditing, so communication might not be too restricted or tense.

Procedures analysts are considered "internal" auditors. When procedures analysts do the functions of an auditor, it is generally because a specific department or function has requested the Policies and Procedures Department to conduct an audit or because the Policies and Procedures Department has a reason to visit a department and ask some specific questions about a topic. In some companies, the auditing department will ask for assistance from procedures analysts because of their knowledge and expertise in business processes, policies, and procedures. The procedures analyst makes an excellent internal auditor because he has management support and he can function effectively within rules and standards.

►For the purposes of this chapter, when the term, "auditor," is used, it will refer to an "external" auditor.

PROCEDURES ANALYST AND AUDITING

Auditing policies and procedures creates an wonderful opportunity for a procedures analyst. Up to this point, the procedures analyst has not had the opportunity to revisit the published policies and procedures. In the first compliance method, the "Self-Assessment Checklist" (Chapter 8, *"Developing Self-Assessment Checklists"*) was used by members of the target audiences to do a "self-inspection" of a specific policy or procedure. Next, the five continuous improvement tools (Chapter 9, *"Using Continuous Improvement Tools to Measure Compliance"*) provided the procedures analyst an opportunity to collect data (or to have data sent to him) to be used in constructing statistical charts and diagrams.

None of these tools has permitted the procedures analyst the opportunity to conduct extensive interviews with users or do a "walk-through" of the daily functioning of the business processes, policies, or procedures. The procedures analyst will have the opportunity to revisit business processes, policies, and procedures in three ways:

1.   Using the "Review Plan" from Chapter 6, *"Creating a Review and Communication Control Plan."*

2.   Using the "Improvement Plan" from Chapter 11, *"Conducting Profitable Continuous Improvement Activities."* The procedures analyst will become involved with continuous improvement activities as suggestions and feedback are submitted to him. He will also do his own investigations into problems, issues, and concerns of managers, process owners, or users.

3.   In auditing, the procedures analyst has an opportunity to conduct one-on-one interviews with those using the business processes, policies, or

procedures, i.e., the target audiences. The procedures analyst gains first-hand experience when conducting an audit. The procedures analyst uses many of the tools, techniques, and ideas of the professional auditor.

The procedures analyst is never totally isolated from policies and procedures because he is accountable for them from inception to retirement (i.e., the life cycle of a policy or procedure). He should be monitoring them through the plans and tools presented in this book. The procedures analyst will become involved again with continuous improvement activities as suggestions and feedback are submitted to the Policies and Procedures Department.

AUDITING METHODS

The method of auditing is open to the procedures analyst and I might add the literature is coming up with new names every day. There are several possibilities including operations auditing, process auditing, quality auditing, and systems auditing that can be considered. While "systems auditing" was selected as the tool of choice for these examples, you can select any of the four types of auditing listed below or any other type that you may have used in other tasks or projects:

1. Operations Auditing is concerned with organizational structure, procedures, accounting and other records, reports, and standards of performance (such as budgets and standard costs).

2. Process Auditing is a verification by evaluation of a manufacturing or test operation against documented instructions and standards.

3. Quality Auditing is a systematic and independent examination to determine whether quality activities and related results comply with quality standards.

4. Systems Auditing is the verification of the operations and business processes performed and used by individuals responsible for business processes, policies, and procedures. Another auditing function is called, "compliance auditing." *Compliance auditing* is the verification of the implementation of written policies and procedures. Auditors check to see if activities are being done by the book (Arter, 2000). Compliance audits and systems audits appear to be synonymous.

SELECTION OF SYSTEMS AUDITING AS THE 7TH COMPLIANCE METHOD

"Systems Auditing" was selected as the seventh compliance method because the procedures analyst is responsible for an infrastructure, or system, of policies and procedures. Systems auditing seemed to be the closest to the goals and objectives of the procedures analyst. The other three auditing methods were not selected because their focus was either too broad or too narrow and they are limited to the time devoted to the review and evaluation of published policies and procedures. As a systems auditor, the procedures analyst audits specific business processes, policies, and procedures. The purpose of the systems audit is to evaluate the:

1. Effectiveness, efficiency, and adequacy of policies, procedures, standards, forms, and reports

2. Conformance of business processes to policies and procedures

3. Conformance of the actions of target audiences with business processes, policies, and procedures

4. Ability of users to learn and understand applicable business processes, policies, and procedures

ROLE OF PROCEDURES ANALYST AS SYSTEMS AUDITOR

The systems audit has the following characteristics:

1. The procedures analyst conducts systems audits because he is:

   a. Normally the most knowledgeable person in an organization about business processes, policies, and procedures.

   b. A systems thinker, thinks "out of the box," and concentrates on the "big picture."

   c. Supported by management.

   d. A good speaker, listens well, and does not face the usual negativity (as the external auditor) from the auditee because he has probably worked closely with the auditee and his department in the development of operational processes, policies, procedures, and forms.

2. The scope of the systems audit includes a specific business process, policy, procedure, or a grouping of these documents.

3. The procedures analyst conducts brief pre-audit and post-audit conferences, if requested by management.

4. The procedures analyst uses tools like flow charts, questionnaires, checklists, and "procedures used as checklists."

5. Audits are performed through personal interviews (aided by a questionnaire), telephone interviews and surveys, video conferences, email, and mail-in questionnaires. Other methods can be used at the discretion of the procedures analyst.

6. Audits can be performed any time after a policy or procedure is published and implemented. Audits are normally requested by the auditee's management but audits can also be initiated by the procedures analyst when there is reason to do so, e.g., a trigger from a review plan, significant feedback from users, a major problem a customer wants investigated, or as a routine part of continuous improvement activities.

7. Audits can be repeated as often as the auditee's management requests it because the procedures analyst is internal to the organization; the traditional auditor is external to the organization and can only repeat audits when requested and paid.

8. Any employee can request an audit to be performed of his area, function, department, or organization.

9. Audit results can consist of flow charts, answers to questionnaires or checklists, marked up policies or procedures, filled-in forms, and logs.

10. Audit results are presented to the auditee during a post-audit conference but without the expectation that the auditee will take corrective or

preventive action. The procedures analyst normally coordinates changes to policies and procedures as a result of an audit. The post-audit conference is a courtesy briefing.

11.   Detailed audit results are kept for further evaluation during continuous improvement activities.

12.   The procedures analyst will follow up with the auditee after improvements are made to existing policies and procedures to ensure the auditee is satisfied with the changes. A new audit can be conducted at the request of the auditee and his management to ensure that the latest changes and improvements have been well received.

TOOLS OF THE AUDITOR

The procedures analyst can use many of the tools of the auditor including an audit plan, a pre-audit conference, a questionnaire, a "procedure as a checklist," an audit report, a post-audit conference, and a follow up meeting. The procedures analyst may choose to alter the manner in which the traditional auditor uses these tools to match the way he approaches problems and issues. The procedures analyst might not use the same terminology of the auditor. When the roles of the auditor and the procedures analyst are compared later in this chapter, the differences and similarities of the two roles will be explained in Table 10-1. In this next section, each tool used by an auditor is discussed; at the end of each subheading, the method by which the procedures analyst uses these tools will be discussed.

AUDIT PLAN

The *audit process* provides objective confirmation of products and processes to certify adherence to standards, guidelines, specifications, and procedures. Audits are performed in accordance with documented plans and procedures. This *audit plan* is defined as a plan of action by which the audit will be performed including resources and schedule. Audit results are documented and submitted to the management of the audited organization, to the entity initiating the audit, and to external organizations identified in the audit plan. The audit plan should include the following components:

1.   Introduction, scope, objectives, goals, success criteria, plan of action, and organizations involved in the audit

2. Project processes, documents, and forms

3. Time frame for the audit team to observe project processes

4. Required reports and distribution process

5. Dates of follow up visits of reports

6. Requirements and objective audit criteria

7. Audit procedures and checklists

8. Audit personnel (includes an audit leader and a team of auditors)

►The procedures analyst does not need to prepare a detailed audit plan. He will do most of the steps of the plan but will not formally document a plan. The procedures analyst may notify the auditee of the intended details of the audit through email or telephone. If a formal audit report is requested by the auditee, then the results of the interview process must be thoroughly documented. The procedures analyst conducts interviews with departmental personnel on a daily basis when collecting information about new or revised policies and procedures. He knows how to approach departments and gather information. The concept of auditing is not new to the procedures analysis: *It is just another form of analysis and research* (the first phase of the "Policies and Procedures Improvement Cycle" (PPIC)).

PRE-AUDIT CONFERENCE

The pre-audit conference is used to establish a rapport between the auditee and the auditor (and team, as applicable). The audit plan is discussed and the ground rules of the relationship between the auditee and the auditor (and team) is established. A schedule is established for meetings to discuss findings, solutions, and recommendations brought forth by the auditor and his team. A beginning and ending date for the audit is also established. An ending date is often more crucial than the beginning date because it puts closure on a project.

►The procedures analyst may either conduct a short meeting with the auditee or email information. A formal pre-audit meeting is not necessary when the relationship is already strong between the procedures analyst and the auditee. If the relationship is not strong, or if the procedures analyst has not had the opportunity to communicate with the department being audited, then a pre-audit meeting should take place to make introductions and to get acquainted with each other.

THE QUESTIONNAIRE

The questionnaire is one of the tools the auditor can use to conduct an audit. The main value of a questionnaire lies in the conversation and information it produces, not in the questionnaire itself. Questionnaires are not the only tool used to complete an audit because questions should generate more questions and answers. A questionnaire is only a guide, it should not control every question. The individuals answering the questions of a questionnaire should answer "Yes" or "No" if the answer is clearly one direction or the other. Other answers include "Not Applicable" and "No Answer." When conducting an audit, the auditor should take notes on the questionnaire and update the questions after the audit is complete so the questionnaire can be reused at a later date and not have to be recreated.

► The questionnaire is probably the primary tool of choice for the procedures analyst because it is similar to the "Self-Assessment Checklist" as described in Chapter 8, "*Developing Self-Assessment Checklists.*" Like the checklist, the questionnaire is developed by the procedures analyst. The main difference is that the procedures analyst can conduct interviews with selected individuals with a department or function and ask questions from the questionnaire. When other questions arise, these new questions should be recorded right on the questionnaire for future reference purposes.

PROCEDURE AS A CHECKLIST

While questionnaires are often the tool of choice by the auditor, the auditor has the option of using a published policy or procedure as his review document when interviewing the auditee and his organization. The document is structured in an outline format and should be easy to follow when asking the auditee questions. Even if the policy or procedure is not clearly outlined or is not in a standard writing format, the purpose and process work flow should be evident. The auditor can ask general questions based on the purpose and business process workflow. The auditor may find the "procedure as a checklist" more beneficial than a questionnaire when:

1. Audit personnel are relatively inexperienced and/or there are variations between individual audit techniques.

2.   One or more members of the audit team are technical in nature and do not have prior audit experience relevant to the scope of the audit.

3.   Circumstances demand more than the ordinary evidence required to demonstrate the validity of the audit activity.

4.   The auditor determines that a step-by-step procedure would be more advantageous in the performance of a particular audit.

➤The procedures analyst may prefer to use the "procedure as a checklist" especially if he was involved in the writing of the initial procedure. His familiarity with the subject will make it an easy task to interview an auditee about his conformance to business processes, policies, procedures, standards, forms, reports, or other documents. Note that you can also use a "policy as a checklist" or "process as a checklist."

THE AUDIT REPORT

The audit report is the formal part of an audit and it represents the auditor's scope, goals, findings, and conclusions. The report format should be discussed in advance by the auditor with the auditee. The audit report is used to communicate the results of the investigation. The audit report should be user-friendly so the reader can readily understand what is being reported. The report should provide correct and clear data that will be effective as a management aid in addressing important organizational issues. The audit report should focus on system errors and non-conformities, not facts and data and other nit-picking errors. Statements that identify systematic problems and show cause-and-effect relationships are the most effective in promoting improvement of a system. The report will not attempt to fix problems "on the spot."

A standard format should be used. Reports can be effective if they help, not hinder, improvement efforts. Reports should be organized and written in a way that promotes improvement. For more information about audits and standard audit formats or templates, locate references in your local library as well as online bookstores such as Amazon.com and Barnes and Noble. Search on words like "audit," "auditing," "systems audits," or "audit report."

➤The procedures analyst is an employee of the organization and is considered an internal auditor. He does not normally require a formal report because the findings and conclusions are retained for future improvement activities. The procedures analyst can use flow charts, checklists, check sheets, and marked-up policies and procedures as audit documentation.

POST-AUDIT CONFERENCE

The post-audit conference is used by the auditor to present the final audit report to the auditee and his management. This meeting can take place on the last day of the auditor's assignment or several weeks later after the auditor has had a chance to write his audit report. The auditee is expected to review the report and return comments to the auditor. The auditee and his management may take action in one of three ways (Russell, 1996):

1. <u>Corrective Action</u>. An action taken to eliminate the cause(s) of existing non-conformities (problems) to prevent recurrence.

2. <u>Preventive Action</u>. An action taken to eliminate the cause(s) of potential non-conformities (problems) to prevent recurrence.

3. <u>Remedial Action</u>. An action taken to alleviate the symptoms of existing non-conformities or any other undesirable situation.

With the stress of the work environment and the fast pace of organizations, it is likely that managers will take <u>remedial action</u> when necessary and incorporate either corrective or preventive action if a situation arises that necessitates immediate changes. The norm of the audited department will be to put aside the results until there is time to incorporate the suggestions of the auditors.

►The procedures analyst does not need to present formal findings to the audited organization. He can present a courtesy report of the findings with an estimated date when the suggestions in the report might be completed and incorporated into revised business processes, policies, and procedures. The auditee will be given the opportunity to work with the procedures analyst in the development of improvements to the existing policies and procedures. The procedures analyst makes a powerful auditor; he is internal to the organization and has the ability and authority to make the necessary improvements based on the results of an auditing activity. He can also incorporate the findings from the external auditor as deemed necessary by the auditee and his management.

FOLLOW UP AFTER IMPROVEMENTS

In accordance with the audit plan, the auditor will follow up with the auditee at a time set during the post-audit conference to:

1. Obtain the auditee's written response to the report.

2. Evaluate the adequacy of the response.

3. Verify that corrective, preventive, or remedial actions have been accomplished as scheduled.

4. Determine that the actions were effective in preventing recurrence.

Follow up action may be accomplished through written communication, review of revised documents, a shortened re-audit after the reported implementation date, or by other appropriate means.

➤The procedures analyst will follow up with the auditee and his management after improvements are made as a result of the systems audit of the organization. The procedures analyst does not expect the auditee to make corrective actions on his own; he will work with the auditee to make improvements as necessary. When there is a Policies and Procedures Department in the company, it becomes the role of the procedures analysts to assist other departments with changes and improvements.

In Table 10-1 below, the similarities and differences of the practices of auditors and procedures analysts are analyzed. You will find the intent of the goals and objectives are very similar, only the terminology is different. The primary difference is in what the procedures analyst does with the results. As an internal employee, he can make a bigger impact on the organization and its policies and procedures infrastructure than the external consultant, who is viewed as an outsider to the organization.

The procedures analyst has the upper hand because he can use a review plan, communication and training strategies, a compliance plan, and improvement plan to ensure that his findings have a good chance of being implemented. He has the advantage of asking the auditee(s) to be a part of the cross-functional team that will study the areas of concerns that were raised during the systems audit. The procedures analyst can use metrics to measure the effectiveness of his efforts.

TABLE 10-1: *Similarities and Differences of Auditors' and Procedures Analysts' Roles*

AUDITOR PRACTICES	PROCEDURES ANALYST IN AN AUDITOR'S ROLE	
	SIMILARITIES	DIFFERENCES
Identifies system failures and operating deficiencies	Objectives are the same	
Examines, verifies, and reports findings	Examines and verifies that business processes conform to policies and procedures	Retains findings for continuous improvement activities, NOT for the auditee to review and make corrections on his own
Verifies conformance to policies, procedures, practices, and standards	Objectives are the same	
Prepares audit plan		Does not use formal audit form; may use a policy or procedure as his guideline for questions
Conducts pre-audit conference		Conducts brief on-on-one meeting with auditee or sends email with purpose and objectives. Sends an overview of what he plans to do during an audit and what he plans to do with the results. Explains the purpose and benefits of his actions
A lead auditor conducts the audit and uses a team of auditors if the audit complexity warrants it	Procedures analyst often leads effort; team may be used if audit complexity warrants it	

Uses questionnaires and checklists during audits	Objectives are the same	A copy of the current policy or procedure may be used as a reference to support questions
Findings are not shared with auditee until the post-audit conference		Detailed findings are normally held for continuous activities
Prepares audit report for presentation to auditee's management		Formal report not used; mostly notes and flow charts are retained for continuous improvement activities
Conducts post-audit conference to discuss results of audit report		Procedures analyst reviews summary of findings with auditee at post-audit meeting, if requested by auditee
Conducts follow up of auditee's response to audit results		Procedures analyst does not ask for a response to results; he may request the auditee to be a part of the team that studies suggested improvements
Portrays good listening, speaking, negotiating, and selling skills	Objectives are the same	

AN EXAMPLE OF A QUESTIONNAIRE FOR THE "*Purchasing System*" CASE STUDY (Refer to Table 10-2)

A questionnaire has been selected as the method to illustrate how the procedures analyst conducts a systems audit. The *Purchasing System* case study presented in Chapter 3, "*Focusing on a Case Study to Apply the Principles of this Book*," is used as a model for developing the questionnaire for the systems auditor. The power of this book is in examples like this questionnaire.

STARTING AUDIT

The procedures analyst will commence the audit by reviewing all pertinent documentation available that is used by the Purchasing Department. This could include flow charts, policies, procedures, forms, reports, logs, meeting minutes, lessons learned, or other documents identified as useful.

The procedures analyst will prepare a questionnaire based on this documentation. He will discuss the purpose of the audit with the auditee and his management. He will arrange a time schedule for interviews and conduct the audit. He will use the questionnaire to direct his questions to the auditee. During the interview, he will draw flow charts to aid in understanding the processes and work flow, take extensive notes, and ask new questions to gain knowledge about the *Purchasing System*. When the audit is complete, he will present an overview of the findings to the auditee in a post-audit meeting, if requested by the auditee and his management. The procedures analyst will file the new documentation with the existing documentation of the *Purchasing System* for future use.

The procedures analyst will conduct continuous improvement activities to incorporate changes to the *Purchasing System* procedure. He will update his review plan as discussed in Chapter 6, *"Creating a Review and Communication Control Plan,"* and conduct the necessary communication and training to deploy new changes to the business processes, policies, and procedures of the organization.

During the audit, the procedures analyst will be concerned with the main functions of the *Purchasing System* as discussed in Chapter 3, *"Focusing on a Case Study to Apply the Principles of this Book."* including:

1. Determination of need for an item (s) from any requester within the organization

2. Receiving requisitions into the Purchasing Department

3. Verifying the information on the requisition with the current procedure on processing purchase requisitions

4. Purchasing management approval of purchasing requisition and the assignment of a buyer

5.   Buyer reviewing purchase requisition(s) and adding it to his workload

6.   Researching the purchase requisition by reviewing Purchase Order history, blanket order contracts, or supplier catalogues

7.   Contacting appropriate suppliers

8.   Obtaining preliminary "verbal" orders from the suppliers

9.   Requesting formal bids using the Request for Quotation (RFQ) form

10. Negotiating prices and selecting a supplier

11. Preparing the purchase requisition to be transformed into a purchase order

12. Generating and issuing Purchase Orders

13. Specifying shipping conditions and routing

14. Following up on delivery status

15. Securing evidence of receipt of materials and services

16. Verifying the inspection reports as a result of a delivery being inspected

17. Checking invoices to ensure there is no discrepancy between the price on the packing sheet and the price on the purchase order

18. Maintaining files for a purchase. This purchasing file could include purchase requisitions, requests for quotation, purchase orders, receivers, and invoices

19. Creating a Purchase Order history file for future orders

The investigation of each of these functions will produce information of value as the procedures analyst does an extensive analysis in preparation of the systems audit for the *Purchasing System* process and procedure.

INSTRUCTIONS FOR DEVELOPING THE QUESTIONNAIRE

The questions for this questionnaire have been derived from the functions above and from the flow chart and procedure for the *Purchasing System* process. The questionnaire should be developed so that a "No" answer describes a problem and that a "Yes" answer is a positive response. The auditee can also answer "NA" or "Not Applicable" or can refrain from providing an answer, i.e., "No Answer." The procedures analyst can make comments in the "Notes" section at the end of the questionnaire by writing, "See notes," in the comments' column. Additional questions can be generated from discussions. These new questions should also be noted in the "Notes" section. When the audit is completed, the procedures analyst can return to his work area and make the suggested changes to the questionnaire before he forgets the comments and the way they were said.

While audits might be a one-time event for external auditors, the procedures analyst (acting as a systems auditor) can conduct internal audits as often as both groups think the audits are necessary. For instance, the procedures analyst may audit the *Purchasing System* in January and then again in July after changes and improvements have been incorporated. The audit review cycle can also be added as a category to the review plan as introduced in Chapter 6, "*Creating a Review and Communication Control Plan.*" In June, the procedures analyst can remind the management of the specific organization that he will start preparing to do an audit for them that will start at some prearranged date in July.

USING THE QUESTIONNAIRE

The auditor will use the questionnaire as a guide for questions that are directed at the auditee and members of his team. The same questionnaire should be used for participants of the audit. If a question is asked that generates a new question, then the question and the answer should be noted for this audit and future audits. If the auditee stumbles on a question, then the auditor should try to paraphrase the question: *The more questions answered, the better the results*. If new questions are added during questioning, the auditor should make sure that they become a part of the total sample.

The auditee also has the option of not answering if he is uncomfortable with any of the questions. The auditee should never be forced by the auditor. Forcing an auditee to respond can lead to disastrous results for the auditor. The auditor has to be extra careful not to offend the auditee.

TABLE 10-2: *Purchasing System Questionnaire* (paraphrased from Lindberg, 1972)

Purchasing System Questionnaire					
Auditor Name:				Date:	
Questions	Yes	No	NA	Not Answer	Comments
1. Is a department or a single organizational unit engaged in purchasing? If yes, prepare a departmental organization chart identifying positions and reporting relationships. If no, is the purchasing function completely decentralized? If yes, identify responsibilities and describe the purchasing system used.					
2. Does the present degree of centralization or decentralization of purchasing appear justified? If no, list reasons in comments or make reference to notes at the end of the questionnaire.					
3. Do written purchasing policies and procedures exist? If yes, have purchasing policies been established at the (a) corporate level; (b) divisional level; (c) local level; and (d) departmental level. Describe exceptions in comments.					
4. Have any purchases recently been made outside the prescribed purchasing routine? If yes, does the circumvention appear justified?					
5. Are any accounting functions performed by the purchasing department or by purchasing personnel?					
6. Does the purchasing department serve as a source of information from suppliers, competitors, and so on?					
7. Are there purchasing functions that have adapted to data processing? If yes, have specific programs been written and made operational? If no, are their areas that should be computerized?					

192

8. Is the gross dollar value of all purchases made this year known?					
9. Is the percent of total purchases (purchase orders and dollar value) handled by the purchasing department known? If yes, put in comments.					
10. Have you made a distribution of purchase order value, that is, distributed by number and dollar value? If yes, put it in the notes.					
11. Does the purchasing department have a voice in the selection of materials, supplies, specifications, and so forth? If no, has it too little voice?					
12. Is expediting deliveries a major problem?					
13. Are overdue deliveries regularly expedited or taken note of in the receiving process and acted upon?					
14. Are all purchases delivered to a central receiving location, as opposed to direct delivery to the requester?					
15. Is batching of small orders routinely done; that is, are blanket purchase orders of commonly used, low-unit-cost items, provided?					
16. Are purchasing activities subdivided so no individual has the responsibility for an entire purchasing transaction from beginning to end?					
17. Are orders ever divided among a number of suppliers? If yes, is any advantage offered by the division?					
18. Are purchase order drafts used; that is, are combination orders and order payment forms employed?					
19. Is there an approved supplier list for purchased items?					
20. Is the documentation up to date and in the hands of users? See the list of questions below for a "yes" answer:					

If yes, do the procedures cover the following? A. Requisitioning. B. Bid requirements and method of supplier selection. C. Authorizations and signatures required. D. Organizational and operational relationships with (1) accounting department; (2) receiving department; and (3) inventory planing and control departments. E. Necessary forms, reports, and files. F. Supplier evaluation. G. Buyer evaluation. H. Legal considerations including trade regulation laws, use of uniform commercial code, warranties, product liability considerations, and nonperformance. I. Purchases from local suppliers. J. Use of blanket orders, systems contractors, or purchasing agreements.					
21. Is each purchase transaction based on the provision of a purchase requisition, and is approval of the requisition required by a duly authorized person(s) before a purchase order is made up?					
22. Are there policies that outline the conditions under which supplier selection can take place outside the purchasing department?					
23. Are purchase requisitions ever marked rush, emergency, or as soon as possible? If yes, is it known what percent of purchase orders are so marked?					
24. Are bids received from the same suppliers each time?					
25. Are exceptions to the lowest bid allowed? If yes, how are such exceptions controlled?					
26. Are purchase order blanks pre-numbered and properly controlled?					
27. Do managers who approve requisitions appear to have enough information to make intelligent approval decisions?					

28. Are routing considerations (delivery costs, freight allowances, premium rates) given adequate attention in the evaluation of competitive bids?					
29. Are transportation allowances verified?					
30. Are efforts made to ship by the most economical methods?					
31. Is price included whenever possible in the purchase order?					
32. Are prices of items not pre-priced, verified after receipt of purchase confirmation?					
33. Are purchase orders written so that materials received can be easily identified and checked?					
34. Is the policy for acceptance of gifts from suppliers explicit?					
35. Does the company investigate conflict of interest such as ownership by purchasing agent of stock in suppliers?					
36. Are material price variances used as a measure of purchasing agent performance?					
37. Are quality control analysis reports used as a measure of purchasing agent performance?					
38. Are all purchases made on purchase orders channeled through the purchasing department? If yes, should they be, for example, on-site, small inventory levels (rack jobbers), etc.?					
39. Are receiving tickets pre-numbered and is a permanent record kept in the receiving department or is a copy of the purchase order sent to receiving as authorization to accept goods to speed processing?					
40. Are returned purchases cleared through the shipping department?					
41. Are invoices checked in the Accounting Department against purchase orders, receiving reports, and inspection reports?					

42. Is there a definite responsibility, as supported by evidence, for checking invoices for prices, extensions, and freight charges? If no, list exceptions in notes.					
43. Are purchases made for employees cleared through the Purchasing Department in a routine manner?					
Notes: (Number the comments; list additional notes on the back of this questionnaire)					

RESULTS OF QUESTIONNAIRE

For our hypothetical example above, we will assume that five questions were answered "No," two questions were answered "NA," and three questions were left blank (or "No Answer"). The "Yes" answers can be written as positive comments in the Audit Report. The "No," "NA," and "No Answer" answers can be explained in an "Issues" or "Improvements" section in the final audit report (or the format selected by the procedures analyst). Each of these "Non-Yes" answers should become a part of the improvement activities for the procedures analyst. Also, if there were any comments with the "Yes" answers, they should be added to the folder for improvement activities for the *Purchasing System* procedure. The assumed responses to this questionnaire include all "Yes" answers except the following "No" answers, "NA" answers, and "No Answers."

The five "No" answers are:

1. Is the documentation up-to-date and in the hands of users? Do they understand it?

2. Are there policies that outline the conditions under which supplier selection can take place outside the purchasing department?

3. Are all purchases delivered to a central receiving location, as opposed to directly delivered to the requester?

4. Is the policy for acceptance of gifts from suppliers explicit?

5. Are quality control analysis reports used as a measure of purchasing agent performance?

The two "NA" answers are:

1. Are Purchase Order drafts used; that is, are combination orders and order payment forms employed?

2. Does the company investigate conflict of interest such as ownership by a purchasing agent in stock of its suppliers?

The three questions left blank ("No Answer") are:

1. Do managers who approve requisitions appear to have enough information to make intelligent approval decisions?

2. Are transportation allowances verified?

3. Are material price variances used as a measure of purchasing agent performance?

These questions and answers will be retained by the procedures analyst and used during continuous improvement activities in Chapter 11, "*Conducting Profitable Continuous Improvement Activities.*" A synopsis of the answers with possible recommendations will be presented to the auditee either in a short post-audit conference or through email, if requested by the auditee and his management. The auditee will be informed that he and his organization can participate in the improvement activities either by becoming a part of the cross-functional team that will investigate the audit results or by acting as "subject matter experts" when asked questions about policies and procedures.

The auditee's department can also conduct internal improvement activities that can be used to support the activities conducted by the procedures analyst. Occasionally, the auditee's department will implement internal procedures that support the organization's policies and procedures infrastructure. For example, "desk-level" instructions may be written for a clerical person to operate a computer or for an accounting assistant to process a payroll check. Also, a receptionist may create a log to record the return of badges.

CHECKLIST FOR CHANGE:

✓ Systems audits provide the procedures analyst with a valuable tool for examining and verifying conformance to business processes, policies, and procedures.

✓ Systems audits are used for examining, verifying, and reporting the compliance of major business processes, policies, and procedures.

✓ The procedures analyst makes an excellent auditor because he is internal to the organization. He can make changes and improvements easier and quicker than an external auditor. An external auditor can only suggest changes. The internal auditor can find ways to incorporate necessary changes and improvements as they are reviewed internally by both employees and management.

✓ The procedures analyst uses many of the tools of the traditional auditor for systems audits.

✓ The results of the audit for the procedures analyst can be used when conducting continuous improvement activities; the results will not be presented to the auditee to conduct corrective and preventive actions. When the external auditor presents his audit report, he expects action by the auditee in the form of corrective and preventive actions. The difference between the auditor and the procedures analyst is that the auditor can <u>expect</u> actions to happen — the procedures analyst can take the necessary steps to ensure the changes and improvements are incorporated!

APPLYING WHAT YOU HAVE LEARNED:

Select the audit approach you want to take. Work with your management and with the management of departments within your organization to select major business processes, policies, and procedures that could become audit candidates. Select an area to audit. Discuss the expected actions and results with the management of the selected area. Obtain names of individuals to interview (i.e., auditees). Explain the benefits of the audit and probable results to the auditee and his management. Establish a time line for the audit. Set up meetings to discuss progress, issues, and concerns. Conduct the audit. Discuss high-level audit results with the auditee during one-on-one meetings

198

with the auditee, if requested. Invite the auditee and his management to participate in continuous improvement activities.

ACHIEVE 100% COMPLIANCE:

The systems audit is introduced in this chapter as the preferred auditing choice for the procedures analyst. The results of the systems audit provides support and potential areas for improvement for continuous improvement activities of a specific business process, policy, or procedure. Ideally, when the suggestions become changes and improvements, the level of compliance will increase.

REFERENCES:

Arter, Dennis, *Beyond Compliance*, Quality Progress Journal, ASQ Quality Press, Milwaukee, Wisconsin, June 2000.

Burton, John C; Palmer, Russell E; Kay, Robert S., *Handbook of Accounting and Auditing*, Warren, Gorham & Lamont, Boston, Massachusetts, 1981.

Lindberg, Roy A and Cohn, Theodore, *Operations Auditing*, AMACOM, New York, New York, 1972.

Russell, J.P. and Regel, Terry, *After the Quality Audit*, ASQC Quality Press, Milwaukee, Wisconsin, 1996.

Software Quality International, *Auditors Training Course*, Upland, California, April 25 - 28, 1990.

Part Three

INCORPORATING IMPROVEMENTS
AND ACHIEVING COST SAVINGS

Part Three shows how the results of the compliance methods discussed in Part Two can be used to make improvements to existing business processes, policies, and procedures. Savings of millions of dollars can be achieved through creative problem solving. Chapter 13 focuses on ways the procedures analyst can assist his organization to become "proactive" and "forward-thinking." Chapter 14 helps the procedures analyst "Look to the Future" by showing him how to do a career assessment and become a part of the solution, not the problem.

Chapter 11

Conducting Profitable Continuous Improvement Activities

In recent years, a new management truth has emerged. Companies pursuing quality initiatives like Six Sigma, the Malcolm Baldrige Award, ISO Quality Standards, Capability Maturity Model, or Total Quality Management (TQM) as a competitive strategy have found that improved quality, increased productivity, reduced costs, and greater customer satisfaction are interconnected. Leading businesses now think differently about their processes. Processes are no longer viewed as just manufacturing processes. Business processes constitute a significant portion of organizational cost. Until recently, improvement activities were focused on manufacturing processes and not business processes.

Management is finding that there are many processes that use material, equipment, and people to provide outputs and services. These non-manufacturing business processes are more important to competitiveness than manufacturing processes. Organizations have shifted their focus to the improvement of business processes and how to they are going to ensure profitable continuous improvement activities become the vision and norm for the company. Benefits of improved business processes, policies, and procedures have moved beyond operational and tactical effectiveness to strategic effectiveness and positioning. There are six strategic benefits that can be achieved from business process improvements:

1. Improved customer satisfaction

2. Improved business processes, policies, and procedures

3. Reduced cost and cycle time

4. Improved service levels and response times

5. Enhanced quality and flexibility

6.   Improved employee productivity and morale

IMPROVEMENT DEFINED

Improvement means to enhance quality, i.e., conformance to requirements, by improving value and by achieving excellence for the customer. *Process improvement* is the application of improvement activities to business processes, policies, and procedures. Repeatable, or continuous, improvement activities can be achieved when the "Policies and Procedures Improvement Cycle" (PPIC) introduced in Chapter 1, *"Introducing the Policies and Procedures Improvement Cycle"* is applied. Improvement activities are applied in the fourth phase of PPIC, "Report & Improve."

PROCESS IMPROVEMENT — STRATEGY & GOALS

Process improvement is a major undertaking for any company. Improving business processes will be a major factor to maintaining a competitive advantage as organizations fight to become recognized in their industry and strive to be number one. Competition will be intense. Continual change, or improvement, is needed to stay even or ahead of the competition. Organizations have to recognize that "continual change" is here to stay and must constantly work toward building a new mind-set open to changes and improvement. Management's commitment can be achieved by ensuring process improvement initiatives are a part of the company's strategic goals.

Successful companies are driven by the vision and values of their leaders. The executive leadership must create and publish a vision that can be clearly understood by the entire organization. The vision must become so ingrained in the minds of employees that everyone understands what it means and how it drives the direction of the company. With a strong vision of what business process improvement can do for a company, a CEO can give employees the freedom to explore new ideas and concepts, and the power and resources to make decisions and implement changes brought about by business process improvements.

Developing a worthwhile business strategy and process vision relies on (1) A clear understanding of organizational strengths and weaknesses, coupled with an understanding of market structure and opportunity and (2) Knowledge about innovation activities undertaken by competitors and other organizations. The improvement process is a never-ending journey. Each new process starts with commitment from management.

Creating a strong and sustained linkage between strategy and the way work is done is an enduring challenge in complex organizations. Strategies must be aligned with processes. Process improvement is most valuable in a strategic context because the streamlining of processes is useful in areas that really matter to the business. Change is more likely to be successful if the effects of the change benefit the business and its employees and focus on what matters to customers and management. The organization's goals for improvement include:

1. Exceeding customer requirements

2. Improving an organization's image and employee morale

3. Creating a common vision and mission

4. Improving communication and bridging responsibility gaps

5. Providing training for the required new skills

6. Standardizing and streamlining processes

7. Resolving problems before they become crises

8. Improving the design and documentation of processes, products, and services

9. Incorporating recognition and rewards systems to reinforce desired behavior of employees

10. Management modeling the business processes, policies, and procedures, and setting an example for the rest of the organization

> Process change without strategy and vision seldom goes beyond streamlining, and frequently ends as failure.

The most difficult lesson for management to learn is that real improvement takes time to accomplish. Improvement does not happen overnight: *It is ongoing and continuous.* The urgency of the need, the obviousness of the cause, and the clarity of the solution have little to do with getting things straightened out. Process improvement just does not happen: *It has to be planned.* Improvements should not be made without reason. The second most difficult lesson for management to learn is proving that improvement has been incorporated into business processes, policies, and procedures. The procedures analyst can have a major influence because he is accountable for business processes, policies, and procedures over their life cycles.

"PROVING" IMPROVEMENT

Improvement means nothing unless you can prove that improvement has been achieved. You ask, "*How is this done?*" The simplest way to "prove" improvement is to show an improvement in time or cost, depending on the goal. For example, if the cost to process 10,000 four-part purchase requisition is $900.00 and the cost to process 10,000 three-part requisition is $500.00, then you could claim a savings of $400.00 per form if the process can be improved to eliminate the need for the extra part. Three ways to "prove" improvement are explained below:

1. By Number or Value. Five quality tools were introduced in Chapter 9, "*Using Continuous Improvement Tools to Measure Compliance.*" The execution of each tool resulted in a type of comparison, i.e., a relationship, a value, or a number. If a positive comparison can be shown, an improvement can be justified.

    For instance, a control chart is calculated for Process "A" and is shown to be out of control. If an improvement is made for Process "A" that brings the control chart in control, an improvement can be claimed. This is a simple example — business processes and statistics are much more involved and every consideration must be discussed before the final report can be prepared.

2. By Cost or Time. Time or cost can be compared using the five quality tools introduced in Chapter 9, "*Using Continuous Improvement Tools to Measure Compliance.*" Conducting a cost benefit analysis is an excellent way to show a side-by-side, step-by-step comparison of two processes, policies, or procedures. The process cycle time and costs can be easily compared. The results will be clear using this kind of analysis in Chapter 12, "*Saving $1 Million with Cost Benefit Analyses.*" Chapter 12 details a cost benefit analysis that compares the *Purchasing*

System procedure in Chapter 3, *"Focusing on a Case Study to Apply the Principles of this Book,"* with the *Purchase Card System* procedure at the end of this chapter.

3.   <u>By Cost of Quality</u> (COQ). The COQ is method used by quality professionals for "proving" improvement. Refer to Appendix "B" for an explanation and example of using the COQ for demonstrating clear proof for "proving" improvement has taken place. Follow through with the examples and you will appreciate the processes and variables necessary to "prove" an improvement.

When improvement is proved, increased compliance will be achieved. Without this proof, compliance cannot be proved or achieved. We can show that an improvement did actually occur, or that quality is achieved because a customer's requirements were met, but we still must continue to use the compliance methods developed in Chapter 7, *"Establishing a Compliance Plan,"* to achieve compliance of our published policies and procedures. Performing ongoing compliance measures is one of the major themes of this book. Meeting requirements, satisfying the customer, and lowering costs are great results but none of them is useful information if the compliance of published policies and procedures has not been achieved.

ESTABLISHING AN IMPROVEMENT PLAN

The procedures analyst should establish a general improvement plan for continuous, ongoing improvements to business processes, policies, and procedures. The plan should be endorsed by the CEO and management, contain a vision and mission statement that focuses on business process improvement, and provide direction for the selection of major business processes, policies, and procedures that need improvement. The procedures analyst should make the improvement plan available to all employees through a communication campaign. An improvement plan should be written clearly and in a format that can be read and understood by all employees. There are nine areas that the improvement plan should address. Each area will be addressed below.

SECTIONS OF AN IMPROVEMENT PLAN

1.   <u>Management Commitment</u>. The need for a continuous improvement plan should be discussed with management; the benefits can be

presented with an emphasis on the need for process streamlining, cost and time reduction, improved quality and flexibility, and enhanced service levels. The procedures analyst can ask the CEO to write a statement of commitment and ask them to affix his signature to the first page of the improvement plan. This endorsement will show commitment to anyone who reads the document.

2.   <u>Company Vision, Mission, Strategy, and Objectives</u>. Statements that relate business processes, policies, and procedures to the company's strategic goals should be included and explained.

3.   <u>Policies and Procedures Department's Strategy and Objectives</u>. The procedures analyst should write a separate statement of the strategy and objectives of the Policies and Procedures Department; the tie from management's strategic goals should be addressed. This policies and procedures statement should be printed, framed, and hung on a wall within the area where the procedures analysts' work. This same statement should be included in the "Improvement Plan." Examples of strategic goals for the Policies and Procedures Department include:

a.   Writing effective policies and procedures that can be measured

b.   Adhering to the "Policies and Procedures Improvement Cycle" (PPIC) by ensuring continuous improvement activities are iterative

c.   Providing communication in a variety of formats for clear understanding and applicability

d.   Providing diversified training and mentoring for business processes, policies, and procedures

e.   Measuring business processes, policies, and procedures using quality tools

f.   Using the results of the execution of quality tools to report and make improvements to business processes, policies, and procedures

g. Promoting ongoing continuous improvement activities

h. Helping the organization evolve into a "forward-thinking" and "proactive" company

i. Striving to become current in new technologies, techniques, and methods as they are applied to business processes, policies, procedures, and forms

4. Cross-Functional Team. A cross-functional team is a team of individuals from areas that impact or are supported by a business process, policy, or procedure. The selection of these team members is based on criteria like knowledge of the areas being studied, heavy use of documents used in selected areas of study, creative thinking, listening skills, strong reputation among his peers, and high productivity. Where possible, one or two team members should be selected from each area.

For instance, in the case of the *Purchasing System* procedure, members of the team could include users who complete purchase requisitions as well as those who process the order, i.e., Purchasing Assistants, Buyers, Purchasing Clerks, Receiving Department personnel, and Accounting Department representatives. Several representatives could be selected from those users who have a high number of requests to the Purchasing Department over a specified time frame such as three months.

5. Listing of Business Processes, Policies, and Procedures for Improvement Purposes. Major business processes, policies, and procedures should be identified and ranked according to importance and use. This list can be prepared using the current list of published policies and procedures. Documents can be prioritized in conjunction with management's comments and other factors like the vision and mission of the company, the results of the compliance plan, and suggestions from process owners, users, or customers.

The Pareto analysis (Chapter 9, "*Using Continuous Improvement Tools to Measure Compliance*") can be used to rank the top 80% of the business processes, policies, and procedures. These business processes, policies, and procedures should be verified that they are tied to the company's strategy, vision, and mission statements and that these topics matter to management. The prioritized list should be circulated first to process owners and users for comment and review, and then to senior management for review and approval. Adjustments should be made based on their comments. When the list is completed, preparations should be made to begin the improvement process.

6. <u>Improvement Tools</u>. There are several quality tools that can be used to make improvement decisions including brainstorming, cause-and-effect analysis, affinity diagrams, flow charts, statistical process control, checklists, scatter diagrams, run charts, Pareto charts, control charts, or histograms. These tools can be used in conjunction with business process streamlining tools. Other tools can be selected depending on your success with these tools.

7. <u>Streamlining Tools</u>. There are twelve cornerstone streamlining tools used for improving business processes, policies, and procedures (Harrington, 1991). Refer to the next section for a complete description of these tools. H. James Harrington's twelve tools are an excellent addition to the tools that have already been suggested in this book.

8. <u>Corrective Action</u>. Employees are encouraged to talk about their problems because opportunities for correction come to light from employees who are more familiar with the operations in their own areas and not just from defects found through inspections, reviews, and audits. These problems must be addressed immediately. If problems suggested by employees are addressed and resolved in a timely manner, employees are more likely to bring forth more problems. Employee feedback is critical to the success of the policies and procedures infrastructure.

Management's Commitment

Management's commitment is very important to any improvement plan. Management can show support for the improvement plan established by the procedures analyst by:

1. Showing interest, providing the resources required, and working closely with the procedures analyst and supporters

210

2. Developing common objectives that support the proposed changes

3. Breaking down walls that stand between departments and functions

4. Searching out improvement opportunities

5. Setting up department improvement teams to support the processes being evaluated

6. Changing their own thinking to get a total process perspective

7. Providing the necessary training and education to support the new business processes, policies, and procedures

8. Anticipating the impact of process changes on their organization and preparing for them and establishing systems and reviews to ensure that the progress does not degrade

STREAMLINING TOOLS & CONTROL POINTS

When you think improvement, think of ways to make things better, to enhance value or quality, to streamline, or to cut fat and waste. While there are many methods and techniques for making improvements, H. James Harrington developed streamlining tools that are known as the "12 Cornerstone Tools" for streamlining business processes, policies, and procedures. These tools are summarized below. Refer to his 1991 book for a complete description of their use.

1. Bureaucracy elimination. Removing unnecessary administrative tasks, approvals, and paperwork. These elements are usually observed on the flow chart for a business process, policy, and procedure.

2. Duplication elimination. Removing identical activities that are performed at different parts of a process, again, these are normally observed on the flow chart.

3. Value-added assessment. Evaluating every activity in the business process, policy, or procedure to determine their contribution to meeting customer requirements.

211

4.   Simplification. Reducing the complexity of the process; for instance, this could be as simple as reducing the number of steps or tasks to accomplish an activity.

5.   Process cycle-time reduction. Determining ways to compress cycle time to meet or exceed customer expectations and minimize costs.

6.   Error proofing. Making it difficult to do an activity incorrectly; for instance, a computer program can be created that can only be completed one way through the use of validation tests. A control point that has the power to completely stop a process is a form of "error proofing." Control points are discussed in the next section.

7.   Upgrading. Making an effective use of capital equipment and the working environment to improve overall performance.

8.   Simple language. Reducing the complexity of the way we write and talk, making our documents easy to comprehend by all who use them.

9.   Standardization. Selecting a single way of doing an activity and having all employees do the activity that way all the time. Standardization is only possible with reviews, audits, control points, communication, training, and compliance checking.

10. Supplier partnerships. Assisting suppliers improve their input. The output of the process is highly dependent on the quality of the inputs.

11. Big picture improvement. Helping the cross-functional team look for creative ways to change a process drastically.

12. Automation and/or mechanization. Applying tools, equipment, and computers to boring, routine activities to give employees more time to do creative activities.

CONTROL POINTS

An improvement method that I have used for the past twenty years is the "control point." I am not sure this is the correct term but it describes its purpose well. A *control point* is an individual, form, or some point in the work flow that acts as a "watchdog" or "stopping point" for the processing of business processes, policies, and procedures. For instance, in the *Purchasing System* procedure, the Purchasing Assistant acts as a control point because he can stop any purchase requisition from entering the system if a requester has not adhered to the guidelines in the *Purchasing System* procedure. A control point can also be a form, document, report, or software program. For instance, a form could be designed so that it can only be completed one way or it can contain check points for the user to ensure that he is completing it correctly. When a form is completed online, it is possible to design it to restrict wrong answers from being entered. The control point in this case is the form with built-in validation features. The control point is a good feature to add to the implementation of any business process, policy, or procedure.

►The procedures analyst can try to identify control points in the analysis phase of the "Policies and Procedures Improvement Cycle" (PPIC) so the members of the cross-functional team can come to an agreement on issues and concerns early in the "Analyze & Research" phase rather than after the process, policy, or procedure is approved and published. Even though the control point is considered a part of the implementation process, early cooperation of the cross-functional team members and sponsors can make the process much easier during implementation. The more people that work with you early in a process and agree with the team's analysis and solutions, the better chance the published policies and procedures will be accepted.

AN EXAMPLE — IMPROVEMENTS ARE APPLIED TO THE CASE STUDY

The purpose of this major example is to apply what has been learned in this book and actually select a solution that would greatly improve the current paperwork, labor intensive *Purchasing System* flow chart and procedure. This example ties together many of the principles and themes of this book. The case study, *Purchasing System*, from Chapter 3, *"Focusing on a Case Study to Apply the Principles of this Book,"* will be our focus. Many assumptions are made but I believe that the points presented will help you find creative solutions to your current business processes, policies, and procedures.

HIGH LEVEL VIEW OF EXAMPLE

A cross-functional team will be established in the example to lead you through this example. Meetings will be conducted and solutions will be developed using brainstorming, affinity diagrams, and root cause analysis to identify areas, issues, or experiences relevant to the best solution to the *Purchasing System* business process and procedure. A new flow chart and procedure will be written based on the solution selected. The latest industry standards for the purchase of MRO items will be applied to the solution selected. The team will be considered successful when they have identified a solution, documented a flow chart, and transferred the information from the flow chart to a procedure draft using a standardized writing format. The cross-functional team will continue to meet until a policy or procedure is coordinated, written, and published. The current team can celebrate and disband. Additional teams will be developed, as needed, for future improvement activities.

In Chapter 12, *"Saving $1 Million with Cost Benefit Analyses,"* we will compare the two procedures (i.e., original *Purchasing System* procedure and the new *Purchase Card System* procedure) and calculate the cost savings realized when a major improvement effort identifies a new, better, and faster process. The *Purchasing System* has been altered significantly as it was the result of a complete re-engineering effort. The content of this procedure is based on *Purchase Card System* guidelines currently in use by Mettler Toledo, Inc., in Worthington, Ohio. The primary difference is that I added a writing format and a few logical inferences that could be made from the *Purchase Card System* guidelines to accommodate the seven sections of the writing format. The example contained in the remainder of this chapter includes a scenario, establishment of a cross-functional team, analysis of the results from a compliance plan, team meetings, identification of solutions, selection of a single solution, a revised flow chart, and a revised procedure (though a completely re-engineered procedure looks more like a new procedure).

➤START OF EXAMPLE

1.   SCENARIO

The original *Purchasing System* procedure was written and approved by users and management; it was published, communicated, and trained. A review plan was designed for tracking internal and external changes to the procedure. A compliance plan was established and seven compliance methods (i.e., a self-assessment checklist, scatter diagram, run chart, control chart, histogram, and Pareto chart) were identified to monitor the stability and compliance of this procedure. A senior manager requested that this *Purchasing System* procedure be reviewed for improvement purposes because there have been complaints about how long it takes to process a purchase requisition from internal and major external customers and suppliers. The procedures analyst must take this request seriously and take the necessary steps to satisfy the request of the senior manager.

The procedures analyst has placed this procedure on top of his improvement list because of the attention it had been receiving from process owners, users, and management within the company. This procedure deserves the attention it is getting not only because a senior manager wants it reviewed but also because it matters to the customer and it affects the vision and culture of the company. The procedures analyst will establish a cross-functional team to write an improvement plan and start reviewing the procedure for possible improvements.

2.   CROSS-FUNCTIONAL TEAM

The procedures analyst will serve as the leader and facilitator of this team. He will select team members from those individuals who played an important role in the *Purchasing System* business process and procedure. By referring to the flow chart in Chapter 3, *"Focusing on a Case Study to Apply the Principles of this Book,"* the individuals most affected would include Purchasing Assistants, Purchasing Managers, MRO Buyers, Receiving Department Representatives, and Accounting Department Representatives. Several users, and their managers, who process the highest number of purchase requisitions, will also be invited to be members of this team. The supervisors who manage the company stationery supplies and maintenance supplies can also be invited to participate.

►The goal of the cross-functional team is to involve as many different participants as feasible while at the same time ensuring that the individuals selected are knowledgeable or subject matter experts for the specific business process, policy, or procedure being reviewed. The procedures analyst will set the charter and the ground rules for the regular team meetings. He will offer training that will include team building, listening and presentation skills, and a summary knowledge of quality tools.

The cross-functional team will use the results of the execution of the seven compliance methods from Chapters 8 to 10 to begin their analysis of the *Purchasing System* procedure. A flow chart will be developed based on the results. The strategic goals and objectives of the company will be examined to determine if the procedure satisfies these goals or if a new and better solution is needed. If a new solution is identified, the flow chart will be adjusted to match the new process. The current procedure will be revised based on the new flow chart. The 40-step plan of action (Chapter 2, "*Writing Effective Policies and Procedures*") for writing effective policies and procedures will be applied when coordinating, writing, and approving the revised procedure. The procedure will then be published, communicated, trained, and added to the review plan (Chapter 6, "*Creating a Review and Communication Control Plan*") for continual monitoring.

3.   ANALYSIS OF AVAILABLE DATA

There are four kinds of data available to the team for reviewing the *Purchasing System* business process and procedure. First, the review plan (Chapter 6 - Review Plan). lead us to identify two new laws that affect the *Purchasing System*. Second, we have the results from the five quality tools (Chapter 9) Third, we have the documentation of the flow chart and the procedure (Chapter 3). Fourth, the team members have been asked to collect relevant material such as forms, logs, reports, and filled in forms (e.g., purchase requisitions, purchase orders, receivers, or request for quotations) and bring them to team meetings for further analysis. The team will use the streamlining tools (Chapter 11) to evaluate the existing flow chart and procedure. The procedures analyst will remind the team to consider the use of control points as a way to enforce phases along the path of the procedure when, and if, it is revised. One mistake to avoid is to assume that just because a senior manager said that the procedure has problems, it does not mean that it needs improvement. Your investigation should determine if the senior manager is just being paranoid or that there is really a problem.

The results from the application of the seven compliance methods are summarized in Table 11-1. The primary results are derived from the examples in Chapter 9, "*Using Continuous Improvement Tools to Measure Compliance.*" For each compliance method, the results are briefly discussed along with several possible interpretations of this information. These interpretations are brief. In a real situation, the procedures analyst should spend adequate time reviewing the results of the execution of the compliance methods. The cross-functional team members could be invited to a meeting to discuss these interpretations. An adequate analysis will lead to a better solution being selected.

A summary of the "Interpretation" statements will follow. This summary can be used to support the selection of the final solution. The cross-functional team can design a checklist and "check" off each of these statements as they are satisfied.

216

TABLE 11-1: *Results of Application of Seven Compliance Methods*

TOOL	RESULTS OF THE EXECUTION OF THE TOOL
Self-Assessment Checklist	On the average, 71% of the individuals completing requisitions for MRO items thought they completed the purchase requisition satisfactorily (refer to Appendix "A" for these results). This percentage figure was obtained by calculating the average of the results returned by the users that completed the "Self-Assessment Checklist." ➤Even when the users completed the "Self-Assessment Checklist" they did not rate themselves as 100%; this can suggest that the purchase requisition is probably hard to understand and needs further investigation to find ways to simplify the process. The fact that the users completing the checklist did not indicate that they were doing the process perfectly every time (100% rating) indicates that the users are serious about getting the best possible process (the more problems they find, the greater the possibility that the process will be reviewed for improvement purposes). The normal response when users "self-inspect" themselves is to say that they are perfect. This answer can have a negative effect for the users, e.g., if the users have no problems with a process, the procedures analyst might place it at the bottom of his prioritized list of policies and procedures to review.
Scatter Diagram	A strong correlation was found between training hours and the time to complete the requisition, i.e., as the training hours increased, less time was needed to complete the purchase requisition. ➤One conclusion is to increase training hours; however, then the training costs would increase. The team needs to investigate the requisition process and find ways to reduce the number of required fields on the requisition. If the requisition process is simplified, the training hours could be reduced which in turn, would certain reduce the training costs.

Run Chart	The volume of purchase requisitions being rejected by the Purchasing Department has decreased over time.
	➤This result seems to indicate that the users became more efficient in completing the requisition over time. Another conclusion is the Purchasing Department became more efficient in their review process or they relaxed the rules by correcting mistakes themselves and not returning the requisition to the requester (the requester cannot learn unless he sees his mistakes) for correction.
Control Chart	The process for reviewing purchase requisitions was shown to be out of control.
	➤For this example, it has been identified that the cause of the "assignable cause" was due to the complexity of the form design of the purchase requisition and this caused many mistakes early in the requisition process as well as later in the process when the requisition was processed by the Purchasing Department.
Pareto Chart	Typographical (typo) and spelling errors were the most significant errors encountered when the Purchasing Department processed Purchase Orders.
	➤The *Purchasing System* is a manual process and these kinds of errors can be expected. These results could point the team toward finding a solution that could simplify the process within the Purchasing Department. Too many people handle the requisition and the technology for processing the orders is out-of-date.
Histogram	Purchase requisitions were being rushed through the system for special requests from senior management. This "rushing" caused other purchase requisitions to be delayed.
	➤It would seem that the *Purchasing System* is being circumvented and there are no guidelines for "rushed" purchase requisitions. A new procedure may be necessary.

Systems Audit	The users did not think that the *Purchasing System* procedure was up-to-date nor that everyone was following the guidelines for MRO purchases. The users thought that some individuals were circumventing the Purchasing Department by using petty cash, checks, or personal credit cards.
	►These results confirm the results of the other six compliance methods: *the requisition takes too long to process from the point of need identification to receipt of the order.* The team should review all of the comments of those interviewed during the systems audit, rank the findings, and begin the improvement process.

A summary of the results of the execution of the compliance methods methods point to the following concerns about the *Purchasing System* process and procedure:

1. The *Purchasing System* process and procedure have too many variables and steps. Multiple errors and delays can cause the process to take too long and even lead to failure, i.e., a purchase requisition being rejected and the requester not having his need filled.

2. The *Purchasing System* process takes too long to process an order; for instance, the users thought that there had to be a better way to process orders for a single item that may cost less than $10.00 or to process orders for items they want right away.

3. The *Purchasing System* is a paperwork, labor intensive, manual process and too many errors were being incurred when documents were being filled in manually without validation features.

4. The Purchase Requisition form has too many fields to complete and the instructions for completing the form seem vague.

5. Users are finding ways to circumvent the *Purchasing System* procedure and order traceability is being lost.

6. The purchase requisition is taking too long to train and the training costs are exceeding the training budget.

7.   Managers have been using their position to "rush" orders through the Purchasing Department.

8.   The Purchasing Department is correcting obvious errors for the users and not returning the requisitions. The users are not being given the opportunity to improve their learning process by correcting their own mistakes.

9.   The Purchasing Department is using terminals, typewriters, printers, and computers that are out-of-date and not able to handle the current needs of a large organization.

These results seem to indicate that a better solution is needed for the purchase of MRO items. The cross-functional team will need to find ways to improve, or re-engineer, the current paperwork, labor intensive, *Purchasing System* procedure to satisfy these concerns.

From a thorough investigation of the interpretations made in Table 11-1, the cross-functional team made the following detailed analysis of the compliance results.

1.   The results from completed "Self-Assessment Checklists" indicate that most of the users were comfortable with the way they completed the purchase requisition (this indicates bias as they were doing a self-inspection of the way they followed the *Purchasing System* procedure). At the same time, the Purchasing Assistants were rejecting many requisitions. This conclusion could indicate that the users were "hurrying" through the lengthy requisition process and not adhering strictly to the *Purchasing System* procedure. Another conclusion is that the Purchasing Assistants were not familiar with, or have not been thoroughly trained, in the use of the *Purchasing System* procedure. Rejections became commonplace for the Purchasing Assistants.

2.   The results of the continuous improvement tools indicated that there was either a problem with the training methods and/or the *Purchasing System* procedure was too complex, or both.

3.   General consensus pointed to a lengthy *Purchasing System* process with too many variables (e.g., finding the right requisition form to use,

finding a manager to sign a requisition, convincing the Accounting Department to fund the purchase, routing the requisition to the Purchasing Department, and so on) that were slowing the process to a snail's pace or causing the requisition to be rejected and returned.

4. From an analysis of the flow chart and procedure for the original *Purchasing System* procedure, it seemed like there were too many steps involved when requesting, placing, receiving, and paying for orders. The steps may not have been clearly described in the procedure and the training may not have covered all the steps necessary to process a requisition with few or no errors.

5. The *Purchasing System* procedure was labor intensive and each step is manual with the exception when a carbon-interleaved Purchase Order form is printed as the result of input to a computer network.

6. The Purchase Order form is manually typed into a terminal where the computer network generates a Purchase Order. A spell checker was available but it was not turned "on" because it was considered to be a crude database of a selected number of words. This manual operation was causing many typos and spelling errors that were being noticed by customers receiving the orders.

7. The users would inadvertently use an obsolete purchase requisition, the users were not adequately informed about new requisitions, and the users did not know what to do with their "old" forms.

8. The users did not receive training on how to review published catalogues when requesting items that they had never ordered, or had not been ordered recently. This lack of knowledge often resulted in poorly worded descriptions on the requisition. The buyer was forced to follow up on each requisition.

9. The multi-part forms (i.e., 3-part purchase requisition, 5-part purchase order, 3-part request for quotation, and 4-part receiver) have unnecessary fields to complete. Each form had at least ten fields that were repeated on each form. When fields are repetitious on several forms, it typically indicates that forms could be combined.

10. Some of the potential requesters of MRO items were never available to be trained on the documentation, processes, and procedures. They were busy "putting out fires," "rushing" orders for senior management, or they did not know how to use their time efficiently.

11. Training was difficult within the Purchasing Department due to the rotation of purchasing staff, employee turnover, and low morale.

12. Senior managers were receiving special treatment from the purchasing personnel when they insisted that their purchases be placed ahead of other purchases that had come in earlier.

13. There were no procedures or guidelines for handling "rush" or "emergency" orders. The cross-functional team thought that a new section could be added to the current procedure describing "rush" and "emergency" orders.

14. The MRO buyer was not using the most current purchasing laws to his advantage when ordering items costing less than $500.00. In the current purchasing law, a verbal purchase order is acceptable for orders under $500.00. A written Purchase Order is required for orders over $500.00. The MRO buyers were requesting a Purchase Order for each order.

15. There were internal purchase requisition guidelines and logs being used by the Purchasing Assistants that were not being shared with everyone in the department, not even the procedures analyst.

16. The methods used by the Purchasing Manager for selecting the appropriate MRO buyer was not always clear or consistent. There were no internal guidelines or procedures for this selection process.

17. The MRO buyer applied the same purchasing process to MRO purchases as he does to other orders regardless of dollar amount. Thus, an order for $39.50 would receive the same attention and documentation as an order for $100,000.

18. The Receiving Department is inspecting all orders regardless of size or dollar value for carton and content damage. They would write up

extensive damage and inspection reports for orders of any value. They did not distinguish between $100 orders and $100,000 orders.

19. Payment to a supplier was being held if there was even the smallest error. The Accounting Department is too strict on supplier payments and suppliers often did not get paid for 10 weeks. Reputable suppliers have complained to the senior management team in the Purchasing Department about the organization's poor payment policy.

4.   TEAM MEETINGS

Team meetings were conducted once a week for two hours over a period of two months. The procedures analyst prepared an agenda and distributed reading materials two days ahead of each meeting. Each team member was expected to be prepared before the meeting started. We will assume that the team members reviewed all of the materials available. Co-workers and industry contacts were consulted about information they might have about a solution to the *Purchasing System* procedure. The Purchasing personnel decided that they would brainstorm with their own department as well as see what others who work with or support the Purchasing Department have to say about simplifying the purchase of MRO items.

The team applied H. James Harrington's twelve streamlining tools (Harrington, 1991) to each solution to determine how many tasks or steps could be reduced or eliminated.

5.   SOLUTIONS IDENTIFIED

The cross-functional team considered seven solutions that are described in Table 11-2. The solutions were derived from an analysis of known "contracting" options for the procurement of low dollar items as well as one creative solution that combines all of the purchasing forms into one.

Results of the compliance methods, network contacts, articles from the National Association of Purchasing Managers, Purchasing Magazines, Purchasing Books, Purchasing Law, and the team's brainstorming resulted in the following solutions. Each solution will be briefly described. A reason for accepting or rejecting it is included. One solution will be selected and explained in Section 6. The actual solution will be a combination of solutions.

TABLE 11-2: *Suggested Solutions to the Improvement of the Purchasing System*

SOLUTION	DESCRIPTION OF SOLUTION
Blanket Orders for MRO Items	A blanket order is a purchase order that covers a large quantity over a period of time. Blanket orders are useful when the quantity is known and the exact items to be ordered are known. ►This solution only works when you can forecast what you will be ordering; with MRO items, the order quantities are never certain from one time to the next. This is not a good solution because you cannot forecast MRO items.
Combination Forms	A single form could be designed to be a combination of a purchase requisition, purchase order, request for quotation, and receiver. The form would replace the four forms currently used in the *Purchasing System*. As the price on the MRO orders never exceeds $500.00 and purchasing law states that verbal purchase orders are acceptable for orders under $500.00, the buyer does not have to generate a hard copy Purchase Order for the supplier. ►This solution reduces the printing of 4 forms (15 parts) to just 1 form (4 parts). The total value of this "Modified Purchase Order" could not exceed $500.00. This solution was actually the solution I used for the *Purchasing System* when it was originally developed in a manufacturing company on the west coast. We were able to save $1 million a year because of the high volume of forms printed and processed. While this was my original solution when I had first conceived of this book, I have since changed my mind and have selected a better solution, one that did not exist when the "Modified Purchase Order" was conceived, designed, and implemented.
Systems Contracting	A systems contract is a type of agreement that is required to support resupply systems of standard merchandise. These orders are for small dollar amounts with large quantities. ►This solution is not feasible because it deals with large quantities and MRO purchases are generally small quantities.

Kanban	The term "kanban" is Japanese for a "numbered card" that is used in business to designate a system in which materials are replaced as they are used. The kanban card travels with the material and becomes a resupply signal when the material reaches a predetermined trigger point. ►This solution is useful in a manufacturing process as a way to schedule production material and regulate inventory. The kanban card is also useful in any non-manufacturing process where a regular smooth flow of material is required. However, the nature of MRO items suggests that you cannot regulate or forecast MRO supplies. Thus, this solution would be ruled out.
Purchase Cards (P-Cards)	Purchase Cards (or "P-Cards") are a relatively new solution for MRO purchases. The P-Card system streamlines the labor intensive paper *Purchasing System* process through an electronic exchange of information. Purchase Cards are credit cards that can be issued to anyone authorized to receive a Purchase Card by a Company administrator who has been assigned the responsibility for Purchase Cards. Benefits of P-Cards include automated tracking and reporting, customized reports, improved controls, online requisitions, automatic purchase orders, automatic receiving, improved controls, transaction limits, daily automated approvals, and supplier payment within 24 to 48 hours. ►This solution eliminates 99% of the paperwork, purchasing involvement, management approvals, receiving inspection, and accounts payable. The P-Card appears to be the solution that satisfies all of the concerns of the *Purchasing System*. An order can be placed in minutes versus days or weeks with the *Purchasing System*. The P-Card is an excellent solution. As we will see below, the P-Card can be combined with other solutions like EDI or web systems. As improvements are made to the *Purchase Card System*, the procedure could be modified to increase the transaction maximum from $500 to $25,000.

Web-Based System	Purchases can be made online with, or without a Purchase Card, when a user accesses a supplier's web site. This solution can complement the use of purchase cards. Web-based systems can be used for searching out sources, verifying orders and delivery status, obtaining reports on line, and many other customizable features, depending on the Purchase Card solution selected. ➤Web-based systems appear to be a secondary solution to the Purchase Card. Agreements can be worked out with suppliers that have online ordering capabilities on their web sites to the extent that the company's employees would be required to order online from preferred suppliers who have what the employee wants to purchase. This solution works out for the supplier, company, and employee. A web-based system can also be used in lieu of the *Purchase Card System* solution. Company credit cards can be used or an employee's personal credit card can be used. The employee can request reimbursement through petty cash, check, or expense report depending on the company's policy for reimbursement.
Electronic Data Interchange (EDI)	Electronic data interchange (EDI) is a paperless system for the transmission of purchasing documents between a company and a supplier. ➤EDI is an excellent solution for large companies that need quick response for repetitive orders. Cost benefit analyses must be made to ensure there is a significant cost savings when using EDI for purchasing documents. EDI is best used in manufacturing environments. EDI solutions are not intended for low-volume, low-dollar purchases. This is not a good solution.

6.   SOLUTION SELECTED

Some of the preceding solutions above have excellent features like no inventory, no forms, or no purchasing interface. The best solution for MRO items seems to be the "Purchase Card" coupled with web-based ordering when available. If the supplier does not have a web site and/or does not offer online ordering, the order can be placed over the telephone or FAX. Several of the solutions reviewed were good solutions for manufacturing environments and for the purchase of production items that are for resale. EDI is an excellent solution for larger companies who have a need for quick response from a supplier for large quantities.

A flow chart of the "*Purchase Card System*" solution is shown in Figure 11-1 on the next page. The purchases in this example are limited to maintenance, repair, and operating supplies, i.e., MRO items. The process flow and guidelines used to develop this flow chart and procedure are based on a "real-life" example. This flow chart is used to write the *Purchase Card System* procedure. The written procedure is presented following the flow chart.

The benefits of the *Purchase Card System* are listed below:

1. Average reduction of administrative costs, overtime, and expenses including the elimination of all Purchasing Department activities for MRO purchases except for the negotiation of preferred suppliers for web and non-web use

2. Increased productivity with the elimination of paperwork, approvals, purchasing interfaces, and the reduction of receiving inspection and accounting representatives

3. Improved controls by placing dollar and transaction limits on a cardholder

4. A Preferred Supplier program with volume discounts. The suppliers may be listed in a manual printout of a database, the department may have hundreds of supplier catalogues, or the suppliers may be accessed through the web

5. Sourcing and ordering online

6. Customized reports

7. Automated receiving and tracking

8. Electronic fund transfers of transactions

9.   Significantly reduced process flow costs and flexible billing options

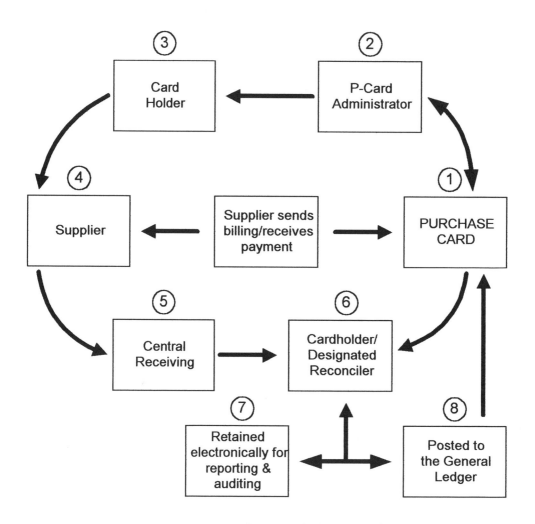

FIGURE 11-1: *Purchase Card System Flow Chart*

7.   <u>PURCHASE CARD (P-Card) OVERVIEW</u> (Refer to Figure 11-1 above)

①   The process starts with a requester asking his manager that a purchase card to be assigned to him. The user completes the necessary paperwork, obtains management approval, and submits the application to the P-Card Administrator for processing.

All employees should not be authorized to receive purchase cards. Individuals who order MRO items frequently (e.g., administrative assistants, secretaries, maintenance personnel, nurses, buyers, leaders, managers, and supervisors) may be authorized to receive P-Cards.

Management should decide who will receive Purchase Cards. The company should write a policy or procedure on this selection process. Since Purchase Cards can be programmed for specific transaction limits, the policy or procedure could provide a table of position titles and their allowed transaction limits.

② The P-Card Administrator processes the request. When the cards are received, the Administrator delivers the P-Card to the requester. The users should inspect the cards to ensure they were printed correctly. Errors should be immediately reported to the Administrator. The P-Card should not be used if any information is incorrect.

③ The cardholder uses his card to place orders with preferred suppliers by calling a supplier or placing the order through the supplier's web site.

④ The supplier processes the order and ships it according to the instructions provided by the requester.

⑤ Receiving accepts the order and places it on a shelf in the Receiving Department for the employee to pick up. The employee can request that the order be delivered from the receiving area to his work area.

⑥ The employee picks up the order and verifies it is what he ordered. When he receives his monthly statement, he reconciles his orders for the month with the statement.

⑦ The P-Card information is processed electronically on the company's computer for reporting and auditing purposes.

⑧ The Accounting Department electronically processes the invoice and makes payment. There is no reconciliation. Reconciliation is done later by the cardholder if he finds any discrepancies when he reviews his monthly statement.

PURCHASE CARD VARIATIONS ON THE SOLUTION

The *Purchase Card System* can have several variations depending on the process flow. This flow would change depending on how the purchases are placed (e.g., telephone, online ordering, or EDI), how the purchases are received (e.g., central receiving, mail room, receptionist, or pick up), or how the purchases are reconciled (e.g., cardholder, departmental financial analyst, or accounts payable). This solution is also dependent on the type of computer used to control the P-Card system. There are many companies that offer "one-stop" Purchase Card systems on the Internet.

In the following section, a procedure has been written based on the flow chart in Figure 11-1 and the analysis of the eight steps required to process an order (six steps are required to process an order using a P-Card, two additional steps are related to authoring the use of a P-Card). This procedure is based on a "real-life" Purchase Card system used at Mettler Toledo, Inc., Worthington, Ohio. The standard writing format recommended in Chapter 2, *"Writing Effective Policies and Procedures,"* has been used for this procedure. The *Purchase Card System* procedure is the result of re-engineering the *Purchasing System* procedure.

Written Procedure — Purchase Card System (Re-Engineered Purchasing System)

Purchase Card System for Maintenance, Repair, and Operating (MRO) Supplies	Procedure No.	Date
	Revision No.	Page___ Of___

1.0   <u>Purpose</u>

This procedure provides a significant solution to the procurement of maintenance, repair, and operating (MRO) supplies through the use of a specialized credit card called a "Purchase Card" or "P-Card."

2.0   <u>Revision History</u>

DATE	DESCRIPTION	AUTHOR INITIALS
1/10/2000	Original Document	SBP
6/12/2000	Re-engineered Procedure	SBP

3.0   Persons Affected

Employees (also called "Cardholder"), Bank Card Provider, Suppliers, and Customers

4.0   Policy

The policy of the company is to:

4.1   Offer the use of a specialized credit card for the procurement of low-priced, low volume MRO supplies that are not for resale.

4.2   Limit purchase card transactions to $500.00 or less.

4.3   Prohibit the purchase of the following kinds of items when using the purchase card: *capital equipment and materials, travel and entertainment expenses, and goods and services that become part of the company's inventory of goods and services for sale.*

4.4   Inform cardholders that these purchase cards are for business purposes only and any misuse of the card is subject to severe consequences, up to and including, termination of employment.

5.0   Definitions

5.1   Purchase Card (also known as a "P-Card" and "Procurement Card"). A specialized credit card in which employees may purchase MRO supplies without direct purchasing, receiving, or accounting involvement. The card is provided from any authorized bank or credit union. The Purchasing Department has the responsibility of negotiating Purchase Card agreements for the company.

5.2   Maintenance, Repair, and Operating (MRO) Supplies. Expense materials that are used by employees to help them perform their jobs. These can include, but are not limited, to small tools, cleaning supplies, office supplies, consumable items like forms, postage, subscriptions, and other items that are not for resale. The company policy and procedure will specific which items are considered to be MRO supplies.

5.3 <u>Transaction Log</u>. A one-part form used by an employee to record purchases made with the P-Card. This log is generally used by employees to record any online or telephone supplier orders. The log is used to reconcile what the P-Card cardholder ordered, with the actual statement from the authorized "provider" of the credit card. The requester's manager may review the Transaction Log and the bank reconciliation sheets at any time.

6.0 <u>Responsibilities</u>

6.1 The Purchasing Department Executive (i.e., title of person who manages the Purchasing Department) shall ensure compliance to this procedure.

6.2 Employees shall:

6.2.1 Sign and agree to the terms and conditions of the P-Card agreement.

6.2.2 Use the Purchase Card for MRO supplies only.

6.2.3 Limit transactions to $500.00 or less.

6.2.4 Notify the credit card provider immediately of any lost or stolen cards, advise his manager, and the P-Card administrator of the situation.

6.2.5 Use only preferred suppliers authorized by the Purchasing Department when placing orders using the P-Card.

6.3 Managers shall:

6.3.1 Approve employees for using P-Cards.

6.3.2 Identify transaction limits and monthly credit limits for the cardholder.

6.3.3 Provide a list of preferred suppliers to the cardholder including a hard copy version and an electronic reference.

6.3.4 Review weekly and monthly summary statements for budget information and policy compliance.

6.3.5 Review the employee's "Transaction Log" for order activity.

6.3.6 Discipline employees who abuse the use of the P-Card.

6.4 The P-Card Program Administrator shall:

6.4.1 Coordinate new, and existing, accounts for the company's cardholders.

6.4.2 Work closely with the P-Card provider to ensure a smooth flow of operations that are seamless to the cardholder.

6.4.3 Resolve problems and complaints regarding the P-Card by contacting the Card Provider.

6.5 The Purchasing Department shall:

6.5.1 Negotiate a list of preferred suppliers and provide the information to both department managers and to the P-Card Administrator.

6.5.2 Maintain a list of preferred suppliers for both online and offline requests for purchases.

6.6 The Receiving Department shall receive P-Card purchases and place them on a shelf for pick up. They will contact the requester that the order is waiting for their pick up. The requester can also arrange for their order to be delivered directly to their work area.

7.0 Procedures

7.1 Purchase Card Guidelines

The Purchase Card is intended to be an alternative method for the purchase of small dollar value, miscellaneous expenses, materials, and services. Types of Purchase Card requests are office expenses, maintenance and repairs, miscellaneous noncapital equipment purchases, postage, subscriptions, forms, brochures, promotional supplies, dues and memberships, production supplies, and temporary employment agencies. If a supplier sells one of these items and is not listed on the preferred supplier list, you should ask the Purchasing Department if this supplier has been considered or can be added. The Purchasing Department might ask the Quality Department to assist them with supplier qualification tests. If the supplier passes these tests, he will be added to the preferred supplier list.

7.1.1   Exclusions

7.1.1.1   Transactions greater than $500.00

7.1.1.2   Capital equipment and materials

7.1.1.3   Travel and entertainment expenses

7.1.1.4   Goods and services that become part of the company's inventory of goods and services for resale

7.1.2   Important Guidelines

7.1.2.1   The Purchase Card is a charge card and must be used in such a manner that ensures the security and safekeeping of the card. The card is not transferable.

7.1.2.2   The Purchase Card is the property of the company and should only be used for business purposes. Any abuse can result in severe consequences, up to and including, termination of employment.

7.2   Requesting a Purchase Card

7.2.1   When an employee wants a Purchase Card, he will request permission to be authorized from his management. In some cases, management may request justification why this employee needs a Purchase Card. The employee will then have to provide a full justification for the purchase.

7.2.2　The manager will review the need for the request and if granted, the manager will request a Purchase Card from a Purchase Card Program Administrator. The manager will provide the following kinds of information to the administrator:

　　7.2.2.1　Transaction limit per day, week, and/or month

　　7.2.2.2　Transaction limitations

　　7.2.2.3　Purchase Card guidelines

　　7.2.2.4　Signed Purchase Card agreement

7.2.3　The P-Card Administrator will obtain the Purchase Card from the card provider.

7.2.4　The employee's manager will provide guidelines relevant to using preferred suppliers for Purchase Card transactions.

　　7.2.4.1　The employee is expected to notify his manager of any lost or stolen purchase cards and to advise the Purchase Card Program Administrator. Notification is required to release the company from liability for changes incurred by someone other than the cardholder.

　　7.2.4.2　The employee must contact the Purchasing Department for assistance in setting up suppliers as Purchase Card suppliers.

7.3　Using the Purchase Card

7.3.1　When the employee wants to buy a part, tool, or item, he has to find a supplier. Using guidelines from both his management and from the Purchasing Department, he will telephone the order to an authorized supplier or visit the supplier's web site and order online. The employee must ask the supplier if he accepts a Purchase Card as a form of payment.

7.3.2   If the employee wants a new supplier added to the preferred supplier list, he will submit a request to the Purchase Card Administrator for review and coordination with the Purchasing Department.

7.3.3   The employee shall maintain a Transaction Log of all purchases.

7.3.4   When placing an order, the employee shall advise the supplier of the following information:

7.3.4.1   Sales taxes are applied to all transactions unless specified as exempt.

7.3.4.2   Purchase Card transactions are "cash" sales, invoices and Purchase Orders are not required and will not be accepted.

7.3.4.3   The shipping address, including name, building or room number, and phone number of the person to whom the material is to be delivered, and the words, "PURCHASE CARD," should be prominently marked on the outside of all boxes, packing lists, or other shipping containers.

7.3.5   The employee shall obtain a receipt or packing list when goods have been received and verify that the materials and/or services received are what was ordered.

7.3.6   The employee shall resolve all discrepancies with the supplier. Returns and credits of goods are to be handled as separate transactions. They are not to be combined with other purchases.

7.3.7   The employee shall retain the receipts or packing lists and keep a monthly transaction log of card purchases for proper tax documentation and auditing purposes. All receipts and monthly transactions shall be reconciled with the card provider's statements. These receipts should be retained for four years.

7.3.8 The employee shall notify the P-Card Program Administrator of any billing discrepancies on the monthly statement that cannot be resolved with the supplier. The employee will maintain current copies of their month statements and the daily "Transaction Log" for at least six months to ensure that all reconciliations take place as necessary.

7.4 Manager's Responsibilities

7.4.1 The manager shall initiate Purchase Card accounts by filling out the Card Provider's P-Card application.

7.4.2 The manager will identify transaction limits; this limit must be within the manager's approval limits.

7.4.3 The manager will review the monthly summary statement for budget information and approval limits. If the manager suspects a problem, the summary statement should be reviewed weekly, or even daily. The manager is given a separate summary statement listing of the purchases of their subordinates.

7.4.4 The manager will submit a memorandum to the Purchase Card Administrator if there are any discrepancies or questions.

7.4.5 The manager shall maintain the monthly summary statements on file for at least 12 months.

7.5 Receiving Department's Responsibilities

7.5.1 The Receiving Department shall receive Purchase Card purchases. If the paperwork is correct, the words, PURCHASE CARD, will be written on the documentation and boxes. The unopened boxes and packing list will be placed on a shelf for pick up. The requester will be contacted.

7.5.2　The requester will be asked to sign a log that he has picked up his order.

7.6　Accounting's Responsibilities

7.6.1　Any supplier's bills will normally be electronically routed directly to the company's general ledger system whereby the bill is automatically processed and the funds are transmitted electronically to the supplier within a few days.

7.6.2　The Accounting Department shall reconcile any differences or problems with transactions of the requester or the supplier.

END OF PROCEDURE

SUMMARY OF "*PURCHASE CARD SYSTEM*" SOLUTION

This *Purchase Card System* procedure has solved the issues and concerns that management and the users had with the paperwork, labor intensive, *Purchasing System* procedure. This solution has eliminated all manual aspects except for the completion of a "Transaction Log" by the Purchase Card cardholder when placing orders and possibly the original Purchase Card Application paperwork for the Purchase Card provider bank. The Purchase Requisition, Purchase Order, Request For Quotation, and Receiver forms have been eliminated. The Purchasing Department is no longer involved in MRO purchases with the exception of setting up the preferred supplier list for MRO purchases. The Receiving Department is still involved in the receipt of shipments but they no longer inspect the contents or process a receiver. The accounting process is electronic and suppliers can be paid within days instead of weeks or months.

The need for communication and training is reduced because the Purchase Card will become a regular part of the communication and training campaign. Extra classes will not be required. Mentoring and coaching is easy to apply to the Purchase Card cardholders because the Purchase Card cardholders can typically learn in one or two sessions rather than an ongoing mentoring process over many months.

The only real downfall to the Purchase Card is abuse by the users. This is an area that needs to be controlled by management. Statements need to be closely watched so that unneeded items are not purchased or that higher quality items are not purchased when a lower cost item would suffice. Especially in those companies that permit a much higher "buying limit" like $25,000.00, Management and Accounting need to be especially careful that they audit "Transaction Logs" and Purchase Card statements frequently. This auditing practice may deter abuse.

IMPROVEMENT IS CONTINUOUS — REMEMBER THIS!

Improvement is continuous even when measurements point to processes that are in total compliance. You cannot relax for a minute because when you stop improving, you start slipping backward. The improvement process is continuous, there is no stopping point. You will always be faced with personnel changes, skill changes, systems changes, customer changes, requirement changes, or vision and strategy changes. Continuous improvement is a way of life and is the key to staying competitive. Stop or slow this focus, and any competitiveness you gained, will be lost.

➤Profitable continuous improvement can be achieved when the cost is calculated to be a reduction in cost over the process being improved. Without a disciplined method for measuring costs, it would be impossible to determine if an activity were profitable or if a stated improvement is really an improvement.

CHECKLIST FOR CHANGE:

✓   An improvement plan is introduced that enables the procedures analyst to ensure the major business processes, policies, and procedures are routinely reviewed and measured.

✓   The 12 streamlining cornerstones are discussed and applied to the 7 solutions that were identified by the cross-functional team. These streamlining tools led to the re-engineered *Purchase Card System* procedure.

✓   The use of control points is introduced as a mechanism for creating a focal point that could act as a "watchdog" for the process, policy, or procedure.

✓   Techniques for calculating the "Cost of Quality" (COQ) for policies and procedures are presented along with an example of a cost of quality calculation. An example of the COQ for policies and procedures is presented in Attachment "A."

✓ A cross-functional team is established to study the seven solutions identified as possible solutions to the paperwork and labor intensive *Purchasing System* procedure.

✓ Seven solutions are presented as an alternative to the original *Purchasing System* procedure. The *Purchase Card System* was selected as the primary solution. A *Web-based System* was selected as a supplemental solution for the authorized Purchase Card holders to buy online from preferred suppliers.

✓ A *Purchase Card System* flow chart and an eight-step descriptive analysis are presented.

✓ A *Purchase Card System* procedure is written as a result of analysis of the flow chart and the descriptive analysis of the flow chart.

APPLYING WHAT YOU HAVE LEARNED:

Establish an improvement plan and obtain management approval. Verify that the plan's methods are in alignment with the company's vision and strategy. Select and prioritize the business processes, policies, and procedures that matter the most, to your customers and management. Create and publish an improvement plan. Create cross-functional teams and search out improvement to the business processes, policies, and procedures listed in your improvement plan. Communicate your results. Promote your department and success stories.

ACHIEVE 100% COMPLIANCE:

The introduction of the improvement plan is a major step to achieving 100% compliance. Large-scale business processes, policies, and procedures require revision on a periodic basis depending on a variety of factors like new tax laws, new legislation, or events like a merger, acquisition, or a major organization change. Once these business processes, policies, and procedures are improved, approved, published, communicated, and trained, the procedures analyst can continue his monitoring of published policies and procedures through the use of the compliance plan.

The procedures analyst can assure that published policies and procedures are measured instead of being treated as opinions of the procedures analyst and a cross-functional team. When measurements are taken of newly improved policies and procedures, the procedures analyst can start making comparisons with the original baselined documents to see how much improvement is made. If improvement is achieved, the results of the compliance methods should show an increase in the compliance level.

REFERENCES:

Bhote, Keri R., *World Class Quality*, AMACOM, New York, New York, 1991.

Crosby, Philip B., *Quality is Free*, A Mentor Book, New York, New York, 1980.

Davenport, Thomas H., *Process Innovation*, Harvard Business School Press, Boston, Massachusetts, 1993.

Fearon, Harold E., Dobler, Donald W., Killen, Kenneth, H., *The Purchasing Handbook*, McGraw-Hill, Inc., New York, New York, 1993.

Gitlow, Howard S. and Gitlow, Shelly J., *Total Quality Management in Action*, PTR Prentice Hall, Englewood Cliffs, New Jersey, 1994.

Grieco, Peter L., *MRO Purchasing*, PT Publications, Inc., West Palm Beach, Florida, 1997.

Harding, Michael and Harding, Mary Lu, *Purchasing*, Barron's Business Library, Hauppauge, New York, 1991.

Harrington, H. J., Ph.D., *Business Process Improvement*, McGraw-Hill, Inc., New York, New York, 1991.

Harry, Mikel Ph.D., and Schroeder, Richard, *Six Sigma*, Currency, New York, New York, 2000.

Hart, Christopher, W. L., and Bogan, Christopher E., *The Baldrige*, McGraw-Hill, New York, New York, Inc., 1992.

Hoyle, David, *Quality Systems Handbook*, Butterworth-Heinemann, Oxford, England, 1994.

Hultman, Ken, *Making Change Irresistible*, Davies-Black Publishing, Palo Alto, California, 1998.

Johansson, Henry J., McHugh, Patrick, Pendlebury, A. John, and Wheeler, William A., III, *Business Process Reengineering*, John Wiley & Sons, New York, New York, 1993.

Katzenbach, Jon R. and Smith, Douglas K., *The Wisdom of Teams*, A HarperBusiness Book, New York, New York, 1993.

Mettler Toledo, Inc., Worthington, Ohio: *James Maxwell, Supplier Manager - Systems Purchasing, assisted with the editing of the sections of this book involving purchasing matters.*

Page, Stephen B., *Establishing a System of Policies and Procedures*, BookMasters, Inc., Mansfield, Ohio. 1998.

Peters, Tom, *The Circle of Innovation*, Alfred A. Knopf, New York, New York, 1997.

Poirier, Charles C., and Houser, William F., *Business Partnering for Continuous Improvement*, Berrett-Koehler Publications, San Francisco, California, 1993.

Quality Council of Indiana, *CSQE Primer*, ASQ, Milwaukee, Minnesota, 1996.

Shewhart, Walter A., *Statistical Method from the Viewpoint of Quality Control*, Dover Publications, Inc., New York, New York, 1986.

Tregoe, Benjamin, B., Zimmerman, John W., Smith, Ronald A., Tobia, Peter M., *Vision in Action*, Simon & Schuster Inc., New York, New York, 1990.

Tushman, Michael L. and O'Reilly, Charles A, III, *"Winning Thru Innovation*, Harvard Business Press, Boston, Massachusetts, 1997.

Wind, Jerry Yoram and Main, Jeremy, *Driving Change*, The Free Press, New York, New York, 1998.

242

Chapter 12

Saving $1 Million with Cost Benefit Analyses

Saving $1,000,000 in improvements may sound like a large number but when you consider how savings are computed and the factors used for the calculations, you may be able to make an equally astounding claim for your improvements. *Savings* can be thought of as a positive difference (i.e., a number greater than zero that constitutes either material or labor savings, or both) between the current business process, policy, or procedure (i.e., a baseline) and subsequent improvements over a specific period of time. If a negative number is the result of the comparison, a savings cannot be realized and an alternate solution should be considered. If you have a good reason to select an alternative that does not show tangible savings, then document your justification, and present it along with your report to management. There can be situations where an improvement results in intangible results like improved productivity and quality and still meet the customer's requirements and expectations.

While there are many ways to compute savings, savings in this chapter will be calculated using a technique called a "cost benefit analysis" that examines the material and labor transactions of each step in each process of two or more business processes, policies, or procedures. The term *cost benefit analysis* is defined as an economic analysis which assigns a numeric value to the cost effectiveness of an operation, procedure, or program. When comparing several improvement suggestions, a cost benefit analysis can be repeatedly calculated to find the most cost-effective improvement.

In the cost benefit analysis examined in this chapter, both the *Purchasing System* procedure and the *Purchase Card System* will be compared to show the cost savings of using the *Purchase Card System* instead of the *Purchasing System*. The result of this analysis will be computed in several ways to show you how to report savings to your management. Each procedure will be analyzed to ensure every step has been identified. If the procedures have been written as suggested in Chapter 2, "*Writing Effective Policies and Procedures*," this analysis should be an easy task.

Three costs will be reviewed: *Material, labor, and overhead*. The material and labor costs are administrative in nature and should include every known cost like the speed of a person doing a task, making a phone call, mailing a document, preparing a form, or filing a document. The third cost, overhead (or burden), is added (as a percentage of the sum total of material and labor costs) to the sum of material and labor costs, e.g., if the material and labor costs are $100, the overhead rate is 100%, then the total cost will be $200. Overhead costs can include facilities, computer time, insurance, taxes, inventory, utilities, or maintenance costs. While financial analysts often debate whether computer time should be included in material costs or included as a component of overhead costs, in this chapter, computer time will be considered a part of overhead costs.

Historically, there has been a glaring misuse of cost information. For instance, when the costs of administrative transactions are used to justify the number of people, damage to the business may result. When simplification of a process is used to eliminate employees, the benefits from what those employees should have been doing instead, are lost. For instance, many buyers say that they do not have time to do the analysis and negotiations required to establish better business arrangements with suppliers because they are buried in paperwork. If new methods of doing paperwork cut their time in half, buyers will have the time to do their other work and the rate of business improvement should accelerate. Sales should increase and profits should improve. However, if management views this process of cutting the buyer's time in half as an opportunity to cut the staff in half, then no further business improvements will be possible.

►The purpose of doing cost benefit analyses is to compare the improved costs of business processes, policies, or procedures and show the tangible benefits of spending money and doing business in a certain way, not to justify reductions in resources! The rest of this chapter will focus on doing a transaction comparison of the two purchasing procedures. The net results of these transactions will be compared and guidelines for presenting this information to management will be discussed.

COST BENEFIT ANALYSIS DEFINED

While this chapter focuses on the comparison of a major process and procedure, *Purchasing System* with a totally reengineered process and procedure, *Purchase Card System*, there will be instances where smaller transactions are compared. The type of calculation illustrated in this section can be used with any transaction size. Every cost

244

is listed in the cost benefit analysis in Table 12-1 to illustrate the importance of capturing all costs. Knowing the costs of each step in a process can help to eliminate expensive processes by changing the resources used, changing the processes used, or finding a better solution to current business processes, policies, or procedures.

Justifying a change to management can be a simple task when a detailed cost benefit analysis has been performed. Numbers show the true value of a transaction: recall the phrase, *"data is only an opinion until measured."* If the cost benefit analysis only included high-level tasks, then management would be able to "shoot holes" in most improvement justifications. When every known step is measured, the procedures analyst will have a strong argument for justifying changes to management.

PREPARATION FOR A COST BENEFIT ANALYSIS

There are eight steps involved in the preparation of a cost benefit analysis for business processes, policies, or procedures:

1. Identify the two (or more) processes or documents (e.g., business processes, policies, or procedures) to review. A total cost is calculated for each document and then compared. These calculations should be done separately and then compared side-by-side in a table.

2. List the steps involved to accomplish the business process, policy, or procedure by reviewing the current published document or flow chart. These steps can usually be derived from a process flow and from the "Procedures" section of the written procedure (in this instance, it is an assumption that you used the seven-step writing format discussed in Chapter 2, *"Writing Effective Policies and Procedures"*).

    No step should be left out of the cost benefit analysis. Even if an individual does a step that takes ten seconds, it should be recorded. Seconds add up to minutes and minutes add up to hours.

3. Identify the function or job title of the person who performs each step (i.e., role or position). Names of employees should not be used.

4. Obtain the average yearly salary for each identified position. Consult the Payroll or Human Resources Department for this information. As this

information is often confidential, you could ask for the range of a position and then you could use the midpoint of the range.

5.   Determine the standard number of work hours per year of an employee; consult the Payroll or Human Resources Department for this information.

6.   Translate the average yearly salary of each position into a "cost per minute" number as follows:

$$\frac{\text{Annual Salary}}{\text{Standard Work Hours Per Year}} = \text{Cost per Hour}$$

$$\frac{\text{Cost per Hour}}{\text{60 Minutes per Hour}} = \text{Cost per Minute}$$

For example, the cost per minute of a Purchasing Manager's time with an average yearly salary of $60,000 is $0.48 based on 2080 work hours per year. The cost per minute for a Purchasing Assistant with an average yearly salary of $35,000 is $0.28.

7.   Determine the time it takes for a transaction to occur. For a complete analysis of the cycle time for the entire process from start to finish, you can also include the processing time for an employee. For instance, if an employee completes a form and puts the form into the interoffice mail system and it takes 2 days to reach his manager's office, then the mail transaction is listed as 2 days. If this same form sits in the manager's inbox for 4 hours and it takes the manager 10 minutes to sign the form, then the entire transaction time is 4 days, 4 hours, and 10 minutes. In our example in Tables 12-2 and 12-4, only the actual time (in this case, 10 minutes) to process the transaction is shown for purposes of keeping this example simple. When you do the cost studies, these figures will have more meaning to you.

Time studies should be performed for each step listed in the transaction flow. Actual time studies are preferred because subjective numbers can be challenged by management. Four methods for collecting this time include:

246

a. The procedures analyst can monitor a transaction by observing the person who does that transaction over a set period of time. A check sheet can be used to record the exact steps and time it takes to do each step. A watch with a second hand, or stop watch, can be used to record time. This process should be repeated for each step.

b. The procedures analyst could perform a systems audit of a department or function which performs specific transactions. This audit would have the same effect as the first collection method except that the procedures analyst would be able to analyze all the transactions performed in a sequence instead of analyzing a single transaction for a short period of time.

c. The individual who performs a transaction could monitor his own transaction time for a set period of time and report the results to his supervisor and to the procedures analyst.

    This third method is the least preferred because bias can enter into the time recording because the individual can shorten the time it takes to do an activity to make himself look good to his management. He can also guess at transaction times and not even do the analysis which may seem tedious to him.

d. Depending on the time needed to record a transaction, the second and third collection methods could be combined by allowing the procedures analyst the opportunity to verify the transaction times recorded by the individual doing a step.

8. Multiply the "cost per minute" of the individual doing the transaction by the time (in minutes) each transaction step takes. For instance, if it takes a manager 15 minutes to review and approve a form and the cost per minute of a manager is $0.48, the cost of the transaction is recorded as $7.20 for 15 minutes.

Once these variables have been identified, a table of transaction costs can be created for each procedure. The costs can then be totaled and the overhead percentage can be applied. The resulting savings (if any) can be used to create a report for management. A report can be prepared, along with the material, labor, and overhead costs, and forwarded to management.

EXAMPLE OF A TRANSACTION SAVINGS

If it costs $200.00 to process a purchase order and an alternate solution costs $50.00, the positive difference is $150.00. Switching to this alternate solution will save a minimum of $150 per purchase order. While this example ignores many variables, it illustrates the simple math of savings. If 10,000 purchase orders were processed a year, the savings would be $1.5 million ($150.00 x 10,000)! If 5,000 purchase orders were processed, the savings would be $750,000. If these numbers appear ridiculous, consider that 5000 purchase orders a year equates to an average of 19 purchase orders per working day. Considering waste and errors, a figure of 19 purchase orders per working day equates to about 2.4 purchase orders per hour on an eight-hour day! You can begin to appreciate that significant savings can be achieved when improvements are added to business processes, policies, and procedures.

COST BENEFIT ANALYSIS OF TWO PROCEDURES

The original, labor and paperwork intensive, *Purchasing System* procedure from Chapter 3, "*Focusing on a Case Study to Apply the Principles of this Book,*" and the solution, *Purchase Card System* procedure, selected in Chapter 11, "*Conducting Profitable Continuous Improvement Activities,*" will be compared. The resulting savings of the *Purchase Card System* procedure will be projected based on possible purchase transaction volumes. An analysis of each procedure will include four parts:

1. Record a step-by-step analysis of the process and the procedure that includes every possible transaction including the cost of material as it applies to that transaction, i.e., if a form is involved, then the single cost of that form should be recorded. If a document is mailed, the cost of the envelope and stamp should be recorded or if documents are filed in storage for a period of time, then cost of storage should be recorded.

2. Create a table of the variables needed to record the labor and material costs including working hours, the cost per minute of each role that you have identified to be included, and the costs of material used.

3. Add the labor and material costs for a combined total.

4. Calculate the overhead costs of the combined total of the labor and material costs.

TABLE 12-1: *Purchasing System Procedures — Variables and Costs*

VARIABLES FOR COST CALCULATIONS	VALUE	COST PER MINUTE
Work Hours in a Year	2080 hours	NA
Requester (Average salary of a business professional)	$40,000.00	$0.32
Requesters' Manager	$60,000.00	$0.48
Purchasing Assistant*	$35,000.00	$0.28
Purchasing Manager*	$60,300.00	$0.48
Buyer*	$45,200.00	$0.36
Purchasing Clerk*	$25,000.00	$0.20
Receiving Clerk	$30,100.00	$0.24
Accounting Clerk	$30,000.00	$0.24
Cost of 3-Part Purchase Requisition**		$0.09 each
Cost of 5-Part Purchase Order**		$0.15 each
Cost of 3-Part Request for Quotation**		$0.09 each
Cost of 4-Part Receiver Set**		$0.12 each
Cost of File Space/Storage for 7 Years		$0.08/page
Envelope and Stamp***		$0.35/unit
Average Overhead Costs****		100%

Notes:

* National Association of Purchasing Manager's (NAPM) Purchasing Survey, December 16, 1999. The salary of the buyer is the average salary of the sum total of

the salaries of the buyer plus the senior buyer. There was no distinction between a buyer and a senior buyer in our examples, thus, the average salary figure was used.

** A cost of $0.0295 was used for each part of a form for a quantity from 5,000 to 50,000 forms. For example, if there is a four-part form, then the cost is 4 x .0295 or 12 cents (rounded up to the nearest penny) for a single form. These costs were obtained from the State of Ohio Printing Department: *Refer to Appendix "C" for current costs (March 2000)*. The State of Ohio runs an in-house printing operation and does not sell to the public. Costs may be more expensive at local printers. I used these figures because they came from a reliable source. Since this book is not about forms, I did not want to use price quotes from numerous suppliers just to say I had prices. I wanted to use a reliable price.

*** Cost of envelopes and stamps is based on current prices in the United States.

**** Overhead costs include interest rate of money, taxes, insurance, space, occupancy, telephone costs, faxes, computer time, Internet connections, utilities, equipment (storage and moving), forms inventory, scrap and obsolescence, personnel, transactions: *Counting, sorting, moving, receiving, issuing, reconciling, etc., inspection, reinspection, return of defective material, rework, handling damage, loss, and so on.* Keeping this example simple, a 100% overhead rate was selected. The figures from Table 12-1 above are used in Table 12-2 below to describe the costs associated with the *Purchasing System* and the *Purchase Card System* processes and procedures.

The figures for processing purchasing documents will vary considerably from industry to industry. In this example, I deliberately selected a paperwork and labor intensive *Purchasing System* that I had been accountable for at Dataproducts, a manufacturing company, in Woodland Hills, California (i.e., I was the Purchasing Administration Supervisor and I was responsible for the policies, procedures, and forms within the Purchasing Department). The system is labor intensive and manual (i.e., there was no automation except when the purchase orders were printed after entry into a CRT terminal), at least ten people were involved in the entire purchase transaction, and there were five forms involved. I believe this example helps to show the possible steps involved in a detailed system. If I had selected a simple example with few steps, the process would have been more difficult to explain and you would not have understood the importance of showing every detail of a process or procedure in a cost benefit analysis.

TABLE 12-2: *Purchasing System Process and Procedure Costs*

#	ROLES	PROCESS	COST
1	Requester	Fills out purchase requisition and submits it to his manager for approval	30 min @ .32 = 9.60 →Requisition Form = .09
2	Requester's Manager	Evaluates and approves purchase requisition	15 min @ .48 = 7.20
		Returns requisition to requester	3 min @ .48 = 1.44
3	Requester	Delivers or mails purchase requisition to purchasing, if approved	3 min @ .32 = .96
4	Purchasing Assistant	Logs, date stamps, and reviews purchase requisition for completeness according to the guidelines of the *Purchasing System* procedure. Logs receipt onto internal "Transaction Log." Initials purchase requisition if it passes the review process; gives requisition to Purchasing Manager	20 min @ .28 = 5.60 →Transaction Log = .03 2 min @ .28 = .56
5	Purchasing Manager	Reviews purchase requisition, initials it if approved, and assigns Buyer to process the purchase request	5 min @ .48 = 2.40
		Routes purchase requisition to Buyer	5 min @ .48 = 2.40
6	Buyer	Buyer sorts mail and removes the purchase requisition for processing at another time	10 min @ .36 = 3.60
		Selects suppliers, selects sources, checks reputation of sources, checks preferred supplier list, contacts requester for clarification on order, or calls suppliers for price and delivery information. Sends out formal Request for Quotation (RFQ) forms to suppliers for bidding	60 min @ .36 = 21.60 →RFQ Form = .09, Minimum of 3 forms used, cost = .27
		Receives and reviews bids; selects supplier	10 min @ .36 = 3.60
		Awards purchase order to supplier and explains terms and conditions	15 min @ .36 = 5.40 →Telephone calls

		Issues purchase order; adds purchase order number to purchase order log	5 min @ .36 = 1.80
		Gives purchase requisition to Purchasing Clerk for processing	5 min @ .36 = 1.80
7	Purchasing Clerk	Types purchase requisition information into CRT Terminal to generate a PO from the computer	15 min @ .20 = 3.00 ➜Computer time
		Picks up PO's from the printer, sorts by Buyer; and delivers PO's to Buyer	10 min @ .20 = 2.00 ➜PO Form = .15
8	Buyer	Proofreads PO and signs; delivers PO to Purchasing Manager for review and approval	10 min @ .36 = 3.60
9	Purchasing Manager	Reviews and approves PO	5 min @ .48= 2.40
		Gives PO to Purchasing Clerk	5 min @ .36 = 1.80
10	Purchasing Clerk	Splits PO, mails or delivers copies to supplier, receiving, accounting, and keeps a copy for Purchasing file	15 min @ .20 = 3.00 ➜Mailing = .35
11	File space and storage for 7 years	Files documents in a storage area. Cost of file space / and storage for at least 7 years	At .08/page = .80 and 10 pages for an average PO file per year
12	Buyer	Receives PO acknowledgment, reviews for signatures and changes	5 min @ .36 = 1.80
13	Purchasing Clerk	Inserts a "Return Acknowledgment PO" into appropriate PO file	5 min @ .20 = 1.00
14	Receiving Clerk	Receives material at receiving dock, inspects material and signs shipper's manifest. Opens the shipping container and inspects contents. Records inspection results on internal receiving log	15 min @ .24 = 3.60
		Reviews supplier's packing sheet. Prints a copy of the 4-part receiver set from the PO. Fills in information on the Receiver.	5 min @ .24 = 1.20 ➜Receiver = .12

		Splits receiver form and makes distribution to designated departments	15 min @ .24 = 3.60
		Delivers order to the requester	10 min @ .24 = 2.40
15	Purchasing Clerk	Receives PO, stamps a date on it, and files Receiver copy with PO in file	5 min @ .20 = 1.00
16	Requester	Receives material and compares contents with original requisition copy	10 min @ .32 = 3.20
17	Accounting Clerk	Receives, date/stamps, and files PO copy and Receiver copy in the accounting files	10 min @ .24 = 2.40
		Receives and opens mail, sorts invoices in mail, and pulls PO from the accounting file to match invoice	20 min @ .24 = 4.80
		Cross-checks data with PO, Receiver, and Invoice. If all three agree, an invoice is batched for processing	5 min @ .24 = 1.20
		Validates printout of invoices, consolidates multiple PO's into one check; authorizes check to be printed	3 min @ .24 = .72
		Picks up check, stamps signatures on check, attaches check to copy of invoice, inserts it into envelope, and mails it	15 min @ .24 = 3.60 →Mailing = .35 →Check Cost = .03
		Files completed documents and reports in "Closed" file	10 min @ .24 = 2.40
18	File space and storage for 7 years	Cost of file space / and storage for at least 7 years	10 pages @.08/page = .80 per PO file per year
Total Transaction Costs			**$119.67**

The total process costs (material and labor) and overhead costs for this *Purchasing System* business process and procedure are listed below:

1. Cost: $119.67

2. Cost with Overhead: $239.34

The total cost of completing the steps of the *Purchasing System* process and procedure is $119.67. With the addition of the overhead percentage, the cost becomes $239.34 for completing a single purchase from the point of "requesting an item" to "paying for it." One good reason for including overhead costs is to reflect organizational costs like facilities, utilities, computer time, telephone use, fax use, or Internet use. If you can find an easy way to separate out the individual transaction costs for any of the items listed in the overhead component, then you will be able to improve your cost basis for the business process, policy, or procedure.

While these figures seem high, the numbers do not lie. The actual cost of this transaction can only be determined through a step-by-step analysis. Without this analysis, it is only a guess. From Chapter 9, "*Using Continuous Improvement Tools to Measure Compliance*", we learned that "*data is only an opinion until measured and applied.*" Recall that numbers are needed to "prove" that improvement has really been accomplished. Without this data, you only have opinions.

TABLE 12-3: *Purchase Card System — Variables and Costs*

VARIABLES FOR COST CALCULATIONS	VALUE	COST PER MINUTE
Work Hours in a Year	2080 hours	NA
Purchase Card Cardholder (Average salary of a business professional)	$40,000.00	$0.32
Purchase Card Cardholder's Manager	$60,000.00	$0.48
Purchase Card Program Administrator*	$50,000.00	$0.40
Accounting Clerk	$30,000.00	$0.24
Receiving Clerk	$30,100.00	$0.24
Cost of 1-Part Transaction Log**		$0.03
Average Overhead (Same used in Table 12-1)		100%

Notes:

* The Purchase Card Program Administrator has an important position of interfacing with Credit Card Providers and Company Management, thus the salary is higher than the cardholder but lower than a Manager.

** Refer to the second note of Table 12-1 for the cost of a form.

The *Purchase Card System* process and procedure were discussed in Chapter 11, *"Conducting Profitable Continuous Improvement Activities."* The steps for this process start when the Purchase Card cardholder makes a request to buy something. For the purposes of fair comparison, both processes are started at the same place, i.e., *"identifying a need for a part or item."* A transaction analysis for the *Purchase Card System* process and procedure is presented in Table 12-4. The total costs of both procedures will be compared and this information will be used to prepare a report for management. These transaction analyses can also be used by procedures analysts when looking for improvement opportunities, waste reduction, duplication, or errors.

TABLE 12-4: *Purchase Card System Process and Procedure Costs*

#	ROLE	PROCESS	COST
1	Purchase Card Cardholder	Determines need; searches for sources; uses the Internet; checks historical data and past purchases	20 min @ .32 = 6.40 →Computer Time (Overhead)
		Places order through telephone or Internet online form; requests words, "Purchase Card" be placed on all correspondence and shipping containers	10 min @ .32 = 3.20 →Telephone costs and computer time (Overhead)
		Fills out "Transaction Log" of each purchase made	5 min @ .32 = 1.60 →Transaction Log = .03
		Receives fax receipt from supplier or prints receipt from Internet.	2 min @ .32 = .64 →FAX (Overhead)
2	Receiving Clerk	Receives order, marks it as a purchase card order, puts order aside to be picked up by requester, contacts requester for pick up	5 min @ .24 = 1.20
3	Purchase Card Cardholder	Picks up order from the Receiving Department or requests that the Receiving Department delivers the order	15 min @ .32 = 4.80
		Verifies order matches original receipt received from supplier	2 min @ .32 = .64

4	Accounting Clerk	Receives order electronically. (Order is paid electronically.)	→Overhead costs
		Reconciles any differences with either the requester or supplier as necessary	10 min @ .24 = 2.40
5	Purchase Card Cardholder	Reconciles monthly statement with Transaction Log	15 min @ .32 = 4.80 →Transaction Log=.03
6	Purchase Card Cardholder's Management	Reviews monthly statement (of Purchase Card Cardholder's purchases for the month). Audits "Transaction Log" for problems or discrepancies	5 min @ .48 = 2.40
7	Purchase Card Program Administrator	Provides communication with Purchase Card provider and resolves any issues as required	10 min @ .40 = 4.00
Total Transaction Costs			**$32.14**

The costs for this *Purchase Card System* process and procedure are listed below:

1. Cost: $32.14

2. Cost with Overhead: $64.28

The overhead cost will be used for the *Purchase Card System* to compare costs with the *Purchasing System*. Using the overhead cost is especially important for the *Purchase Card System* because 99% of its processes are accomplished electronically (e.g., credit card processing, ordering, buying, receiving, and order payment).

COST COMPARISON: PURCHASING SYSTEM vs. PURCHASE CARD SYSTEM

In Table 12-5 below, the total cost with overhead applied will be used for cost comparisons. Several figures were calculated or assumed for this table. Using the figure of 2080 working hours as the number of hours worked in a year, the total number of " working days" can be calculated as 260. In Column 1, I assumed a daily average of purchases. In Column 2, the annual figure is calculated. In Column 3, the total costs of the *Purchasing System* are calculated and recorded based on the daily purchases in Column 1. In Column 4, the total costs of the *Purchase Card System* are calculated and recorded based on the daily purchases in Column 1. In Column 5, the difference between the two procedures is calculated; the resulting figure is the annual savings, if any. Note that even if overhead costs are not applied, the annual savings are still significant (i.e., the annual savings would be equal to one-half of the figures recorded in Column 5 because the overhead percentage was 100%, or twice the cost of the material and labor for the process).

Table 12-5: *Annual MRO Purchases: Purchasing System vs. Purchase Card System*

MRO DAILY PURCHASES	MRO PURCHASES FOR 1 YEAR	PURCHASING SYSTEM COSTS	PURCHASE CARD COSTS	ANNUAL SAVINGS
10	2,600	$622,284	$167,128	$455,156
20	5,200	$1,244,568	$334,256	$910,312
30	7,800	$1,866,852	$501,384	$1,365,468
40	10,400	$2,489,136	$668,512	$1,820,624

Interpretation of Data

The first observation that appears is the size of the savings. Recall earlier in this chapter, I indicated that saving $1,000,000 is not difficult. The transactions listed for each procedure have been broken into smaller task units. The primary reason for these substantial savings is that the *Purchase Card System* solution is a radical improvement (re-engineering effort) over the manual, paperwork and labor intensive *Purchasing System* process and procedure. From Table 12-5, it appears that a small number of daily documents can produce substantial savings. The best conclusion is that the Purchasing Department should realize that MRO items account for a large number of the orders that come through their department and that adequate resources should be assigned to handle these kinds of orders.

Based on comments from Peter L. Grieco, 1997, the author of a book called, *Purchasing*, these quantities (i.e., daily purchases) may actually be low. He states:

> *"MRO procurement, or the purchasing of material, repair and operating supplies, is an overlooked area of business that is rich with potential savings. It is incorrect to think that office supplies, services of heating or air-conditioning technicians or temporary help do not*

*have a significant impact on the cost of running a business,
manufacturing a product or providing a service. MRO procurement
has a large monetary impact on your business. Some say that 25-30%
of all manufacturing, maintenance, and operating parts can be
accounted for by MRO consumables. Other procurement experts
contend that the process of purchasing and managing these items can
account for as much as 75% of a company's supply chain resources.
This can translate into a financial impact of between $0.35 and $0.50
out of each dollar used to purchase these MRO items."*

SUBMITTING MANAGEMENT REPORTS

Depending on management's requirements for the Policies and Procedures
Department to submit progress reports, the minimum documentation requirement is
a status report. Reports like a weekly status report, special situation report, or a
multi-page document justifying the implementation of a major business process,
policy, or procedure could be prepared. Reporting requirements should be worked out
between management and the Policies and Procedures Department. The procedures
analyst may also wish to provide weekly updates of his progress in status meetings.
He should use every opportunity to "toot his horn" and show the progress and
importance of his efforts. Written reports that show significant savings on major
business processes, policies, and procedures should be presented to senior
management at least quarterly, if not more frequently. Management must be
constantly informed of the progress of the Policies and Procedures so they can remain
loyal sponsors and stay focused. Email could be used to provide more timely updates
to management relevant to major improvements made to business processes, policies,
and procedures.

These reports could be as simple as showing a bar chart with how many policies and
procedures were processed in a week or month time frame, the number of
improvements incorporated, and the net cost savings. These reports could include
information like the following:

1. Listing of the titles of new or revised business processes, policies, and
   procedures that have been added since the last status meeting

2. Bar chart showing cost savings figures and the number of policies and
   procedures processed for a specific time frame

3.　Bar chart showing the level of compliance over the same period of time used in the cost savings run chart above

4.　Projection of new or revised policies, and procedures

5.　Projection of cost savings for the rest of the fiscal or calendar year

6.　Objectives for the following month and subsequent months including strategic goals and plans for achieving higher compliance figures

CHECKLIST FOR CHANGE:

✓　Use cost benefit analyses to compare the costs of business processes, policies, and procedures for the purpose of calculating cost savings.

✓　Understand the eight components of laying out the variables necessary to prepare and do a cost benefit analysis.

✓　Detail as many transactions as possible to ensure the most accurate cost comparison and savings can be calculated.

✓　Prepare a cost savings table to compare the daily and yearly costs of business processes, policies, and procedures.

✓　Achieve savings of more than $1 million when significant improvements are applied to the *Purchasing System* procedure.

✓　Understand when and how to apply overhead costs to cost comparisons.

✓　Use information from cost benefit analyses to justify improvements and continued activities to improve business processes, policies, and procedures.

✓　Prepare progress reports for management.

APPLYING WHAT YOU HAVE LEARNED:

Identify business processes, policies, and procedures to compare using cost benefit analyses. Select every minute detail of each procedure. Calculate and total the labor and material costs of each step. Subtract the costs of the improvement from the most recent baselined business process, policy, or procedure. Calculate daily volumes of your documents. Translate these volumes into annual savings. Report your findings to management. Keep a record of findings to be used in future ongoing continuous improvement activities.

ACHIEVE 100% COMPLIANCE:

This chapter is about savings. When any kind of savings plan is shown for business processes, policies, or procedures, management is more likely to approve plans and objectives for the Policies and Procedures Department to seek out further improvements and work with them to help the company evolve into a "proactive" organization. With the implementation of an improvement plan, achieving 100% compliance is possible.

REFERENCES:

Bemowski, Karen and Stratton, Brad, *101 Good Ideas, How to Improve Just About Any Process*, ASQ Quality Press, Milwaukee, Minnesota, 1998.

Burt, David, N., Dobler, Donald W., Lamar, Lee, Jr., *Purchasing and Materials Management, Text and Cases*, McGraw-Hill, Inc., New York, New York, 1990.

Davenport, Thomas, H., *Process Innovation*, Harvard Business School Press, Boston, Massachusetts, 1993.

Fearon, Harold E., Dobler, Donald W., Killen, Kenneth H., *The Purchasing Handbook*, McGraw-Hill, Inc., New York, New York, 1993.

Grieco, Peter L., Jr, *MRO Purchasing*, PT Publications, West Palm Beach, Florida, 1997.

Harding, Michael and Harding, Mary Lu, *Purchasing*, Barron's Business Library, Hauppauge, New York, 1991.

Harry, Mikel PhD, and Schroeder, Richard, *Six Sigma*, Currency, New York, New York, 2000.

Larkin, TJ and Larkin, Sandar, *Communicating Change*, McGraw-Hill, Inc., New York, New York, 1994.

Lindberg, Roy A., and Cohn, Theodore, *Operations Auditing* (Section on Purchasing), American Management Association, Inc., New York, New York, 1972.

Lockamy, Archie, III and Cox, James F., III, *Re-engineering Performance Measurement*, Irwin Professional Publishing, New York, New York, 1994.

NAPM InfoEdge Journal, "Managing Small-Dollar Purchases," January 1996, Volume 1, No. 7, Tempe, Arizona.

Peters, Tom, *The Circle of Innovation*, Alfred A. Knopf, New York, New York, 1997.

Pilachowski, Mel, *Purchasing Performance Measurements: A Roadmap for Excellence*, PT Publications, West Palm Beach, Florida, 1996.

Poirier, Charles C., and Houser, William F., *Business Partnering for Continuous Improvement*, Berrett-Koehler Publications, San Francisco, California, 1993.

Shewhart, Walter A., *Statistical Method from the Viewpoint of Quality Control*, Dover Publications, Inc., New York, New York, 1986.

Thomsett, Michael C., *Winning Numbers*, American Management Association (AMACOM), New York New York, 1990.

Wind, Jerry Yoram and Main, Jeremy, *Driving Change*, The Free Press, New York, New York, 1998.

Chapter 13

Preparing an Organization to be Receptive to Change

Publishing policies and procedures is not always an easy task. Knowing if an audience has received the information the way it was intended, if the communications deployed have been well received, if training classes were attended, if the training material has been applied to the trainee's work environment, or if the users even received notice of the new policies and procedures are the concerns of every procedures analyst. These concerns, and others, will be addressed in this chapter.

The first step in preparing an organization to be receptive to change is to know your audience (i.e., users) when distributing policies and procedures to them. The subsequent steps will be involved with understanding the characteristics of the audience, e.g., determining the company's culture, identifying management's viewpoint on training, determining if users generally resist change or are fearful of anything management does or say, and finding ways to prepare an organization to improve their receptivity to change. The procedures analyst must know in advance what kind of audience will be using and applying the policies and procedures that are being distributed to them. Identifying your audience can be accomplished in many ways, three of which are listed below:

1. When the policies and procedures are written or revised as a result of improvements, the procedures analyst will coordinate the research and draft documents with all known users or representatives of these users. The cross-functional team members (led by the procedures analyst) that coordinate this research and coordination process are also sponsors of the draft policies and procedures as they are being created. These team members have the responsibility of informing the department management and employees in their local work area about what they are doing with the Policies and Procedures Department. As progress is made with the cross-functional team, the team members should be relaying progress and possible benefits of their work to their fellow

workers and management. These progress updates can be very important in gaining support from users throughout the company. If the cross-functional team has been staffed with team members that represent the users of the target audiences, then these updates can be valuable in promoting user receptivity and reducing the employees' attitude of "resistance to change."

2. The procedures analyst can start the policies and procedures communication campaign before the draft policy and procedure documents are approved and implemented, to prepare potential users in advance for new or revised business processes, policies, and procedures that will be released in the near future.

3. The procedures analyst can work closely with senior management to prepare the organization to be receptive to change. When employees are "resistant to change," any new or revised business processes, policies, or procedures often result in "inaction" on the part of the users. The procedures analyst can play an important role as a "change agent" for the company to ensure policies and procedures are properly communicated, trained, measured, and improved.

    The rest of this chapter will focus primarily on this third method of identifying the characteristics of your audience.

Simplicity, clarity, accuracy, and consistency are key elements to writing policies and procedures that will be readily accepted by target audiences. Procedures analysts tend to overlook the bigger picture of how the organization accepts changes. If change is not readily accepted, even the best written policies and procedures are tough to sell! The procedures analyst must keep an eye on the general mentality of the company's viewpoint toward change. *This viewpoint will make a difference to the deployment of communication strategies and training campaigns.*

For this chapter, we will focus on the larger picture of preparing an organization to be receptive to change. If the general organizational mentality is to resist change, it makes little sense to do a major communication and training campaign of policies and procedures until efforts are made toward changing this mentality. The procedures analyst may be able to determine the company's viewpoint on change through surveys and metrics. Two widely recognized viewpoints include "reactive" and "proactive":

1. Reactive. If a company is reactive (i.e., reacts to change after it happens), then there is a good probability that there will be many employees that do not like change and will tend to resist efforts to incorporate changes of any kind. Just recognizing that there are pockets of employees who resist change will be a major step in helping an organization become receptive to change.

2. Proactive. If a company is proactive (i.e., works to prevent a situation from occurring or recurring) and receptive to change, implementing new or revised policies and procedures will be much easier and the procedures analyst will be able to concentrate on the quality of the policies and procedures rather than worrying about why users resist change!

PROCEDURES ANALYST'S ROLE IN PREPARING AN ORGANIZATION TO BE RECEPTIVE TO CHANGE

The successful implementation of policies and procedures depends on the organization's culture and its receptivity to change. The procedures analyst can influence the way policies and procedures are received, understood, applied, and complied with, if he has uses the plans and tools presented in this book. He can work closely with two specific areas to start gathering information about the organization's culture and strategic goals:

1. Target audiences to understand their needs, values, and beliefs to ensure the appropriate methods of communication, training, and learning are used to assure new or revised policies and procedures are easily accepted and assimilated into their work environment, and

2. Senior management, the President, the CEO, and other high ranking staff to understand how they expect policies and procedures to be communicated and assimilated into the organization. The procedures analyst should focus on developing a strong bond with senior management. This strong relationship will prove valuable for three reasons:

   a. A senior management ally may prove to be a valuable source of information for the procedures analyst.

b. The procedures analyst should be able to seek assistance from senior management for ideas about communication, training, mentoring, improvements, or budgetary restrictions

c. The procedures analyst will hear about company initiatives before they start. This information gives him the chance to participate on company initiatives at their onset rather than after teams have been formed. Working on company initiatives will be useful to the procedures analyst because he can promote the importance of his work to the team members. Examples of company initiatives include Total Quality Management (TQM), ISO Quality Standards, Capability Maturity Model (CMM), Six Sigma, or Value Engineering. The procedures analyst should be an asset to these large scale company efforts because of his knowledge of the company's business processes, policies, procedures, forms, and other company information.

The stronger the bond the procedures analyst develops with management and employees, the easier it will be to implement policies and procedures because these individuals should put more trust into the work of the procedures analyst. If the procedures analyst reports to a member of senior management, bonding with senior management should be easier than if the procedures analyst reports to a lower-ranking manager. In this case, the procedures analyst should work closely with his manager to find a way to communicate with senior management and obtain their support and sponsorship. Without direct support and commitment of senior management, the continuing success of the policies and procedures infrastructure will be dubious.

RESISTANCE TO CHANGE MENTALITY

The perception of policies and procedures depends on how receptive or resistant employees are to change. The culture, management style, vision, and core values of the organization can make the job of the procedures analyst easy or difficult. In a traditional company, management typically resists change and reacts to problems as they occur rather than trying to prevent them from occurring. Managers are faced with daily problems that cause them to stop what they are doing and find solutions. Managers do not have time to mentor an employee after training.

Managers and employees view change differently. Both groups know that vision and leadership drive successful change, but few leaders recognize the ways in which individuals commit themselves to bring about change. Senior managers see change as an opportunity to strengthen the business by aligning operations with strategy, to take on new professional challenges and risks, and to advance their careers. For many employees, however, including middle managers, change is neither sought after nor welcomed — *it is disruptive, intrusive, and upsets the balance.* Managers believe that their actions will produce change. Very often change is only superficial, temporary, or imagined. Real change requires dramatic, committed, and insightful leadership.

When companies try to "think out of the box" and look for ways to become "forward-thinking," they are being "proactive" in their approach. The term *proactive* is defined as acting in anticipation of future problems, needs, or changes. Recalling our discussion in the "Introduction" on the importance of moving away from being "resistant to change," companies need to be able to anticipate change to stay even or get ahead of the competition. Companies now compete on global markets against global competitors. Customer expectations are rising. Attitudes and values are changing. Most important, our minds are changing, stretching to comprehend and cope with the implications of a world economy undergoing revolutionary change. As organizations fight to become recognized in their industry and strive to be number one, competition grows more intense. Continual change is needed to stay even or get ahead of the competition. The companies that succeed will be those that anticipate change and develop strategies in advance.

The procedures analyst should focus on activities and events which help an organization change their way of thinking. If the procedures analyst were to focus on a single element, it would be organizational culture. The development of an efficient infrastructure of policies and procedure is dependent on the procedures analyst's ability to understand and influence the culture through effective communication and training campaigns.

➤From experience, I have found that when I try to understand how the organization thinks as a whole rather than trying to change the behavior of one or two departments or functions, published policies and procedures are more readily accepted and the initial compliance levels are higher than expected. I had often wondered why my policies and procedures were not accepted as readily as I had thought — I found it was because I was being narrow minded and I was not considering the values, beliefs, and culture of the target audiences or the total organization.

ORGANIZATIONAL CULTURE DEFINED

The basic character or style of any organization is what is popularly referred to as its culture. Understanding organizational culture is a necessary part of being successful, but organizational culture is only part of a much broader framework. Culture provides the foundation for a strong and a successful organization. The understanding and application of organizational culture are the hallmarks of a successful organization. For our purposes, *organizational culture* can be defined as a system of values, beliefs, myths, tools, and practices through which we respond to the environment. The culture influences how work is accomplished. The beliefs and values of employees are critical to the success of any organization. If the procedures analyst can influence the culture, then it will be easier to implement a policies and procedures infrastructure in a company.

According to Peter Senge in his book, "*The Dance of Change*," (Senge, 1999) organizational (or corporate) culture:

> *"Provide the ground rules for corporate activities, how we interact with others, and perhaps even how we think. Some people act according to the rules and others react without even realizing rules are affecting them. The basic philosophy, spirit, and drive of an organization have far more to do with relative achievement than do technological or economic resources, organizational structure, innovation, and timing. All these things weigh heavily on success. The golden ring of success is attainable only if the organization wants to reach it.*

> *You cannot create a new culture out of thin air. The values, beliefs, tools, and practices can be studied. Cultures of successful companies can be benchmarked. You can then propose new values, introduce new ways of doing things, and articulate new governing ideas. Over time, these actions will set the stage for new behavior. If people who adopt that new behavior feel that it helps them do better, they may try it again, and after many trials, taking as long as five or ten years, the organizational culture may embody a different set of assumptions, a different way of looking at things, than it did before. Even then, you have not changed the culture but you have set the stage for the culture to evolve."*

The procedures analyst cannot create a new culture, but he can help management and employees with some of the components "culture" strategists seek like an organization built on a structure of teams, continuous learning, and continuous improvement. The procedures analyst can work closely with senior management and employees in creating business processes, policies, procedures, and necessary forms to help with the development of teams, training classes, mentoring programs, and communications that focus on continuous improvement. The procedures analyst makes a good "salesperson" of teams, continuous learning, and continuous improvement because these three components are important aspects of the responsibilities of the procedures analysts. Each of these three components will be further explored later in this chapter in the discussion of the "proactive" organization.

"REACTIVE" AND "PROACTIVE" ORGANIZATIONS

Most companies start out as "reactive" organizations though many would probably not admit it. Companies would prefer to say that they are trying to be "proactive" or that they are "proactive." Some organizations like where they are, some will never get out of the "reactive" mode, and many will operate somewhere in between "reactive" and "proactive" modes. Making a change in culture, or behavior, does not happen overnight. Patience, time, and lots of effort is required on the part of senior management and employees. Organizations evolve — *it could take a lifetime to become a "proactive" organization.* As organizations realize the value of creating a company that is receptive to change, changes themselves will have a higher chance of acceptance. As policies and procedures are written, published, communicated, trained, and deployed, they will be more readily accepted (and higher compliance levels might be achieved) if the organizational culture is considered when developing the communication and training campaigns.

1.   "REACTIVE" ORGANIZATIONS

The traditional organization is typically led by a management team that is "reactive" to problems and situations. Management does not anticipate problems, rather they wait for problems to happen and then they act, or react. Management is constantly "putting out fires" and they never have enough time to do anything right the first time. They work on past issues and problems. They fail to look to the future. The organizational structure is top heavy with management and there is a clear division between management and employees. Organizations are built around a clear system of hierarchical relationships, with greater discretion in decision making further up the hierarchy and within an established chain of command as the primary mechanism for coordination.

Organizations are governed by clear and consistent written rules and procedures that cover all positions, both operational and managerial. Management believes that they control the company and that what they say is right and that employees must do as they say or look for other work. Neither group trusts each other. Communication is limited. Management communicates among each other but not to employees. Employees feel left out and are afraid to speak out in fear of losing their jobs.

Training is viewed as a company benefit or privilege. Training is usually equated to learning and the company often ignores the daily learning in which all employees must participate in if the company is to succeed. Training is frequently conducted by a training group, thereby lifting the burden of training from the managers. Management no longer has to be involved. When the trainee returns to work, there is no effort on the part of the managers or the organization to assist the newly trained employee with the application of his training to his working environment. The information is quickly lost. Managers do not care what their employees are taught, they just want their employees to get back to work. Managers rarely see the worth of these training courses, worse, they do not see how employee training is helpful to their work areas.

The characteristics of a "reactive" organization can be summarized as follows:

1. Primary and overriding purpose is to make money, to produce near-term shareholder return

2. Managers and employees are constantly "putting out fires." Direction is by a "seat-of-the-pants" philosophy

3. Approach is symptomatic, not problematic

4. Reasoning is by experience rather than statistically based

5. Focus is on product, not on process

6. Analysis is by experience, not data

7. Process adjustment is done by tweaking, not statistical process control

8. Managers and employees resist change and believe, "If it's not broke, don't fix it!"

9. Managers are smarter than customers and employees

10. Managers and employees do not trust one another

11. Teams are misunderstood and are almost nonexistent

12. Strategic success comes from large one-time innovation leaps rather than from continuous improvement

13. Goals are based on realistic perceptions

14. Training is a perk or benefit to an employee; training is not meant to have much bearing on the employee's work environment

15. People are a cost rather than an asset

16. To err is human, perfection is an unattainable and unrealistic goal

➤ DOES YOUR COMPANY BEHAVE LIKE THIS OR DOES IT EXHIBIT SOME OF THESE 16 POINTS? If so, then your company probably fits the "reactive" organization profile or somewhere in between "reactive" and "proactive." The procedures analyst has a difficult time working in a "reactive" organization because he is continually being "pushed back" in his efforts by senior management and employees who resist change. When management and employees are constantly "putting out fires" and solving daily "urgent" problems, new or revised policies and procedures are not readily accepted. These policy and procedure documents are often considered a nuisance. The procedures analyst can roll out his communication and training plans but it takes perseverance to measure and audit departments when the procedures analyst knows that policies and procedures are not readily accepted or applied in the company.

2. "PROACTIVE" ORGANIZATIONS

In today's economy and environment, there is a strong move for companies to become "proactive" organizations (other names include learning organization, knowledge-enabled organization, or high performance organization). In the "proactive" organization, management looks ahead and tries to prevent problems from occurring or recurring. Managers and employees form alliances and have respect and trust for each other. These relationships are often bonded through teams. As companies move away from being "reactive" and resistant to change, management begins to realize that they cannot do it alone and they must start involving workers from across the organization through teams. Resistance to change is minimal because of the improved communication and feedback systems that are often implemented as a result of those alliances between management and employees. Organizations are empowered with clear direction and goals.

Continuous learning is likely to be a major initiative in the "proactive" organization. Training is generally offered to all employees with an incentive to further their skills. Plans are put in place to mentor or coach employees when they return from training to ensure that training is incorporated into the work environment. When training is used immediately, the employee learns. Without the immediacy of applying his training to his work environment, the employee loses what he has been taught. When applied, this learning becomes wisdom. With wisdom, employees can apply their knowledge to current or forward-looking projects. These employees become assets for the company (Senge, 1999).

Business processes, policies, and procedures have the best chance of being successfully implemented, communicated, measured, and improved if they are deployed in "proactive" organizations where the overall structure is unified, the culture is "forward-thinking" and "resistance to change" is minimal. The procedures analyst is most successful in this type of environment because he knows his published policies and procedures will be readily accepted and welcomed. He will find quickly that helping organizations change their culture and ways of thinking will be an asset when he publishes policies and procedures because employees will be more eager to accept new ideas and change. The characteristics of a "proactive" organization can be summarized as follows:

1. Management tries to prevent problems from occurring instead of constantly "putting out fires" after they occur

2. Control is localized, not centralized

3. Focus is on process and data, not experience

4. Benchmarking and metrics are routine activities

5. Management and employees work together in teams

6. Focus is on high participation and a team-based network

7. Teams are empowered

8. Forward-looking thinking, thinking out of the box, and systems thinking becomes normal behavior

9. Resistance to change is minimal

10. Clear direction and goals shared by management and employees alike

11. Continuous learning and change are key components to the vision and strategic goals of the organization

12. Training is a necessity, not a luxury

13. Training is expected to lead to an improvement in the work environment, rather than for ideas to "rattle" around in the brain unused

14. Employees are assets, not a cost

15. The customer is paramount

IMPLEMENTING POLICIES AND PROCEDURES IN A "PROACTIVE" ORGANIZATION

Throughout this book, plans, tools, processes, methods, guidelines, and techniques have been discussed that will help the procedures analyst successfully implement business processes, policies, and procedures through the planning of communication, training, metrics, and improvement activities. The success of the implementation of a policies and procedures infrastructure will depend on the organization's culture, attitude, management structure, willingness to change, and eagerness to improve not only the company's business processes, policies, and procedures but also the skills and learning capabilities of its employees. There will always be new challenges, new skills to learn, new technologies, and new ways to earn the respect of its employees to gain the customer's trust, increase sales and profits, and become a model of excellence for other companies. The procedures analyst is successful in a "proactive" organization because he has management commitment and the authority to make significant improvements. There is typically a strong relationship between senior management and the procedures analyst, and this makes the job of the procedures analyst much easier. The procedures analyst succeeds because he:

1. Has the endorsement of senior management for the development, maintenance, and improvement for the policies and procedures program for the company. Management's commitment is shown when they change their vision and strategic goals to give authority to the Policies and Procedures Department to carry out plans to write, coordinate, implement, communicate, train, measure, and improve the policies and procedures infrastructure.

2. Coordinates new or revised business processes, policies, and procedures with the assistance of cross-functional teams. Uses these teams to brainstorm ideas, find root causes to problems and issues, help coordinate the development of the policies and procedures infrastructure, and champion approved policies and procedures.

3. Works closely with senior management to ensure the structure and content of business processes, policies, and procedures are closely aligned with the company's vision, core values, and objectives. Randomly reviews the processes, policies, and procedures to ensure the "policy statements" meet or exceed the intent of the company's vision, core values, and objectives.

4. Assures that training is not equated to learning and implements a training plan that requires trainees to receive "on-the-job" mentoring and coaching following any kind of training. Works closely with management to ensure that employees are being given the opportunity to apply what they have learned. Works with management to obtain feedback on the results of mentoring their employees after their training.

5. Executes review, compliance, metrics, audit, and improvement plans to work toward achieving 100% compliance of business processes, policies and procedures.

PROCEDURES ANALYST AS A "CHANGE AGENT"

A successful procedures analyst can be a catalyst for change in an organization because he can apply his knowledge and successes from the establishment of a successful policies and procedures infrastructure. The procedures analyst serves the role of "change agent" as he assists senior management with companywide change initiatives. A *change agent* is defined as a representative of management who helps to modify, alter, change, or transform business processes, policies, and procedures in a positive way for the organization. The procedures analyst is a good candidate to lead or facilitate companywide team efforts for change because of his knowledge of company business processes, policies, procedures, forms, and the organizational culture. He has a strong relationship with management and he is familiar with departmental politics. He is successful because of professionalism, discipline, persistence, social skills, customer care, and his personal drive to succeed.

The essential skills and abilities of a change agent include the ability to facilitate, lead, listen, and make things happen. The wisdom to know when to push the change versus when to step back and let people accept the change over time is also required. Humility can easily facilitate the implementation of change. Successful change management cannot be achieved without the proper communication strategy. Appropriate new communication methods are required to get people involved and to let them know why the change makes sense (Edosomwan, 1996).

As a change agent, the procedures analyst assists management by leading and facilitating teams working on companywide initiatives. He can make significant contributions because he has extensive experience in company business processes, policies, procedures, and forms. He can gain cooperation from management and employees because of other contacts with them, e.g., writing policies and procedures and designing forms for their department, attending team and staff meetings, conducting audits, or working on company improvement initiatives.

Through the implementation of business processes, policies, and procedures, the procedures analyst makes small, incremental changes to the organization. When major policy and procedure systems are implemented, the procedures analyst can make significant changes to the organizational culture. Put in the right perspective, the Policies and Procedures Department can be portrayed as a successful pilot group for helping an organization make better use of teams, improve productivity, enhance quality, achieve significant cost savings, increase sales and profits, and improve employee morale. As more and more departments achieve success, the organization will grow as a result.

The rest of this chapter is devoted to showing how the procedures analyst can be helpful to senior management in preparing the organization to be receptive to change. Excellent books have been written on this subject, i.e., becoming a "proactive" organization or a learning organization. My intention is <u>not</u> to show you the way to become a "proactive" organization. My goal is to point out some of the activities the procedures analyst could be doing to help his organization become more receptive to change and evolve toward a "proactive" organization.

As the procedures analyst becomes more involved in companywide projects, he will earn a reputation as a "change agent" and may be asked by senior management to assist with "trouble" areas (e.g., departments, functions, or projects that are behind schedule, over budget, or are experiencing problems) as well as work on companywide improvement initiatives. Personally, I enjoy working on companywide projects, working with hundreds of people, and doing projects that help the company succeed. These extra projects can add diversity to your job. I suggest you consider "branching out" and help other areas of the company — you have the experience, so why not share it.

THE MODEL "PROACTIVE" ORGANIZATION

An organization must develop a set of ideal goals when striving to become a "proactive" organization. Management needs a road map to follow — developing these goals on your own is difficult. Hundreds of books have been written on this subject; I have selected three authors (James Belohlav, Warren Bemis, and Peter Senge) and have presented a combined set of goals for designing a proactive, forward-thinking, learning organization. Senior management can pick and choose from this list and create their own goal list, but they cannot escape the necessity to create a similar list of goals for their own organization. Once this list is created and approved, it should be communicated to all employees with an emphasis of how important these goals are to the organization and its future.

If senior management does not have a plan to follow, it will be impossible to achieve a unified organizational design that enables their organization to achieve global dominance. Senior management must use every possible tool at their disposal to create and maintain organizational effectiveness.

TWELVE GOALS OF A MODEL "PROACTIVE" ORGANIZATION

1. As new organizations emerge, a change should occur in the organization. Executive team structures will emerge at the top of organizations and collective intellect and collaborative action will become more evident.

2. Organizations will exist in networks of suppliers, competitors, and customers who cooperate with each other to survive in an increasingly competitive marketplace.

3. Organizations will establish alliances and joint ventures that can be capitalized on and the particular strengths of the individual partners will be leveraged.

4. Organizational boundaries can become fuzzy as various allegiances emerge between and among various departments, functions, and areas.

5. Within organizations, teams will be the norm at all levels. Teams, not individuals, will become the basic organizational building blocks. In most cases, the wider scope of teams will ensure that the output is measurable and meaningful to the people producing it.

6. High performance work teams will emerge that integrate the social and technical systems of work, using both advanced technology-based tools and state-of-the art human system designs. These work teams bring together work, people, technology, and information in a manner that optimizes the congruence or "fit" among them to produce high performance in terms of the effective response to customer requirements and other environmental demands and opportunities.

7. Organizations will be able to create design teams quickly with the aid of technology-supported design tools.

8. Work processes will strive for zero defects and no after-the-fact inspections or reconciliation. Data is entered only once and quality inspection is built into each step of the work process to ensure that mistakes are not exported down the line.

9.   In designing work processes, automation should be incorporated as much as is practically possible. Pushing for maximum effectiveness encourages a work design in which people do those tasks that uniquely use human skills and capabilities.

10. System-level "continuous learning" and "continuous improvement" will be two important principles for new organizations.

11. There will be a general emphasis on developing people who understand the broader strategic issues and specific tasks in an organization.

12. There will be a more balanced emphasis on short-term financial performance.

The future of this model organization is much greater than the sum of its parts. Organizations of the future will be dramatically more flexible and efficient. Management and employees will learn rapidly, and overall, they will adapt quickly to changing environmental conditions and to competitive initiatives. The procedures analyst can show management how the Policies and Procedures Department has been successful and use similar techniques for assisting senior management in their quest to evolve into a "proactive" organization.

ASSISTING AN ORGANIZATION TO BECOME RECEPTIVE TO CHANGE

There are a number activities and events in which the procedures analyst can participate to help the organization evolve its culture and move toward being a "proactive" organization. With extensive experience in process improvement, training, and teams, the procedures analyst will be able to provide insight to management in at least the following three ways:

1.   <u>TEAMS — CATALYSTS TO AN EVOLVING CULTURE</u>

The use of teams is one of the goals of a "proactive" organization. A "forward-thinking" organization performs the majority of its operations through teams. A procedures analyst works with teams on a routine basis and is very successful. He can be a good salesperson for teams because he uses teams in his everyday work. He can show others the success of teams used for policies and procedures. The procedures analyst uses cross-functional teams to analyze, research, coordinate, write, review, write, publish, communicate, train, measure, and improve business processes, policies, and procedures. For this reason, the procedures analyst makes a good promoter and salesperson for using teams to solve problems, brainstorm ideas, or write policies and procedures. The procedures analyst can take the initiative from management to promote the use of teams throughout the organization.

Useful Definitions

> A *team* is two or more persons associated together in work or an activity. *Teamwork* is work done by team members with each doing a part but all contributing to the efficiency of the whole. A *facilitator* is a person who assists a team meeting achieve its stated goals, keeps the team on track, and tries to ensure that all team members participate. As a company evolves and starts using teams as a way of life, facilitators can become a requirement of every team meeting. A team should have common goals, a charter, ground rules, a schedule, and a set of rules for conducting the team meeting.

The procedures analyst can offer to serve the role of leader, facilitator, or serve both roles, in new teams to help the team members understand the importance of teams and teamwork to the success of an organization.

Personal Example:

> *When I worked at Datatape Incorporated, a manufacturing company in Pasadena, California, we had successfully built a company of teams, employees helped each other and we were able to implement new ideas quickly and effectively. A procedure was written on the use of teams in the company. Facilitators were seen as an important part of team meetings. We had special training classes for facilitators and they would be requested to attend as many meetings as possible that fit their schedule. We regularly communicated our successes and celebrated our victories when we implemented a major system or received compliments from our customers. Teams became a way of life at this company. This transition did not take place overnight, it took about 18 months to integrate the company with a network of teams. Through teams, this company became more receptive to change.*

➤As a procedures analyst enacts his communication, training, compliance, auditing, and improvement plans, he is helping the company and the culture to evolve. As new business processes, policies, and procedures are incorporated into the organization, change occurs and positive improvements are implemented. The persistence of the procedures analyst will become a catalyst for other departments to start doing incremental changes within their organization in an effort to help the company and culture evolve, and as we shall see, to help employees learn and continually improve, not only the company but also themselves.

2.   CONTINUOUS LEARNING

When a company learns to utilize and foster the growth of the knowledge and skills of employees across departments and functions, to integrate learning activities into every employee's work, to encourage and reinforce all modes of learning, and to align this learning with the company's strategic business directions, significant progress is being made toward becoming a "proactive" organization. The knowledge and skills of your employees are what differentiates you from your competitors.

Learning is the acquisition of the knowledge and skills necessary to meet individual, group, and company goals. Learning activities can take many forms, including but not limited to, traditional approaches to training. Changes in learning methods must be complemented by strong leadership, flexible organizations, and supportive policies and procedures if the "proactive" organization is to succeed. Becoming a "proactive" organization is not really an option for any company that wishes to succeed, it is their only choice!

> Training is not learning, the application of training to the work environment is learning!

With the stiff competition from companies who are trying to do everything right, companies cannot be fickle. They must continually try to be one or more steps ahead of their competition in every conceivable way possible. Peter Senge made a powerful statement when he said that "training is not learning unless it is applied to an employee's work environment" (Senge, 1999). An organization must learn to apply the full meaning of this statement to become a "proactive" organization.

➤The procedures analyst can be a driving force for ensuring the two behaviors, training and learning, are properly implemented in an organization. If the procedures

280

analyst has established the communication and training plans discussed in Chapters 4 and 5, he will have a good start at incorporating change in the organization. These plans help the users within target audiences learn about business processes, policies, and procedures. As policies and procedures are deployed and mentoring programs go into effect, this concept of "using the information from a training class in one's work environment" will start spreading through the organization. Initiating a companywide mentoring program is a good place for the procedures analyst to start helping the organization become more receptive to change.

Learning becomes "continuous" as policies, procedures, and company initiatives are successfully deployed with the aid of mentoring, coaching, and managing efforts. As employees learn and as the organization evolves toward being a "proactive" organization, employees should become motivated to seek new information through training courses, computer-based training, seminars, local associations, books, or the Internet. With the addition of mentoring and coaching, this training whether it is self-taught or taught in a classroom setting, can lead to learning. Learning can lead to knowledge. Knowledge can lead to wisdom which can be used for making better decisions. Decisions can lead to more training and learning, and the cycle continues.

3.   CONTINUOUS IMPROVEMENT

Continuous improvement is a major undertaking for any company. Improving businesses is a major factor to being competitive as organizations fight to become recognized in their industry and strive to be number one. Continual change and improvement are needed to stay even or get ahead of the competition. Senior management makes a major statement when they incorporate improvement initiatives into the company's strategic goals and communicate these goals to the organization. Creating a strong and sustained linkage between strategy and the completion of work is an enduring challenge in complex organizations. Change is more likely to be successful if the effects of the change benefit the business and its employees, and focus on what matters most to customers and management. As employees observe new practices which lead to better results, credibility will increase and more people will be willing to commit themselves to similar changes. As change occurs from business processes, policies, and procedures, companywide changes can be initiated with the same mechanism by which policies and procedures were implemented, communicated, trained, measured, and improved. Senior management can take the lead from the procedures analyst for establishing communication, training, measurement, improvement, and cost savings programs.

Continuous improvement starts with ideas, networks, personal gains, and business results. This turns into enthusiasm and a willingness to commit and thus the cycle continues. Continuous improvement needs to start slowly on a small scale and grow steadily. Companywide continuous improvement should not be done all at once. Improvement should be gradually implemented, starting with a team, department, branch, or division, and working outwardly into acceptance. Profound change can be self-reinforcing. Chances are, the more constructive the behavior of senior management, the more employees will follow that behavior. Building a culture that is receptive to change (i.e., readily accepting new ideas, concepts, or improvements) is no easy task, there should be no deadline and no predetermined ending point.

> Change starts on a small scale with functions, departments, and branches and spreads to the whole organization. Change does not work if the organization tries to change the organization all at once!

➤The procedures analyst has already been identified as a "change agent" with his assistance to senior management on major change initiatives. Any new or revised published policies or procedures include changes to the current way of doing things. Even if the organization is slow to getting started with a continuous improvement program, the procedures analyst must continue to do what he does best: *Analyze, research, coordinate, approve, publish, communicate, train, measure, and improve business processes, policies, and procedures, and work with management and employees to become more receptive to change.*

> Improvement should be gradually implemented, starting with a team, department, branch, or division, and working outwardly into acceptance by the entire organization.

Your job does not stop if the organization is not cooperative. In Chapter 14, "*Looking to the Future*," we will explore the many activities the procedures analyst can do to earn a respected reputation in his organization, among his peers, and in his industry. Looking forward to the future, the procedures analyst can keep abreast of current technology, methods, guidelines, plans, tools, techniques, journals, and books developed and written by experts of disciplines that support or are impacted by policies and procedures, continuous improvement, culture, or change. He can also improve his education and work toward certifications that will help his career.

OBSTACLES THAT CAN HINDER IMPROVEMENTS

There are some obstacles that can hinder or prevent organizations from achieving the kind of improvements they expect from becoming a "proactive" organization:

1. Lack of senior management commitment to continuous process improvement (this obstacle has stopped organizations from being successful!). From personal experience, I have seen senior managers who they support or endorse a company initiative but would never allow any of their subordinates to participate or attend meetings. They were even known to reprimand employees for participating. This attitude indicates a lack of support — in this particular company, the company initiative was a Total Quality Management program and it eventually failed. When support is given, the procedures analyst should determine if it is really support or just "lip-service."

2. Organizational strategic goals that do not reflect quality initiatives and continuous process improvement.

3. Middle management who fear uncertainty about future roles.

4. Organizations that focus on "fixing" problems rather than preventing them.

5. Lack of focus on business processes, policies, and procedures.

6. Absence of a department that is accountable for business processes, policies, and procedures (i.e., a Policies and Procedures Department).

7. Little training or experience with the plans and strategies that management has outlined for the organization.

8. Untrained or inexperienced procedures analysts in areas like process improvement, developing flow charts, quality reviews, metrics, quality tools, statistics, auditing, communications, training, mentoring, or even writing.

9. Absence of metrics focused on customer value-added processes.

10. Lack, or absence of, communication, training, review, compliance or improvement plans for business processes, policies, and procedures.

IN THE MIDST OF CHANGE

We are in the midst of change. The basis for the rivalry of nations is shifting to economic terms, at least in the industrial world. Competitiveness has become a critical national concern. Both the external and internal determinants of competitiveness require our attention and demand action. We have already witnessed the financial restructuring of much of corporate America. The 1990s have witnessed the beginning of the end of the traditional organization. If we are to succeed, we will need to witness the strategic, managerial, and organizational restructuring of our firms, and the design of new organizational architectures. This is our challenge and this is where the abilities, skills, and insights of the procedures analyst can play an important role.

Change is profound and it will only accelerate in the future. Globalization of markets and technology are having dramatic impacts. A paradigm shift is needed for the mind-set of organizations to compete in world markets. What we did yesterday does not count — what we do in the future will be the guiding light to our careers.

The procedures analyst must become knowledgeable and skilled to succeed in the highly participative, team-based network organization of the future. There is a discussion about career assessment in Chapter 14, "*Looking to the Future,*" about gaining the proper skills and knowledge to succeed in modern, proactive organizations. Intensified competition and ever-increasing customer expectations are forcing organizations to function at a level of effectiveness (high quality at low cost), speed (reduced cycle and product development time), and innovation that is far superior to that of the past.

> My greatest hope is that you can take the plans and tools contained in this book — ideas based on practice — and build better organizations. The choice is yours.

CHECKLIST FOR CHANGE:

✓ Guidelines and suggestions are presented for preparing an organization to be receptive to change.

✓   The procedures analyst plays an important role in assisting senior management with their goal of evolving toward or becoming a "proactive" organization.

✓   The difference between "reactive" and "proactive" organizations is discussed with an emphasis on how the procedures analyst can adapt to both working environments.

✓   Through the development of a strong bond with senior management, the procedures analyst can become a "change agent" for company initiatives and help the organization make a paradigm shift toward continuous learning and continuous improvement.

✓   The procedures analyst can make a significant impact in the evolution of a company's culture by becoming a respected "change agent" for management.

✓   Twelve ideal goals for a model "proactive" organization are presented as a starting point for management to establish a similar set of goals. These goals represent the minimum goals for senior management. Management should add or modify these goals, not subtract from these minimum, core, goals.

APPLYING WHAT YOU HAVE LEARNED:

Decide if your organization is "reactive," "proactive," or somewhere in between. Determine the culture make up, management style, skills and learning capabilities of employees, and any continuous learning, improvement programs, or change initiatives currently in progress. Use this information to decide if there should be any changes to the way published policies and procedures are implemented, communicated, trained, measured, or improved. Develop a strong bond with senior management. Work closely with senior management as a "change agent" to assist them with large scale change initiatives and to help them evolve their organization into a "proactive" and an organization that is receptive to change. Communicate small and large successes.

ACHIEVE 100% COMPLIANCE:

Achieving 100% compliance of policies and procedures is not likely in a "reactive" organization. By working with the culture and people of an organization, the procedures analyst can find ways to improve the way business processes, policies, and procedures are received by target audiences. Preparing the organization to become "proactive" and receptive to change can help the procedures analyst in four ways:

1. In a proactive, forward-thinking environment, the procedures analyst may be able to achieve 100% compliance of policies and procedures.

2. The procedures analyst can work closely with senior management by serving as a "change agent" in helping the organization evolve toward becoming a "proactive" organization.

3. The procedures analyst can help senior management develop goals for the new organization using the twelve goals suggested earlier in this chapter as a model "proactive" organization.

4. The procedures analyst can find better ways to implement new or revised policies and procedures by studying the culture of the company and developing a strong bond with senior management.

REFERENCES:

Belohlav, James A., *Championship Management*, Productivity Press, Cambridge, Massachusetts, 1990.

Deal, Terrence E. and Kennedy, Allan A., *The New Corporate Cultures*, Perseus Books, New York, New York, 1999.

Edosomwan, Dr. Johnson A., *Organizational Transformation and Process Reengineering*, St. Lucie Press, Delray Beach, Florida, 1996.

Harvard Business School Contributors, *Harvard Business Review on Change*, Harvard Business School Press, Boston, Massachusetts, 1998.

Harvard Business School Contributors, *Harvard Business Review on Knowledge Management*, Harvard Business School Press, Boston, Massachusetts, 1998.

Nadler, David A., Gerstein, Marc S., and Shaw, Robert B. and Associates, *Organizational Architecture*, Jossey-Bass Publishers, San Francisco, California, 1992.

Peters, Tom, *Thriving on Chaos*, Alfred A. Knopf, New York New York, 1988.

Poirier, Charles, C. and Houser, William, F., *Business Partnering for Continuous Improvement*, Berrett-Koehler Publications, San Francisco, California, 1993.

Senge, Peter; Kleiner, Art; Roberts, Charlotte; Ross, Richard; Roth, George; Smith, Bryan, *The Dance of Change*, Currency Doubleday, New York, New York, 1999.

Senge, Peter, *The Fifth Discipline*, Currency Doubleday, New York, New York, 1990.

Shewhart, Walter A., *Statistical Method from the Viewpoint of Quality Control*, Dover Publications, Inc., New York, New York, 1986.

Smith, Douglas K., *Taking Charge of Change*, Addison-Wesley, Reading, Massachusetts, 1996.

Swindle, Robert E. and Swindle, Elizabeth M., *The Business Communicator.* Prentice-Hall, Inc., Englewood Cliffs, NJ, 1989.

Tobin, Daniel R., Ph.D., *The Knowledge-Enabled Organization*, American Management Association, New York, New York, 1998.

Vicker, Lauren and Hein, Ron, *The Fast Forward MBA in Business Communication*, John Wiley & Sons, Inc., New York, New York, 1999.

Chapter 14

Looking
to the Future

What does the future hold for procedures analysts? Instead of guessing, I wrote this chapter specifically to address this career question. The information in this book has given the procedures analyst insight into the kinds of activities he could be doing if his career goals included the pursuit of policies and procedures. There is much to be learned, researched, and discovered on your own. I did not give you all of the answers. Assimilating and applying information is easier when you can see it, read it, and think about it. You can read books, journals, take college courses, join local associations, attend seminars, facilitate teams, and get involved with company initiatives. Your skills and abilities need to be recognized. I have found that the more I know and can apply, and the more I help others in my company, the more respect I earn. With respect, authority and recognition are not far behind.

The procedures analyst has enormous opportunities to learn about an organization because of his daily exposure to business processes, policies, procedures, changes, new initiatives, communication and training strategies, and internal and external changes that could affect the infrastructure of an organization.

One prevalent theme throughout this book is that the procedures analyst is not finished with his responsibilities for policies and procedures once they are published, communicated, and trained. The process is continuous. The procedures analyst is accountable for the quality and content of policies and procedures from inception to revision — and rarely to retirement. Policies and procedures are improved and replaced, but almost never removed from the system completely. They could be removed when a major re-engineering effort significantly reduces the number of steps in activities or tasks. In some cases, the policies and procedures will become shorter and in other cases, the policies and procedures may be completely eliminated from the policies and procedures infrastructure.

As discussed in Chapter 13, *"Preparing an Organization to be Receptive to Change,"* the procedures analyst has already been labeled by senior management as a "change agent" for both process improvement that occurs within the framework of the policies and procedures infrastructure and for major change initiatives. Now the procedures analyst must become known, if he is not already recognized, among his peers, management, and employees. He must build alliances with management and employees and find a common bond with them. The procedures analyst must become a logical choice for senior management when they seek out someone to take charge of the changes that are taking place in the organization and as the organization evolves in the future. Thousands of companies have already started this lengthy process of evolving into a "proactive" organization from the traditional "reactive" organization.

> The procedures analyst must take charge of his career, build an image for the Policies and Procedures Department, build alliances with senior management and other groups involved with change, and work toward becoming a "change agent."

The procedures analyst must start "looking to the future" and anticipating the needs of evolving organizations. When management starts to recognize the procedures analyst as a "change agent," many opportunities will open. As the procedures analyst facilitates teams and works with cross-functional teams to analyze business processes and define policies and procedures, he will strengthen his network of contacts as well as earn respect from management. While some procedures analysts are too timid to take this "aggressive" stance and work in ways to improve themselves in the eyes of management, others are eager for this information.

I firmly believe that either you have it (i.e., ability to coordinate, write, communicate, train, measure, improve, revise, and do it all over again) or you do not. The astute procedures analyst will be diligent, prepared, and ready when needed. Unfortunately, I know of some procedures analysts who think they are good at what they do but in reality, they do not have a clue about their job and its importance to an organization. In the world of policies and procedures, I contend that you cannot be a "follower" if you want to succeed. You must take the lead whenever possible and make suggestions for improvements to the policies and procedures infrastructure as well as to the organization. The procedures analyst must strive to earn respect from senior management. A "follower" does not make things happen: he follows the lead of others and usually makes changes to policies and procedures without questioning the content

290

or source. He is not always involved in the collection and review of new or revised content. The "follower" does not question senior management or any manager or supervisor when he knows they are wrong and are going in the wrong direction on business processes, policies, or procedures. If you are a "follower," you must decide if you want to be a "leader." This chapter will help the "leader" become stronger and the "follower" to decide if he wants to become a "leader."

CAREER ASSESSMENT

The procedures analyst must assess where he is in his career. If working with policies and procedures in various roles (i.e., analysts, supervisors, managers, vice presidents), is his life goal, then he must make sure that he keeps improving his knowledge, abilities, and skills in as many areas as possible that will ultimately be beneficial to this goal. He can do this through a variety of means including face-to-face networking, benchmarking, company initiatives, mentoring, and participation in seminars, conferences, and associations, both locally and nationally. Depending on the type of company and industry, there are hundreds of books and journals available. I have discovered a wealth of information about a company's culture and the future direction of organizations through my research for this book. The procedures analyst should take a closer look at the chapters in this book to ensure that he is comfortable with the information.

Since your education and experience level are not known, I have included the table below to show study areas that have <u>proved useful to me</u> in my quest to become the best possible procedures analyst I can and become respected in my company and industry. In addition to the two other books I have written on the subject of business processes, policies, and procedures, I have been working in the field of business process improvements for more than 30 years. I have written these books to share my experiences with those given the responsibility for analyzing business processes and for coordinating and publishing policies and procedures. I can say with confidence that I have experienced almost every possible way of doing a step or task in the creation, coordination, writing, approval, publication, communication, training, measurement, and improvement of business processes, policies, and procedures. I am motivated to be the best at everything I do. This drive has led me to share my experiences with you. In Table 14-1 below, I have listed the resources that I have found most useful. I have tried to equate these resources to the chapters in this book. I did not include all of the resources I used but I have given you a detailed listing of resources that could potentially become your starting point for your learning process.

Table 14-1: *Study Areas for a Procedures Analyst*

CH	TOPIC	SOURCES OF STUDY
	Introduction	• Harvard Business School Review, *Change* • Deal's book, *The Corporate Cultures*
1	Policies and Procedures Improvement Cycle	• Scherkenbach's book, *The Deming Route to Quality Productivity* • Shewhart's book, *Statistical Method from the Viewpoint of Quality Control* • Davenport's book, *Process Innovation* • American Society of Quality Web Site, located at http://www.asq.org
2	Writing Effective Policies and Procedures	• Harrington's book, *Business Process Improvement* • Davenport's book, *Process Innovation* • Tushman's book, *Winning Thru Innovation* • My earlier book, *Establishing a System of Policies and Procedures* • Poirier's book, *Business Partnering for Continuous Improvement* • *Technical Writing* Association, visit http://www.stc.org • *Policies and Procedures* Special Interest Group, visit http://www.stc.org/pics/ppsig/www/index.htm • Milas' book, *Teambuilding and Total Quality* • Harry's book, *Six Sigma*
4	Establishing a Communication Strategy	• Swindle's book, *Business Communicator* • Larkin's book, *Communicating Change* • Vicker's book, *The Fast Forward MBA in Business Communications*
5	Developing an Effective Training Strategy	• *The ASTD Handbook of Instructional Technology* • Carr's book, *Smart Training* • Schank's book, *Virtual Learning* • Training web site, *http://www.astd.org*

7-10	Establishing a Compliance Plan	• Harrington's book, *Statistical Analysis Simplified* • Chang's two books, *Continuous Improvement Tools, Volumes 1 and 2* • Owen's book, *Beating Your Competition Thru Quality* • Russell's book, *After the Quality Audit* • Lindberg's book, *Operations Auditing* • Beeler's book, *Internal Auditing: The Big Lies* • Harry's book, *Six Sigma*
11-12	Conducting Profitable Continuous Improvement Activities	• Harry's book, *Six Sigma* • Harding's book, *Purchasing* (includes section on cost benefit analyses) • Davenport's book, *Process Innovation* • Senge's book, *The Dance of Change*
13	Preparing an Organization to be Receptive to Change	• Senge's book, *The Fifth Discipline* • Senge's book, *The Dance of Change* • Deal's book, *The New Corporate Cultures* • Katzenbach's book, *Teams at the Top* • Harvard Business School Review on *Change* • Harvard Business School Review on *Knowledge-Enabled Organizations* • Tushman's book, *Winning Thru Innovation* • Poirier's book, *Business Partnering for Continuous Improvement* • Scherkenbach's book, *The Deming Route to Quality Productivity* • American Society of Quality Web Site, located at http://www.asq.org
14	Looking to the Future	Each of the fourteen chapters contain references to a variety of books and journals. Refer to the references in each chapter and read those books of interest. Visit the technical writing web site located at http://www.stc.org. Visit the policies and procedures web site that is a branch of the technical writing association located at http://www.stc.org/pics/ppsig/www/index.htm. Follow the various links on these sites for more references.

NA	Education	Useful course topics (e.g., in-house or external training courses including self-help books) include:

Useful course topics (e.g., in-house or external training courses including self-help books) include:

Management Skills
- Management and Supervision
- Communications
- Listening and Presentation Skills
- Team Building and Facilitation
- Meeting Preparation
- Time Management

General Company Experience
- General knowledge in major departmental areas in your company.
- Company vision, mission, and core values
- Organizational structure
- Products and services
- Business processes, policies, procedures, and forms

Quality Management Experience
- Quality Assurance and Quality Control
- Total Quality Management (TQM)
- Process Improvement Methods
- ISO Quality Standards
- Capability Maturity Model (CMM)
- Software Life Cycle
- Six Sigma
- Quality Tools
- Statistical Process Control (SPC)
- Mathematics and Statistics

Computer Skills
- Basic Software Programming
- Flow Charting
- Web Design
- Electronic Data Interchange (EDI)
- Electronic Commerce (E-Commerce)
- Microsoft Suite of Products

NA	Certifications	The information obtained from simply studying for various certification programs will prove valuable. The three areas discussed below will provide a good source of information to any procedures analyst.
		• **Project Management**: Visit www.pmi.org for certification information. You can find information about project management, planning, scheduling, estimating, life cycles, process improvement, quality control, change control, project policies and procedures, and other administrative functions.
		• **Records Management**: Visit www.arma.org for certification information. You can find information about records management systems, communications, management, human resources, forms management, documentation systems, records management manuals, procedures, and administrative functions.
		• **Forms Management**: Visit www.bfma.org for certification information. You can find information about forms control and the history of how forms, both printed and electronic, play an important part of any policies and procedures infrastructure. This is an area often overlooked by procedures analysts who do not hold the role of a corporate procedures analyst, i.e., one who is involved with policies and procedures for the entire organization. Often this corporate role is also responsible for forms management functions.
NA	Associations	You can seek out books on these subjects or join related associations. Every library should have a list of registered associations worldwide. There are two good sources from the *Encyclopedia of Associations* available from most libraries. The two book titles below were found in a local library in Westerville, Ohio, USA. • *National Organizations of the U.S.* • *International Organizations*

JOB POSSIBILITIES FOR THE PROCEDURES ANALYST

A procedures analyst's career can take a variety of directions depending on his goals and desires. He could move into management or non-management positions. For some, management is their goal, but others prefer "back office" work and do NOT want to be burdened with the responsibilities and headaches that come with being a manager. There are positions for management and non-management individuals. You can work in any industry or company. Using the principles presented in this book, you should also be able to demonstrate to senior management how you add value.

In Table 14-2 below, I have listed possible titles for those who are interested in pursuing careers in areas that actively write and develop policies and procedures, support the efforts of a Policies and Procedures Department, or are impacted by process improvement efforts. The list in Table 14-2 is not all inclusive and each column is independent of the other.

Table 14-2: *Job Titles for Procedures Analysts*

NON-MANAGEMENT	MANAGEMENT
Procedures Analyst, Procedures Writer	Supervisor, Manager, Director, or Vice President in:
Business Process Analyst, Process Analyst	• Policy Development • Policies and Procedures • Business Process Management
Staff Writer, Technical Writer, or Writer	• Process Improvement • Strategic Management
Strategic Analyst, Quality Analyst	• Administrative Services • Human Resources • Technical Documentation
Systems Engineer, Consultant	• Technical Writing

THE CHOICE IS YOURS!

You have the tools, methods, and resources, now it is up to you if you want to become known as one of the "best" procedures analysts in the industry. The world is changing rapidly and procedures analysts need to be ready to take on new challenges, new technologies, new management styles and needs, and work with senior management to help your company evolve into a "proactive" organization in the future.

CHECKLIST FOR CHANGE:

✓   The procedures analyst has enormous opportunities to learn about an organization because of his daily exposure to business processes, policies, procedures, changes, new initiatives, communication and training strategies, as well as new laws that may affect your company.

✓   Tools, methods, and resources are presented to help the procedures analyst move forward in his career and become recognized within his company and among his peers.

✓   Resources and guidelines are suggested to assist the procedures analyst become an "expert" in his field and become an asset to any organization by helping with company initiatives and helping the organization evolve into a "proactive" organization.

✓   The procedures analyst can make a difference in an organization when he can apply the principles learned from this book.

✓   Sources, reading materials, journals, associations, and other means for learning are presented to the procedures analyst to help him keep current in his skills and abilities.

✓   The procedures analyst has many job opportunities available because of his broad background in business processes, policies, procedures, and process improvement initiatives. Some possible non-management and management job titles are presented to "open the eyes" of the procedures analyst to show that there are many areas in an organization to apply his skills.

APPLYING WHAT YOU HAVE LEARNED:

Make a decision to pursue a career in business processes, policies, procedures, and process improvement initiatives. Do an inventory of your knowledge, abilities, and skills to determine if you have kept up with current practices and technology. Work with your management to broaden your education, skills, and responsibilities. Become the "best" procedures analyst in your company, among your peers, and in your industry.

ACHIEVE 100% COMPLIANCE:

This chapter will help the procedures analyst gain the knowledge, abilities, and skills necessary to become respected in his company and to be treated as an "expert" in business processes, policies, procedures, and continuous process improvement. The procedures analyst should be able to get on the path toward achieving 100% compliance of published policies and procedures when he does a career assessment and creates a plan for improving his experience, education, and job skills.

REFERENCES:

Beeler, Dewitt L, *Internal Auditing, The Big Lies*, Quality Progress Journal, Milwaukee, Wisconsin, May 1999.

Bhote, Keki R., *World Class Quality*, AMACOM, New York, New York, 1991.

Chang, Richard Y. and Niedzwiecki, Matthew E., *Continuous Improvement Tools, Volumes 1 and 2*, Richard Chang Associates, Inc, Publishing Division, Irvine, California, 1993.

Davenport, Thomas H., *Process Innovation*, Harvard Business School Press, Boston, Massachusetts, 1993.

Deal, Terence E. and Kennedy, Allan A., *Corporate Cultures*, Addison-Wesley Publishing Company, Reading, Massachusetts, 1982.

Deal, Terrence E. and Kennedy, Allan A., *The New Corporate Cultures*, Perseus Books, New York, New York, 1999.

Dobyns, Lloyd and Crawford-Mason, Claire, *Thinking About Quality*, Times Books, New York, New York, 1994.

Harrington, H. James, *Business Process Improvement*, McGraw-Hill, Inc., New York, New York, 1991.

Harrington, H. James; Hoffherr, Glen D; and Reid, Robert P., *Statistical Analysis Simplified*, McGraw-Hill, Inc., New York, New York, 1998.

Harvard Business School Contributors, *Harvard Business Review on Change*, Harvard Business School Press, Boston, Massachusetts, 1998.

Harvard Business School Contributors, *Harvard Business Review on Knowledge Management*, Harvard Business School Press, Boston, Massachusetts, 1998.

Katzenbach, Jon R., *Teams at the Top*, Harvard Business School Press, Boston, Massachusetts, 1998.

Larkin, TJ and Larkin, Sandar, *Communicating Change*, McGraw-Hill, Inc., NY, NY, 1994.

Milas, Gene H., *Teambuilding and Total Quality*, Engineering and Management Press, Atlanta, Georgia, 1997.

Nadler, David A., Gerstein, Marc S., and Shaw, Robert B. and Associates, *Organizational Architecture*, Jossey-Bass Publishers, San Francisco, California, 1992.

Naisbitt, John and Aburdence, Patricia, *Re-Inventing the Corporation*, Warner books, New York, New York, 1985.

Peters, Tom, *The Circle of Innovation*, Alfred A. Knopf, New York, New York, 1997.

Piskurich, George M., *The ASTD Handbook of Instructional Technology*, McGraw-Hill, Inc., New York, New York, 1993.

Poirier, Charles, C. and Houser, William, F., *Business Partnering for Continuous Improvement*, Berrett-Koehler Publications, San Francisco, California, 1993.

Scherkenbach, William W. *The Deming Route to Quality and Productivity*, CEEPress Books, Washington, D.C., 1991.

Senge, Peter, *The Fifth Discipline*, Currency Doubleday, New York, New York, 1990.

Senge, Peter; Kleiner, Art; Roberts, Charlotte; Ross, Richard; Roth, George, Smith, Bryan, *The Dance of Change*, Doubleday, New York, New York, 1999.

Sheets, Tara E. (edited by), *Encyclopedia of Associations*, 35th Edition, Volumes I and 2, National Organizations of the U.S., Gale Group, New York, New York, 1999.

Sheets, Tara E. (edited by), *Encyclopedia of Associations*, 35th Edition, Parts 1, 2, 3, International Organizations, Gale Group, New York, New York, 2000.

Sherriton, Jacalyn and Stern, James L., *Corporate Culture/Team Culture*, AMACOM, New York, New York, 1997.

Shonk, James H., *Team-Based Organizations*, Business One Irwin, Homewood, Illinois, 1992.

Swindle, Robert E. and Swindle, Elizabeth M., *The Business Communicator.* Prentice-Hall, Inc., Englewood Cliffs, New Jersey, 1989.

Vicker, Lauren and Hein, Ron, *The Fast Forward MBA in Business Communication*, John Wiley & Sons, Inc., New York, New York, 1999.

Wall, Stephen J. and Wall, Shannon Rye, *The New Strategists*, The Free Press, New York, New York, 1995.

Wind, Jerry Yoram and Main, Jeremy, *Driving Change*, The Free Press, New York, New York, 1998.

Appendices

A.   *"Purchasing System"* Summary Report Check Sheet
     (Reference Chapter 8, *"Developing Self-Assessment
     Checklists"*)

B.   Cost of Quality (COQ) Explanation and Illustration
     (Reference Chapter 11, *"Conducting Profitable Continuous
     Improvement Activities"*)

C.   State of Ohio "Copy Center "Prices for Forms
     (Reference Chapter 12, *"Saving $1 Million with Cost
     Benefit Analyses"*)

Appendix A

"*Purchasing System*" Summary Report
Check Sheet

Question No	Number of People to Which Checklists Were Mailed	Number of Respondents	Number of "Yes" Answers	% Yes Divided by Respondents
Requester of Purchase Requisition				
1	1000	500	300	60%
2	1000	500	400	80%
3	1000	500	450	90%
4	1000	500	480	96%
5	1000	500	490	90%
6	1000	500	250	50%
7	1000	500	300	60%
8	1000	500	300	60%
9	1000	500	350	70%
10	1000	500	100	20%
11	1000	500	490	96%
12	1000	500	400	80%
13	1000	500	500	100%
14	1000	500	350	70%
15	1000	500	250	50%
16	1000	500	400	80%
17	1000	500	475	95%
			Average % =	**73%**

Purchasing Assistant				
18	4	4	4	100%
19	4	4	3	75%
20	4	4	1	25%
21	4	4	2	50%
22	4	4	4	100%
23	4	4	3	75%
24	4	4	3	75%
25	4	4	3	75%
26	4	4	4	100%
27	4	4	4	100%
28	4	4	2	50%
29	4	4	2	50%
30	4	4	3	75%
			Average % =	**61%**
Buyer				
31	50	45	40	89%
32	50	45	25	56%
33	50	45	20	44%
34	50	45	35	78%
35	50	45	40	89%
36	50	45	15	33%
37	50	45	15	33%
38	50	45	35	78%
			Average % =	**72%**

Receiving Department				
39	30	30	30	100%
40	30	30	26	87%
41	30	30	22	73%
42	30	30	25	83%
43	30	30	10	33%
44	30	30	25	83%
45	30	30	15	50%
46	30	30	20	67%
			Average % =	**72%**
			All Averages % =	**67%**

Appendix B

Cost of Quality (COQ)
Explanation and Illustration

The *Cost of Quality* can be defined as those costs it takes to comply with the customer's requirements. Quality can be applied to any industry, product, or service whether it is a product sold by the company, documentation used by the company, or an advertisement placed in the local newspaper. The cost of quality can be calculated for any product or service. As COQ can be applied to any process and not just a manufacturing process; we can calculate COQ for published policies and procedures. Some managers intuitively grasp the fact that poor quality is costly and there is a great financial reward in preventing defects at the earliest possible stage or eliminate defects all together. Other managers see poor quality as a nebulous concept with little payback potential.

The cost of quality provides a starting point for management to compare courses of action and focus on decisions. For many, it is a wake up call. Most companies do not know the true cost of their own quality. Many executives estimate their cost of quality to be less than 5% of sales. Executives are often shocked to find that the cost of quality is really 15 to 25% of sales. They think the costs are represented by customer returns, waste, rework, inspection costs, testing costs, or rejects. They are surprised to hear that costs also include late paperwork, lack of planning, excessive overtime and employee turnover, pricing or billing errors, or a loss of market-share (Harry, 2000).

"Lost" revenue is just that — lost, it is real money that shareholders and corporations are entitled to, but will never see. Worse yet, the customers pay the price for a company's inability to run its business in a quality manner. Since quality saves companies money — and lots of it — it makes sense to produce a product or service with virtually no defects by doing it right the first time.

There are three components to the cost of quality:

1. <u>Prevention Costs</u> are the costs of all activities undertaken to prevent defects in design and development, purchasing, labor, and other aspects of beginning and creating a product or service. Examples include quality

planning, process planning, process control, design reviews, product qualification, supplier evaluation, supplier surveys, training, tool control, housekeeping, personnel reviews, procedure writing and reviews, or time and motion studies.

2.   <u>Appraisal Costs</u> are costs incurred while conducting inspections, tests, and other planned evaluations used to determine whether produced hardware, software, or services conform to their requirements. Examples include document checking, drawing checking, measurement control, statistical analysis, receiving inspection and test, materials consumed, equipment calibration, personnel testing, procedure checking, expense reviews, audits, or preventive maintenance.

3.   <u>Failure Costs</u> are costs associated with things that have been found <u>not</u> to conform or perform to the requirements, as well as the evaluation, disposition, and consumer-affairs aspects of such failures. Examples include redesign, reinspection, repair costs, return costs, retesting, employee turnover, corrective action costs, excess inventory, warranty expense, scrap, recalls, late time cards, customer complaints, or bad debts.

If these categories seem unclear to you, you are not alone. You can use any category as long as the cost is recorded. Some find the COQ is an easy concept to comprehend while others find it so nebulous that they do not see the potential payback.

AN EXAMPLE — COST OF QUALITY FOR POLICIES AND PROCEDURES

If you were to calculate the "cost of quality" for published policies and procedures, you could devise a tabulation check sheet for collecting information about each of the activities relevant to the selected process, policy, procedure. A check sheet can be devised for the *Purchasing System* and another one for the *Purchase Card System*.

The total costs of each procedure should be totaled. The COQ of the *Purchase Card System* should be subtracted from the COQ of the *Purchasing System*. The net result should be recorded. If the figure is positive, then you could use this information to support other methods you have used to ensure that the improvement is consistent. If the figure is negative, then you may wish to recheck your numbers and identify if there are "missing" cost items within the COQ original calculations.

The possible costs associated with the above two procedures are listed below.

1. <u>Prevention Costs</u>. Planning, researching, team meetings, telephone calls, video conference meetings, procedure writing, reviews, approvals, forms design and printing, company manual design and printing, publication, distribution, communication, or training costs. These activities are covered in Chapters 1 to 6, 11, and 12.

2. <u>Appraisal Costs</u>. Filling in forms, checklists, logs, performance compliance methods, audits, testing, reviews, and statistical analysis. These activities are covered in Chapters 7 to 10.

3. <u>Failure Costs</u>. Business processes that take longer to perform than the estimates included in the policies and procedures, forms that are discarded because new forms listed in the policies and procedures are not being used, statements that are misinterpreted can lead to wrong conclusions, or inaction. These activities are covered in Chapters 2, 11, and 12.

The total COQ should be calculated when the policies and procedures are published and after they are improved to ensure improvement is achieved and sustained. The comparison of the COQ at different stages in the life of a policy or procedure is another way to measure conformance to requirements, or compliance to baselined policies and procedures.

For instance, if the COQ for processing a purchase requisition is $1,000.00 and the cost of quality after making improvements to the process is $900.00, then you can claim that you have improved the process. If the cost of the improved process turns out to be $1,200.00, you cannot claim that you made any kind of improvement. The procedures analyst could be embarrassed from an improvement that shows a higher COQ instead of a lower one after an improvement is implemented. Efforts should then be taken to determine if there was a mistake in the collection of costs or if there are other costs that could be recorded.

COST OF QUALITY CONCLUSION

The cost of quality is an excellent method for determining the prevention, appraisal, and failure costs of business processes, policies, and procedures. Using the COQ alone, or as the sole basis for a justification for improvements, is not recommended. The COQ calculation is suggested to be used as supporting evidence to the results obtained through cost benefit analyses or other means. There are several problems with using the COQ as a sole indicator of costs for business processes, policies, and procedures. These problems include (Harry, 2000):

1. Costs do not increase in order for quality to improve, given a "Prevention" approach versus a "Detect and Fix" mentality

2. Many significant quality-related costs cannot be captured by most types of accounting systems

3. The conventional COQ theory ignores costly and avoidable inefficiencies that occur in the engineering, manufacturing, accounting, and service sectors of companies

An organization should not have to inspect to achieve quality. Defects should be eliminated at the root source through better processes and better products and service design focused on meeting the needs of the customers. When we aim for this higher standard, we are forced to abandon minor adjustments in how we run our processes and consider entirely new ways of doing business.

Appendix C

State of Ohio
Copy Center Prices
March 2000

For Carbon or Carbonless Forms
Per Image Price

IMAGE COUNT	SINGLE IMAGE PRICE
1-100	$0.0385
101-250	$0.037
251-500	$0.0355
501-1,500	$0.0340
1,501-2,500	$0.0325
2,501-5,000	$0.0310
5,001-50,000	$0.0295
50,000 Plus	$0.028

Examples:

Formula: No. of Forms multiplied by No. of Parts in Form multiplied by Single Image Price = **COST OF FORM.**

1. 500 Forms of 4-Part Carbon Interleaved Forms = 4 x 500 = 2000 Images: 2,000 Images x 0.0325 = **$65.00 for 500 forms**.

2. 5,000 Forms of 5-Part Carbonless Forms = 5 x 5,000 = 25,000 Images: 25,000 Images x 0.0295 = **$737.50 for 5,000 forms**.

Glossary of Terms

Affinity Diagram. A quality tool that allows a team to generate many ideas and issues creatively and to organize them in natural groupings to understand the essence of a problem.

Assignable Cause. A data point on a control chart that is outside of the control limits. These data points are causes that an employee can do something about. They are detectable because they are not always active in the process. We can see assignable causes because they have a stronger effect on the process than chance or common causes that are an inherent part of every process.

Audit. Process used to identify system failures and operating deficiencies so the auditee (i.e., person or group being audited) may initiate appropriate corrective or preventive actions. An audit is a planned, independent, and documented assessment to determine whether agreed-upon requirements are being met. An examination of records to verify their accuracy is usually performed by a person other than the person responsible for the record.

Auditee. An organization, group, or person to be audited. An auditee includes any unit or activity within an organization that is audited.

Auditor. A person qualified to perform an audit assignment. An auditor designated to manage a quality audit is called a "lead auditor."

Audit Report. A signed, written document which presents the purpose, scope and results of an audit.

Baseline. A snapshot in time of a process, policy, or procedure. A baseline is a specification or product that has been formally reviewed and agreed upon, that thereafter serves as the basis for further development, and that can be changed only through formal change control procedures (i.e., for the procedures analyst, change can only occur through a formal, documented system of policies and procedures).

Benchmark. A standard against which measurements or comparisons can be made. An improvement process in which a company measures its performance against the best-in-class companies and determines how these companies performed specific tasks, how they accomplished specific performance levels, and how they can use this information to improve their own performance.

Block Diagram. A simple flow chart that provides a quick, uncomplicated, view of a process. This flow chart technique uses rectangle boxes to describe the activities or tasks in a business process. The block diagram is the simplest kind of flow charting and does not involve any frustrations or headaches when trying to use "just the right" symbol to represent an activity, decision, delay, or storage device.

Brainstorming. A quality tool used by a team to generate a high volume of ideas on a topic by creating a process creatively and efficiently that is free of criticism and judgment. This group problem-solving method brings out many ideas in a short time.

Business Process. A process consists of a group of logically related tasks or the organization to define the results that support the organization's objectives. A process places an emphasis on what, not how. A process is always behind every policy or procedure.

Capability Maturity Model (CMM). A description of the stages through which software organizations evolve as they define, implement, measure, control, and improve their software processes. This model provides a guide for selecting process improvement strategies by facilitating the determination of current process capabilities and the identification of issues most critical to software quality and process improvement. The CMM is one of the primary standards used by software companies to certify maturity to external customers. The Software Engineering Institute (SEI) in Pittsburgh, Pennsylvania, is responsible for the maintenance of these standards.

Cause-and-Effect Diagram (also called a "Fishbone" diagram). A quality tool that permits a team to identify, explore, and graphically display, in increasing detail, the possible causes related to a problem or condition to discover its root cause(s). The diagram focuses on causes, not symptoms.

Change. To make a difference in some manner, to alter, to undergo a modification, or to transform. Some synonyms include adapt, alter, improve, modify, or vary. Organizational change includes the inner shifts of people's values, inspirations, and behaviors along with other shifts in business processes, policies, and procedures.

Change Agent. A professional dedicated to continuous improvement activities and can make change happen. Change agents must have the skills and ability to diagnose a given situation and develop acceptable solutions. Senior management of an organization often sponsors the procedures analyst to be come a "change agent" because of his extensive knowledge of systems, business processes policies, procedures, and forms.

Checklist. A quality tool for gathering data and soliciting responses to questions. The checklist provides a form of feedback to business processes and published policies and procedures. The procedures analyst often designs checklists and distributes them to users to "inspect" their own work as they do it.

Check Sheet. A quality tool that tallies or records observations. A check sheet can be used for various purposes such as gathering data for later analysis, finding out how often something is happening, finding out what kinds of problems are arising, and verifying that something you believe is occurring, is actually occurring. A check sheet is a good starting point for evaluating most problems. A check sheet can show patterns and trends that can be clearly detected and shown.

Coaching. A process in which a manager gives employees feedback on how well they are doing particular duties. An effective coach is one who plays a supportive role all the time, not just once in a while.

Commitment. A pact that is freely assumed, visible, and expected to be kept by all parties. Management commitment of the policies and procedures infrastructure is essential to the continuing efforts of the procedures analyst. Without this commitment, the policies and procedures function is "certain" to fail.

Common Cause. A data point within the control limits of a control chart. Common causes are found in every process. These are causes that the employee can usually do nothing about because they are built into the process. Common causes are continuously active in a process.

Communication. Communication is a process of providing information with the aim of achieving a shared meaning. Communication changes behavior. Communication is an instance of transmitting; it is a technique for expressing ideas effectively (as in speech) or a technique for the transmission of information (as in print or telecommunication).

Communication Methods. Media used to disseminate policies and procedures, examples include printed manual, email, network, Intranet, video, or CD-ROM.

Compliance. To conform or to apply to a rule. The rule in this case is a standard or baseline of a business process, policy, or procedure. Achieving compliance can literally mean that everyone in a target audience agrees with and follows a specific policy or procedure. Compliance can mean achieving stability in a business process and it can be defined as a "comfort level" to management.

Compliance Methods. Tools or methods used to achieve 100% compliance of policies and procedures. Examples included in this book are the check sheet, checklist, run chart, scatter diagram, control chart, histogram, Pareto chart, and systems audit. A compliance plan uses compliance methods to measure business processes, policies, and procedures.

Compliance Plan. A plan of action to select *compliance methods* (e.g., checklists, continuous improvement tools, or audits) to help achieve stability within the business processes, policies, and procedures and work toward the achievement of 100% compliance of policies and procedures. This plan consists of compliance methods that will become the backbone of the plan of action. These methods will be repeated over and over to make continual improvements to a business process, policy, or procedure.

Continuous Improvement. The ongoing improvement of products, services, or processes through incremental and breakthrough improvements. Continuous improvement is an operating philosophy that works to make every process in an organization more effective and efficient.

Continuous Improvement Tools. Tools refer to charts, flow charts, diagrams, matrixes, or presentation techniques used to measure the compliance of policies and procedures; as well as for conducting work shops, brainstorming sessions, team meetings, or other continuous improvement activities. The term, "quality tools," is another term used in this book to describe continuous improvement tools.

Control Chart. A quality tool that describes acceptable and unacceptable variation within a process. Control charts are a graphic display (a line graph) of results over time and against established control limits of a process. A control chart tells when to correct or adjust a process and when to leave it alone. Common causes are data points inherent in every control chart. Assignable causes are data points that only occur in control charts when the process is out of control.

Control Limits. The upper and lower limits, or boundaries, of a control chart. A process is considered in control if all data points fall within the upper and lower limits. If any data points fall outside these limits, then the process if out of control.

Control Point. An individual, form, software program, or other point in a process, policy, or procedure that acts as a "watchdog" or "gatepost" for the processing of business processes, policies, procedures, and forms. Control points are selected by the procedures analyst and the cross-functional team that are studying a process, policy, or procedure.

Corrective Action. Action planned or taken to prevent the recurrence of errors. In this book, corrective action is associated with audits. Normally, corrective action activities are not expected when the company has a procedures analyst because the procedures analyst is responsible for incorporating changes in the business processes, policies, and procedures.

Cost of Quality (COQ). Costs dedicated to or incurred that correct, validate, and identify quality aspects of products and processes. The COQ is the price of doing it wrong (costs of not conforming to requirements) and the price of inspecting and checking (cost of procedures, appraisals, and compliance) added together.

Cross-Functional Team. A group of individuals from various functions in a company that come together to study business processes or existing policies and procedures. The cross-functional team is used by the procedures analyst to analyze, research, write, coordinate, publish, distribute, communicate, train, measure, and improve business processes, policies, and procedures.

Customer. The recipient of a product (or service) provided by a supplier. An *external* customer is a person or organization who receives a product, service, or information but is not part of the organization supplying it. An *internal* customer is the recipient of another person's or department's output (product, service, or information) within an organization.

Cycle Time. The amount of time it takes to complete a particular task. Shortening the cycle time of critical functions within a company is usually a source of competitive advantage and a key quality improvement objective.

Defect. A flow in a system, or system component, that causes the system or component to fail to perform its required function. A defect, if encountered during execution, may cause a failure of a system.

Defects Per-Million-Opportunities (DPMO). The total number of defects per unit divided by the total number of opportunities for defects per unit multiplied by 1,000,000. This number can be directly converted into a sigma value.

Feedback. Information provided for evaluation and improvement.

Finding. A finding is typically associated with audits. A *finding* is an audit conclusion that identifies a condition that has a significant adverse effect on the quality of goods or services produced. An audit finding contains both the cause and effect of a situation and is normally accompanied by several specific examples of the observed condition.

Flow Chart. The flow chart is a universal method for analyzing and improving business processes. The flow chart is defined as a method of graphically describing a current process, or a proposed new process, by using simple symbols, lines, and words to display pictorially the activities and sequences in a process.

Frontline Employee. Individuals who report to frontline supervisors. They operate machines, deliver a service to customers, assemble or transport goods, process information, deliver mail, answer telephones, and so on.

Frontline Supervisor. Lowest level of management usually overseeing 15 to 50 people, or frontline employees.

He. A male gender term. While writers try to avoid the use of gender terms like "he" or "she," sometimes it is difficult to avoid. The word, "He," is generally used in literature, rather than "She" or "He/She" or "He or she."

High Performance Organization. High performance work teams become executive teams at the top of an organization. They integrate the social and technical systems of work, using both advanced technology-based tools and state-of-the art human system designs. These work teams bring together work, people, technology, and information in a manner that optimizes the congruence or "fit" among them in order to produce high performance in terms of the effective response to customer requirements and other environmental demands and opportunities.

Histogram. A quality tool that lets you envisions or see what is happening in a process. A histogram (a bar chart) is a process variation and decision-making bar chart tool that focuses on business process improvement efforts.

Improvement. To increase the value of, to make something more useful, to make things more acceptable, to get closer to a standard.

In Control. A condition that identifies a stable process. The data points stay inside the control limits. Common causes exist and assignable causes are absent.

Infrastructure. An infrastructure refers to a system of resources, facilities, documents, hardware, software, forms, reports, tools, and anything needed to ensure policies and procedures are effective. When the reference is made to a policies and procedures infrastructure, it refers to all the policies, procedures, processes, standards, practices, forms, reports, logs, people, training, tools, equipment, software, hardware, facilities, and the underlying framework needed to support a policies and procedures system in an organization.

International Organization for Standardization (ISO). The organization that publishes and administers a series of international standards (ISO Quality Standards) for the manufacturing and distribution of goods and services.

ISO Quality Standards. International standards for quality systems management. These standards specify requirements and the minimum specifications required for the design and assessment of a management system, the purpose of which is to ensure that suppliers provide products and services that satisfy a specified requirement.

Knowledge-Enabled Organization. In this kind of "proactive" organization, employees acquire the knowledge and skills they need from many different sources, within and without the company. They openly share their own knowledge and skills with others and they all work

318

toward achieving personal and company goals. The other two "proactive" organizations are the high-performance and learning organizations.

Lip Service. An avowal of advocacy, adherence, or allegiance, expressed in words but not backed by deeds. When a manager says he supports a company activity and then fails to show any kind of support, he is said to be giving, "lip service."

Learning. To enhance capacity through experience gained by following a track or discipline. Learning is not acquired following training. Learning can be achieved when the trainee is able to apply the newly acquired information to his work environment through the assistance of his manager, mentor, or coach. Learning always occurs over time and in "real life" contexts, not in classrooms or training sessions.

Learning Organization. An organization skilled at creating, acquiring, and transferring knowledge, and at modifying its behavior to reflect new knowledge and insights. Other behaviors include "systems thinking," "thinking out of a box," or "forward-thinking." In this book, the learning organization is a type of a proactive organization.

Lessons Learned. A phrase quality expert, Joseph Juran uses to describe a structured approach to analyzing past experiences in an endeavor and applying the results of that analysis to improving the quality of future efforts.

Lower Control Limits (LCL). The lower boundary of a control chart above which points plotted can vary without the need for correction or adjustment.

The Malcolm Baldrige National Quality Award. Examination criteria for the evaluation of the strengths and areas for improvement in the organization's quality system and of quality results. The goals of the Malcolm Baldrige Award are to help to stimulate American companies to improve quality and productivity for the pride of recognition while obtaining a competitive edge through increased profits; recognize the achievements of those companies that improve the quality of their goods and services and providing an example to others; establish guidelines and criteria that can be used by businesses, industrial, governmental and other organizations in evaluating their own quality improvement efforts; and provide specific guidance for other American organizations that wish to learn how to manage for high quality. Winners exemplify performance excellence.

Measure. A unit of measure.

Measurement. The act of determining a measure. A measure is the dimension, capacity, quantity, or amount of something.

Mentor. A relationship of two people, who may or may not report to one another, who pay special attention to each other's development.

Method. A reasonably complete set of rules and criteria that establish a precise and repeatable way of doing a task and arriving at a desirable result.

Metric. A standard of measurement. A metric is a quantitative measure of the degree to which a system, component, or process possesses a given attribute.

Out of Control. A condition in which the points plotted on a control chart goes outside the control limits. This condition also indicates that an assignable cause is at work, disrupting the process. Common causes also exist.

Pareto Analysis. The analysis of defects by ranking causes from the most significant to least significant. Pareto analysis is based on the principle, named after the 19th century economist Vilfredo Pareto, that most effects come from relatively few causes, that is, 80% of the effects come from 20% of the possible causes. Pareto analysis is commonly known as the "80/20" rule. The Pareto diagram is the picture part of the Pareto analysis.

PDCA Cycle. A four step process for quality improvement. In the first step (PLAN), a plan for improvement is developed. In the second step (DO), the plan is carried out, preferably on a small scale. In the third step (CHECK), the effects of the plan are observed. In the last step (ACT), the results are studied to determine what was learned and what can be predicted. This four-step approach to team problem solving was initiated by quality guru, Walter Shewart, and later refined by quality guru, W. Edwards Deming.

Plan. A method created for making or doing something or achieving an end. A plan always implies mental formulation and sometimes graphic representation.

Policies and Procedures Department. The department, or function, responsible for writing effective policies and procedures, and for achieving compliance through communication, training, review, compliance, audit, and improvement. The individuals who work in this department are called "Procedures Analysts." This department can be a one-person operation or have fifty people with layers of management. Procedures analysts work in this department. This department can have different names, but the functions are the same.

Policies and Procedures Improvement Cycle (PPIC). A four-step process for writing effective policies and procedures that can be measured. In the first step (i.e., ANALYZE & RESEARCH), the business process is analyzed and researched. In the second step (i.e., PUBLISH & COMMUNICATE), the policies and procedures are approved, published, communicated, and trained. In the third step (i.e., CHECK & AUDIT), the policies and procedures are measured and audited. In the last step (i.e., REPORT & IMPROVE), the results of the measurement process are documented and evaluated and the results are transformed into improvements. This cycle parallels the problem-solving method called the PDCA Cycle. Refer above to a definition of this phrase.

Policies and Procedures Infrastructure. A framework of policies and procedures at an organization. This framework represents all policies and procedures written in an organization as well as those systems that support or are impacted in any way. This infrastructure is discussed in detail in *"Establishing a System of Policies and Procedures."*

Policy. A general strategy or guideline. A policy is a predetermined course of action established as a guide toward accepted business strategies and objectives. Policies create expectations and guides for action. In most organizations, the policy document will provide the general guidelines for procedures and work instructions.

"Proactive" Organization. A type of organization that has evolved from the traditional "reactive" organization that focuses on preventing problems from occurring or recurring. Examples of "proactive" organizations are learning organizations, knowledge-enabled organizations, or high-performance organizations. The "proactive" organization should be every company's goal to stay even or ahead of the competition. Refer to Chapter 13, *"Preparing an Organization to be Receptive to Change,"* for a detailed discussion.

Procedure. A plan of action for achieving a policy; it is a method by which a policy can be accomplished and it provides the instructions needed to carry out a policy statement. Procedures provide the means by which the actions (provided by a policy) can be carried out by management and by employees. A procedure is the result of one or more business processes.

Procedures Analyst. The term, "procedures analyst," is used in this book to represent that person or group of persons responsible for coordinating the efforts needed to establish a policies and procedures infrastructure, and for doing the needed steps. These steps could include the researching, writing, coordination, publishing, implementing, communications, training, doing compliance activities, auditing, and conducting continuous improvement activities as a result of compliance activities. The procedures analyst generally works within a Policies and Procedures Department.

Process. A sequence of steps performed for a given purpose, for instance, the software development process. Any activity or group of activities that takes an input, adds value to it, and provides an output to an internal or external customer. Processes use an organization's resources to provide definitive results. Notice the difference in this definition and the meaning of a business process.

Process Improvement. Process improvement is the application of improvement activities to business processes, policies, and procedures.

Process Owner. The owner of a process, individual, or group of individuals, who is accountable for a business process.

Quality. The degree to which a system, component, or process meets specified requirements; it can also refer to a system, component, or process that meets customer or user needs or expectations. According to three quality experts, Juran, Deming, and Crosby, quality can be defined as meeting requirements, fitness for use, or anything the customer wants. The definition of quality differs as to the intended audience, e.g., the internal or external customer.

Quality Assurance. All the planned and systematic activities implemented within a quality system to provide adequate confidence that an entity will fulfill requirements for quality.

Quality Control. Operational techniques and activities that are used to fulfill requirements for quality.

Quality Management. All activities of the overall management function that determine the quality policy, objectives, and responsibilities, and implementation by means like quality planning, quality control, quality assurance, and quality improvement within the quality system. Quality management refers to the activities you carry out within your organization to satisfy the quality related expectations of your customers.

Quality-Related Costs. Those costs incurred in ensuring and assuring satisfactory quality, as well as the losses incurred, when satisfactory quality is not achieved.

Quality Tools. Used interchangeably with "Continuous Improvement Tools." Quality tools refer to charts, diagrams, matrixes, diagrams, or presentation techniques used to measure the compliance of policies and procedures.

"Reactive" Organization. A traditional organization that "reacts" to problems rather than preventing them from recurring or occurring.

Re-engineering. A method that can be used for revisiting a business process. Literally, it means to scrap the old and start over with a "blank sheet of paper." Long established policies and procedures are abandoned with the intent of taking a "fresh" look at the underlying business processes required to create a product or service, and delivery value to a customer. Re-engineering procedures can result in the elimination of documents from a system. In the case study presented in this book, the *Purchase Card System* had the effect of eliminating four forms and completely rewriting the original procedure, *Purchasing System*.

Review and Communication Control Plan. Shortened to "Review Plan," the review plan is a summary of reminders so that the procedures analyst can stay current with potential changes to policies and procedures. The review plan helps to monitor internal and external changes that happen within or to an organization that may affect the content of policies and procedures.

Role. A unit of defined responsibilities that may be assumed by one or more individuals.

Root Cause. A fundamental deficiency that results in a nonconformance and must be corrected to prevent recurrence of the same or similar nonconformance. The identification of root causes is the objective of the "cause-and-effect" diagram.

Run Chart. A quality tool is used as an analysis tool to collect and interpret data over time, to create a picture of what is happening in the situation you are analyzing, to find patterns yielding valuable insights, and to compare one period of data with another, checking for changes.

Scatter Diagram. A quality tool used to look at how strong the relationship is between two variables.

Self-Inspection. Defined as to inspect, or to view closely, a task or activity originated by the same individual. Self-inspection is used with the "Self-Inspection Checklist" referenced in Chapter 8, *"Developing Self-Assessment Checklists."*

Senior Management. A management role that generally reports to the Chief Executive Officer, President, or Chairman of a company. The primary focus of this group of managers is the long-term vitality of the organization, rather than short-term project and contractual concerns and pressures. Senior management is responsible for the vision, mission, and strategic goals and objectives of a company.

Six Sigma. Six Sigma is a business process that allows companies to improve their bottom line by designing and monitoring everyday business activities in ways that drastically minimize waste and resources while increasing customer satisfaction. Six Sigma asks questions that lead to quantitative answers that produce profitable results Six Sigma guides companies into making fewer mistakes in everything they do. Six Sigma is a statistical way of measuring quality. Six Sigma is equivalent to 3.4 defects per million units of output .

Software Engineering Institute (SEI). The Software Engineering Institute at Carnegie Mellon University in Pittsburgh, Pennsylvania, provides leadership in advancing the state of the practice of software engineering to improve the quality of systems that depend on software. The Capability Maturity Model (CMM) comprises one of SEI's best known products, a software process framework that continues to have a significant effect on the work of the software engineering communities worldwide.

Standard Deviation. A special calculation for control charts that describes how closely measurements (i.e., data points) cluster around the middle of a normal curve. A standard deviation describes a situation in which a variation in a product is due to chance causes alone.

Statistical Process Control (SPC). The application of statistics for the control or a process or system. Statistics create the foundation for quality, which translates to profitability and market share. Statistics help summarize data, provide insight into variability, and clarify decisions and help understand risks. Process control charts have saved considerable wasted effort in many business processes. At times, process control charts' trend analysis has identified potential problems before the internal or external customers were aware of them. Analyzing process control charts significantly helps to put your business processes in a problem-prevention operating mode.

Statistics. Involves numerical or quantitative information and the methods of dealing with that information. The information is called *statistical data* and the methods are called *statistical methods*.

Strategy. Set of intentions as expressed in a strategic plan. The plan states the company's mission, the scope of its operations and goals, and the actions required to fulfill its goals in the broad context of its competitive environment.

Subject Matter Expert (SME). An individual who contains the skills and abilities to be considered the best in a subject. This individual may also be a process owner.

Subordinate. An individual who works for another person. An employee who works for a supervisor is a subordinate. A supervisor can also be a subordinate to a manager, and a manager can be a subordinate to a vice president.

System. A system is a collection of business processes supported by an infrastructure to manage and coordinate functions within an organization.

Systems Audits. The verification of the operations and business processes performed and used by individuals responsible for business processes, policies, and procedures.

Target Audience. Audience is defined as the users of the system like employees, customers, suppliers, or any group that uses a process, policy, or procedure, or is impacted by these documents. The term *target* is used as an adjective to describe an audience that has been selected for a purpose. For instance, a target audience could be a single department such as the payroll department or it could refer to several departments or functions that use a business process, policy, or procedure being published. The target audience could also refer to all employees.

Team. A group of people (two or more), often drawn from diverse but related groups, assigned to perform a well-defined function for an organization or a project. Team members may be part-time or full-time participants of a team. Teams can be for a short-term duration of one day or for several years. The biggest downfall of teams is not setting a deadline, or success factor, when the team should be disbanded. Many teams go on and on.

Tools. Tools refer to diagrams, charts, flow charts, forms, software programs, and so on.

Total Quality Management (TQM). A management philosophy that utilizes employee empowerment and continuous improvement to meet the wants, needs, and expectations of the customer. TQM is the application of quantitative methods and human resources to improve the material and services supplied to an organization, all the processes within an organization, and the degree to which the needs of the customer are met, now and in the future.

Training Trap. Many companies are "trapped" by the tendency to offer training as a benefit and not as a "learning experience" that can be applied to an employee's work environment. When viewed in the context of the work place, training takes on a new meaning. The "trap" is taking training for granted and taking training classes for any reason without an obvious or time-relevant relationship to an employee's work environment. The "trap" can be avoided by taking training that is relevant to an employee's job duties and responsibilities and by assuring that a manager or a mentor is assigned to help the employee apply the new information to his work place.

Upper Control Limit (LCL). The upper boundary on an average control chart below which the plotted points can vary without need for correction.

User. A user is an individual who "applies" a business process, policy, or procedure. The members of a target audience are users. The terms, users, audience, and target audiences are used interchangeably. The term, "target audience," refers to more than one target audience, e.g., the Accounting Department and the Human Resources Department.

Variation. The extent to which things vary, one to the next. Reducing variation in inputs, methods, and outputs is a primary goal of statistical process improvement.

Vision Statement. A vision is the integration of a company's strategic goals into day-to-day management decisions. A vision helps to define the direction of a company and establishes the basic processes to be followed in achieving the vision.

325

Walk-Through. A type of review where the procedures analyst, or a team, physically visits the area under research to observe the operations first-hand and to ask questions.

Writing Format. A logical, structured format that provides consistency, coherency, and organization to a policy or procedure. The writing format is generally considered to be the heart of all policies and procedures because without it the published policies and procedures would not have any continuity or structure to them.

Index*

*NOTE:

Frequently used words like policy, procedure, processes, procedures analyst, teams, organizations, or audiences were left out of this INDEX because each occurs in more than half the pages in the book.